Traditional Asian Plays

Also by James R. Brandon

THE PERFORMING ARTS IN ASIA
ON THRONES OF GOLD: THREE JAVANESE SHADOW PLAYS
THEATRE IN SOUTHEAST ASIA

Traditional
Asian Plays

Edited and with an Introduction
by James R. Brandon

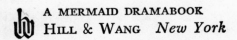
A MERMAID DRAMABOOK
HILL & WANG *New York*

Preface

Most translations of Asian drama consider the written text alone. Yet when a play is staged, words are couched in song, percussion instruments punctuate dialogue, whole scenes can be performed as dance, and symbolic gestures may express the meaning of a moment simultaneously with dialogue. So the most accurate and authentic translation of an Asian play is one which deals with the complete performance. This collection of plays, therefore, is designed to suggest to the reader, and the prospective director, a total theatrical experience. All translations are recent, and most were written specifically with performance in mind. Each version—tested in a premiere English-language production in the United States—incorporates stage directions, costume information, music cues, and interpretive comments. These are, in other words, production scripts.

I have written brief and fairly subjective introductions for the plays and the genres which they represent, but the place of each play within the whole repertory is discussed so the reader can see in what ways the play selected is typical of its genre and in what ways it may be unusual. The English-language production is also described and departures from traditional practice noted. Needless to say, there are other ways a script could be produced. The reader who wants to know more about a theatre form is urged to consult standard works; some of the most recent and accessible are listed in the introductions as Suggested Reading.

Many people have contributed to the translations in this book: translators, adaptors, directors, and sponsoring institutions. They are identified for each play. In addition we all owe a debt to the unnamed performers—most of them theatre students—who mastered the intricacies of traditional Asian theatre forms for these productions. They and their audiences have shown conclusively that the great plays of Asia can be studied, performed, and enjoyed by spectators in the West.

I am deeply indebted to Mrs. Bonnie R. Crown for her friendship and her encouragement during the several years when this manuscript was being prepared. The Asian Literature Program of The Asia Society commissioned the book and generously contributed funds toward its preparation. For this support I am most grateful.

J.R.B.

Contents

Introduction

We are faced with a dilemma when we attempt the hazardous undertaking of comparing Asian and Western drama. We can note the similarities between East and West and the ways in which, despite differences of place and time, the actions of dramatic characters are seen to spring from the same fund of human emotions. The innocent love of Charudatta for the courtesan Vasantasena in *The Toy Cart* does not surprise us; Benkei's many stratagems on behalf of his master in *The Subscription List* are motivated by feelings of loyalty we can easily appreciate. Thus in this sense, drama is universal.

But this simplistic view does little to illumine the nature of Asian plays. Were all plays alike, there would be no point in reading or producing the plays of Sophocles and Shakespeare and O'Neill, let alone the plays of Asian writers whose names we scarcely recognize. The great plays of the West continue to appeal to audiences centuries after they were written because each is a unique expression of a moment in human history. It would seem that our greatest rewards in experiencing the plays of Asia (whether we read them or see them performed) will come when we attempt to understand their uniqueness. For most of us, classical Asian plays require perception in several dimensions that are new to us. This need not be difficult, and for our efforts the returns in extra pleasure can be breathtaking.

One such new dimension is the Asian social, religious, and economic milieu that the dramas reveal. Most of us are not familiar with Asian customs and beliefs. In Japanese *Noh,* for example, we see the tenets of Buddhism manifested in play after play: restless spirits walk the earth, life is impermanent, and all passes to dust. The warrior's code, *bushido,* is the basis of the actions of countless heroes in Japanese *Kabuki.* Indian

1

concepts of kingly authority (and of sensual bliss) are implicit in Sanskrit plays. Prince Suton, in *Manohra*, is presented as an incarnation of the Buddha in a previous life. The world-view of the play is one in which man and his acts are not separate from the spiritual. Rather, through a righteous god-king, earthly acts are seen as an ordered part of a total, all-inclusive Buddhist universe. Characters in Chinese opera are motivated by Confucian concepts of a strongly hierarchical social order. The clown figures that are found in many types of traditional Asian drama may serve as a safety valve for popular discontent, as folk buffoons, or as critics of aristocratic suppression. Without arguing whether the drama is best considered a reflection of the society that produced it or whether, in a more modern vein, it provides a means of communicating with an audience, traditional theatre in Asia does offer us an exceptional insight into the lives of Asian peoples.

An Asian play may also have the dimension of a religious act. This dimension, long absent from our own theatre, is only now beginning to be re-evaluated, perhaps through the influence of Antonin Artaud more than any other single person. Performances in India and Thailand begin with offertory dances to honor the gods. The Thai *lakon jatri* performer is a medium for spirits. In Japanese Noh and Kabuki, at New Year's and on other occasions, very ancient ceremonial dances are performed to invoke the gods. In the most common type of Noh play, the protagonist is the spirit of a man or woman, or in some cases of a tree or other object of nature, temporarily manifested upon the stage. In one of the plays in this collection, *Ikkaku Sennin,* the hermit is able to imprison the dragon gods of rain and then, at the play's conclusion, assume the form of a ferocious demon. He can do this because of religiously derived magic powers. The function of religion varies from one play form to another (it is least important in Chinese opera) and from play to play. But overall, the tie between theatre and religion is extremely important and is manifested in varying degrees throughout Asian drama.

Also, the ways Asian audiences relate to a performance are very different from Western practices. For example, we are in the habit of controlling and focusing our attention; we go to the theatre for a relatively short time (two or, at the most, three hours) and during that time, at least in theory, we concentrate entirely on the stage. Viewing time is short and intense. But in most of Asia, viewing a play is casual and may go on for a very long time. The longest Sanskrit plays run to ten acts. A group of Noh plays on a single bill would, until recently, last eight hours or more. Kabuki began before dawn and continued throughout the day until sundown. As it is physiologically impossible to attend to any action continuously for eight to twelve hours, Asian audiences leave and enter when they wish; they attend to what particularly interests them and ignore what does not. Plays tend to be staged at a slower, more relaxed tempo than in the West. This tends to be true even with shorter plays, or when excerpts from long plays are staged independently. A plot is more likely to be episodic, to develop in a linear fashion, rather than to be woven together symphonically like the usual Western play of one to two hours. (The totally unified nine-hour play can be written—for instance, *Mourning Becomes Electra*—but it can only be a rarity.) None of the plays in this collection is inordinately long, yet a certain easy-going quality is often apparent.

The dimension of Asian theatre that we in the West are least equipped to appreciate, and the one I feel is the most crucial by far, is its dimension as artistic form. Whereas Western theatre is grossly content-centered, Asian theatre balances form and content much more evenly. We can trace our Western predilection for content back to Aristotle. While he acknowledged that the theatrical experience encompassed both form (music, diction, spectacle) and content (plot, character, thought), he unhesitatingly pronounced the elements of form to be of no concern to the playwright. Music, diction (or elocution), and spectacle (or staging) were the proper sphere for the stage practitioner, and hence not worthy of serious concern. The work of the poet was to arouse certain emotions—pathos and terror—and hopefully purge or sublimate them through the proper arrangement of incidents and composition of words. Staged or unstaged, a play was the same to Aristotle. The proper concern of the poet, in other words, was content. And since Aristotle most teachers of literature and critics have quite naturally tended to see things in the same light. Form has been thought of as art for art's sake, frivolous, or brittle, or without depth. And if form was given attention, it was mainly because form could enhance meaning. "Form follows function" tells it all.

But since the time of the Greeks we have known no truly happy marriage of form with content in Western drama. We all recognize the ultimate of narrowness in the realistic and naturalistic movements in the theatre in the past hundred years. Of course the plays of Shaw, Ibsen, Chekhov, Tolstoy, or Miller are structured, but it is not for their structure that they have been valued. Though we recognize the excesses of this period, in fact we have not changed our views so very much. We still tenaciously cling to our worship of literary content.

In essence, the appreciation of form is the appreciation of beauty. It entails an artistic or aesthetic reaction to performance. While not all of the elements of form in an Asian performance will be immediately apparent to us, some are readily recognizable. Music is an integral element of all traditional Asian theatre. Entrances and exits are timed to music; battle scenes are choreographed to fit the musical phrases of an accompanying melody; in some genres, especially in China, song replaces spoken dialogue for long sections. Movement and gesture are patterned into artistically pleasing forms until, when fully integrated with music, they become dance. Elocution is stylized as well. In many genres a stage assistant moves about unobtrusively, bringing and removing properties or helping with costume or make-up. Often a chorus or a narrator appears on stage, adding not only to the aural beauty of performance but to the visual composition as well.

Because theatre in Asia is conceived of primarily as a performing art, the text is not accorded priority, and there is little tendency to look first at a play in terms of its meaning. The theatrical art is regarded as a whole. Thus the meaning of a play may be stated through elements of form, or conversely, certain meanings will imply expression through certain forms. For example, certain movements in Chinese opera symbolize meanings which remain completely unexpressed in the text of the play. In Japanese Noh the climax of a play is a dance, not a scene with dialogue, and the dancer, not the poet, is its chief creator. Music in Chinese opera, in Kabuki, in Thai *lakon jatri,* is artistically pleasing and meaningful, indicating which type of scene is about to unfold, or which character is to appear, or which emotion is being expressed.

Meaning and form are closely allied in these instances. In other cases music, dance, elocution, and spectacle may be enjoyed and appreciated for their own sake, quite apart from any connotative meaning which may be attached to them. So, at a Noh performance, some spectators close their eyes and listen hypnotized to the cadences of music, while others sit enthralled by the exquisite perfection of a particular dancer's technique, and so too, others will follow the text in a printed score, scarcely looking at the performance. The Chinese opera buff may watch the eloquent hand gestures that display the water sleeves of the costume, or he may care about nothing until a difficult vocal passage is reached, and then he will become totally engrossed in the singer's technique. A Kabuki audience takes obvious delight in the stunning color, rhythmic patterns of movement, opulence of costuming, and music when a procession of twenty-five or more courtesans, attendants, merchants, or samurai make their way through the auditorium toward the stage on the raised ramp, even though the entrance is not significant in terms of plot. The purity of a sung note, the quality of a stage pose, the timing of a gesture, the shaping of a phrase—the knowledgeable spectator responds to them as the aesthetically aware person responds to perfection of form in any art. In Asian theatre, color, rhythm, harmony, and balance are legitimate concerns of artist and audience. Regrettably, the printed word can only convey so much, but it is hoped that the plays in this collection will suggest to the reader at least something of the exciting fusion of artistic form with content that vivifies the traditional theatre of Asia.

Suggested Reading

The Dramas and Dramatic Dances of Non-European Races (New York: B. Blom, 1964) is a reprint of William Ridgeway's 1915 classic, the first book in the West to consider Asian theatre on its own terms. Faubian Bowers' *Theatre in the East* (New York: Grove Press, 1960) introduces the major types of theatre in Asia. Leonard Pronko traces the influence of Asian theatre on the West, from Yeats to Artaud, in *Theater East and West* (Berkeley: University of California Press, 1967).

Indian Sanskrit Drama

The most ancient of the major theatre forms in Asia is the Sanskrit theatre of India. Dating any early Indian theatrical event is difficult and at best little more than a guess. However, the majority of the several dozen most important Sanskrit plays were written by court poets and were first staged at court theatres during the period from 300 B.C. to A.D. 700. The major source of information on Sanskrit drama and theatrical practice, aside from play scripts, is the *Natyasastra,* compiled by several unknown authors, probably by A.D. 200, though by tradition ascribed to one Bharata, a professional performer and troupe manager. This very long work gives a detailed exposition of every aspect of theatre art: shape and size of theatre buildings, pre-performance religious rituals, play construction, aesthetics of the drama, dance and gesture, music, and elocution. Presumably it was based partly on actual Sanskrit theatre practice, but its maze of energetically constructed categories is in part theoretical. Other important works on Sanskrit dramaturgy were written in later centuries, but all are derived from the *Natyasastra.*

The finest Sanskrit plays were written by Bhasa, Shudraka (who wrote *The Toy Cart*), and Kalidasa (whose *Shakuntala* is the Indian play best known in the West). Harsha and Bhavabhuti are also admired, but by their time (the sixth and seventh centuries) the drama had begun a decline from which it never recovered. Sanskrit ceased to be a living language. The dead hand of an inflexible dramatic code stifled new creativity. Court patronage ended under Islamic rulers. By perhaps the twelfth century the plays were no longer performed and, as with Greek tragedy, a great living tradition of theatre had died.

No one today can say with certainty how the Sanskrit plays

were staged. However, the traditions of theatre music and of dance have lived on. Folk dance-plays have been discovered in isolated villages where, apparently, very ancient traditions of performance have been preserved. The *Natyasastra* and other treatises have been restudied, and the poses of dancers carved on temple reliefs that date from the classic period provide a wealth of information on earlier dance style. Using these materials, modern Indian directors stage revivals of Sanskrit plays that aim at re-creating the ancient style of performance.

The single most impressive quality of Sanskrit drama is the richness of technique and the enormous variety of detail with which traditional topics and themes were handled. Some dramas are essentially panoramas of Indian life performed in five to ten acts. Ten-act plays were *mahanataka,* or great *nataka.* The plays are either about mythological figures (*nataka*) or legendary harem intrigues (*natika*). Some long plays (*prakarana*) are concerned with the lives of common people and are set not in royal courts but in humble homes; their plots are invented and do not come from the *Ramayana,* the *Mahabharata,* or from mythology. The one-act play was a recognized form: low-caste rogues could be handled (*prahasana*), or the subject might be erotic or humorous (*vyayoga*). There were even monologues (*bhana*), in which a character walked through town conversing on topical subjects with various people he met. Unlike the Noh, the *wajang* of Indonesia, or Greek tragedy, no standard type or structure characterizes Sanskrit drama. Instead, wide ranges of dramatic types were composed within a Sanskrit theatrical style.

Sanskrit plays were written by people connected with royal courts—perhaps even by kings themselves in some cases—and they were written with sophisticated audiences in mind. The plays are basically in prose, but at moments of heightened emotion the language shifts to lyric verse that expands or elaborates on an established emotion—much like an aria in Western opera. Only high-ranking figures speak Sanskrit, the elevated language of the court. For example, in *The Toy Cart*, Sanskrit is spoken by the hero Charudatta, the courtier, the future king Aryaka, Sharvilaka, the judge, and the courtesan Vasantasena. Lower-ranking characters and women (other than courtesans and queens) speak vernacular languages, collectively called *Prakrits*. In the earlier plays, like *The Toy Cart*, language is direct and used for dramatic purposes.

Although in most Sanskrit plays plot and character are important, the major purpose of the drama is not the portrayal of human action. The aim is rather to portray emotional states (*bhava*) in such a way that aesthetic delight (*rasa*) will be aroused in the cultivated spectator. The *Natyasastra*, and other later works, identify eight major emotions, or *bhava*, that can be embodied in the situations of a play: erotic, comic, pathetic, furious, heroic, terrible, odious, and marvelous. Eight *rasa* correspond to the eight *bhava*. A ninth *rasa*, corresponding to spiritual peace or serenity, transcends all others and is the highest goal of Sanskrit theatre.

In the *Natyasastra* plot is analyzed in three different ways, but one striking statement emerges from the otherwise confusing description: the next to the last part of a play should be a pause (*vimarsa*). How remarkable. For this is where we would expect a strong build to a climax, or perhaps the beginning of the resolution of the story, but in any case not a pause. It is consistent with the *rasa* aesthetic, however, for this gives major characters opportunity to fully express their feelings, and it gives the audience time to savor the situation before the action of the play continues. Sanskrit dramatic theory does not suggest that empathetic reaction is an aim of the theatre, unlike Aristotle, who places empathy at the center of tragic theory. Empathy, it would seem, is too emotional, too gross, too uncontrolled to be compatible with the *rasa* aesthetic, which is based upon reflection and educated appreciation.

Sanskrit plays were also considered a form of moral education. It was not proper to portray the fall of a hero, either through his own faults or through the machinations of a villain, for that would illustrate the failure of virtue. The *nataka* presented heroic deeds of royalty and the *prakarana* exalted true love, friendship, and virtue among commoners. Rules of right conduct restricted heroes and heroines to certain limited spheres of action, which were clearly defined in dramatic treatises. The jester, the third major character type, was allowed much greater individuality. In all plays he was a disfigured Brahman priest, a confidant of the hero, a glutton, and a fatalist. But he is given many individual characteristics by different playwrights. It may seem undesirable to restrict the range of expression of characters, which was an important consequence of the many rules laid down for playwriting, but it meant the cultivated spectator knew the rules of the game. And the spectator had to know the rules if he was to savor the delicate nuances of a performance, if he was to experience *rasa*.

The arts of mime, dance, music, elocution, and visual spectacle were as much a part of the drama as the words of the characters, according to the *Natyasastra*. The actor and actress were to use the body in an almost endlessly elaborate system of codified gestures and movements. Movements of the head, eyebrows, nose, cheek, chin, neck, breast, eyes, and feet are catalogued. And for hands, the sign-language of the *mudra* (or *hasta mudra*) was used. Hand positions and movements specified emotional states, actions, the object or subject of an action, animals, inanimate objects, and even grammatical parts. The fullest development of *mudra* sign-language is found in Indian dance. In one form of dance (*padam*) the performer portrays each word of a song with a hand sign as the song is sung. One therefore both hears and sees the words. The exact extent to which *mudras* were used in classical Sanskrit drama is not clear, but they were part of the total system of movement.

We cannot speak confidently about how songs were incorporated into Sanskrit performances. The *Natyasastra* mentions that songs accompanied movement on and off stage and also conveyed a number of different emotions. Singers sat on stage with the musicians, but we do not know which songs they sang and which songs the actors sang. The verses in play texts were probably sung or chanted.

Costume, make-up, and properties—the visual elements of staging—were part of the actor's technique. Through costume and make-up the actor delineated character. Properties were sometimes real, sometimes pantomimed (for example, an actor could mime holding an umbrella instead of holding a real one). Another acting technique shows once again the importance of the concept of *rasa*, for it describes how the actor is to express emotional states (*bhava*) so as to arouse an appropriate *rasa* reaction in the audience. Making the body perspire, the skin bristle, and the face turn red or lose color are given as examples of what the actor could do.

Plays were evidently performed on several types of stages, their size and shape varying according to the occasion and place. Caves or palaces may have been constructed of wood and cloth on occasion, but in general, apparently little or no scenery was used. The stage was most likely a raised wooden platform with pillars marking off certain areas. Drawn curtains were used to close off the backstage area from the view of the audience but not to begin an act or to close it.

Suggested Reading

Theatre in India (New York: Theatre Arts, 1962), by Balwant Gargi, is an interesting introduction. Arthur B. Keith's *The Sanskrit Drama* (London: Oxford University Press, 1924) is still the best work on the drama. More recent views are found in I. Shekhar, *Sanskrit Drama: Its Origin and Decline* (Leiden: E. J. Brill, 1960). There are many translations of Sanskrit plays, but suggested recent ones are: P. Lal, *Great Sanskrit Plays in Modern Translation* (New York: New Directions, 1964); H. W. Wells, *Sanskrit Plays from Epic Sources* (Baroda: University of

Indian Sanskrit Drama

Baroda Press, 1968); and Johannes van Buitenen, *Two Plays of Ancient India* (New York: Columbia University Press, 1968). Arthur W. Ryder's famous early translation of *Shakuntala* is available in a Dutton Everyman Paperback (1959).

The Toy Cart

An Indian Sanskrit Play

BY KING SHUDRAKA

English transcreation by P. Lal

The Toy Cart (Mrichchakatika) is attributed to King Shudraka, who probably lived in the fourth century A.D. The play may have been written by the king's court poet, however, and merely ascribed to Shudraka. It is the most famous example of the *prakarana* type of play, the extended drama about commoners that has an invented plot.

The qualities of richness and variety are everywhere evident in this work. The play is in ten acts, each act containing several scenes; the action of the play shifts from one location to another without pause. Nowhere in Sanskrit drama is there such a wide range of characters: villainous brother-in-law of the king, good-hearted merchant, courtesan, pompous judge, cart drivers, gamblers, and thieves. And, as Balwant Gargi says in the notes to his production of the play, "nowhere in the entire ancient Hindu drama do we find such individualized sinewy characters."

The action of the play, in spite of its two interrelated plots, is easy to follow. The first plot concerns the developing love between the merchant Charudatta and the well-bred courtesan Vasantasena. Charudatta is poverty stricken and feels he cannot ask for her favors. This obstacle is overcome in Act Five by Vasantasena's tactful reassurance that she cares for Charudatta despite his poverty. A secondary plot, beginning in Act Six, concerns the cowherd Aryaka, who, it has been prophesied, shall become king in place of the despot on the throne. The two plots are related, for Charudatta helps Aryaka to escape from his royal pursuers. Around these two plots a wealth of incident is arranged: assignations, nighttime thievery, a comic gambling game, a semifarcical trial, a near murder, and a near execution. The major plot was well known before Shudraka's time. Bhasa's earlier four-act play *Charudatta* handles the same story. It seems that Shudraka took the plot of the merchant and the prostitute and incorporated into it the political subplot. It must have been a surprising play for the audience of courtiers. The intertwining of the two rather separate plots gives the play an unusual kaleidoscopic quality, as acts and scenes shift first to one then to the other group of characters.

The name of the play is a departure from tradition. Usually the title of a *prakarana* play was made up of the names of its two leading figures, but Shudraka found inspiration for the play's title in a minor incident in which Charudatta's son plays with a toy cart made of clay (a scene which is not included in this version).

The erotic and comic *bhava* are clearly the most important emotions portrayed in the early acts of *The Toy Cart*, while in the later acts the heroic, pathetic, and odious *bhava* supplant them. An audience would not be induced to experience the ninth *rasa*, that of serenity and peace, except quite briefly at the play's conclusion. This is considered a deficiency by a number of Indian critics. Certainly the play is long on action and short on serenity. The same critics suggest that *The Toy Cart* is realistic and therefore not genuinely Indian. If we look at the play from the narrow Western view that sees realism in staging as synonymous with the reality of common life, then this criticism is justified. The gambling scene, the nighttime housebreaking, and the carriage rides through the crowded streets are plebeian indeed. They concern ordinary people and are set in the streets of the town and in the homes of the humble. But it would seem that precisely these scenes call for extensive pantomime, stylized gesture, and even symbolic movement. We would commonly call a prison scene such as the one in the last act realistic, but from what we know of Sanskrit theatrical techniques, it is almost certain that Sthavaraka was not costumed as a prisoner, nor was he shown on stage inside a specially constructed prison chamber, and certainly he did not leap "from a high window in the palace jail overlooking the square" as Shudraka's stage directions indicate. In spite of subject matter, then, the play belongs within the mainstream of Sanskrit drama, with all the conventional nonrealistic theatre practices that this implies. Balwant Gargi shows, in the notes to his production of *The Toy Cart*, that the characters, though plebeian, are still part of the Hindu metaphysical world. He writes, "The characters are pulling in opposite directions, the negative and the positive, in a constant search for balance. The uncouth, course, and selfish Sansthanaka is the opposite of the noble, gentle, and generous Charudatta. Both are extremes—one of evil, the other of good. Charudatta meditates and feels; Sansthanaka senses and acts. Throughout the play they retain a balance. Virtue cannot thrive in a void; it requires the presence of evil. The chain of moral law binds priest and sinner, judge and culprit, policeman and prisoner. They are each others' antitheses, yet essential for their mutual existence as the justification of their opposites. Charudatta's wife and Vasantasena (the courtesan) are the spiritual versus the physical. Together they make a complete wife."

The version of *The Toy Cart* published here is based upon a transcreation by P. Lal, as directed at the University of Washington by Balwant Gargi. This translation is written in remarkably colloquial and vivid English. For performance, the traditional opening scene between the stage manager and his wife, an actress of the troupe, was added, as well as an introductory dance suggested by the religious rituals which the *Natyasastra* describes as preceding a performance of a Sanskrit play. The stage manager reappears between scenes to move properties. Sometimes he reacts to the action as well.

The ten-act text required cutting to reduce its playing time. Several verses were dropped, and minor incidents not related to the two main plots were cut. The sections with Charudatta's wife and son were deleted. Some minor characters were combined. The director eliminated some decorative similes and metaphors to simplify the English phrasing.

Since the original tradition of Sanskrit performance died centuries ago, there is no "authentic" mode of performance for *The Toy Cart*. In this performance the director used Indian folk theatre techniques, with which he is particularly familiar. In many respects they correspond with what we know of classical dance techniques. Richly decorated costumes and ornately made hand properties were used—as they are in Indian village theatre—to create striking visual effects.

The play was performed in the Penthouse Theatre at the University of Washington, the first arena stage built in the United States. In the center of the open stage area a round, inner platform about a foot high was built. This area served for designated locales—Vasantasena's house, the court, the garden—while the lower level circling it was used for processions in the street. Four entrances to the arena stage gave the large cast of thirty-eight easy access to this central playing area. Fluidity of staging was designed to match the fluidity of the play's construction. No scenery was used.

Some actual properties were used, but most were imagined and portrayed through mime (a technique described in the *Natyasastra*): throwing mud clots, pouring water, weaving flower braids, opening doors or windows. The cast was encouraged to create objects through both visual and aural suggestion. According to the director, "words were actionized and actions were vocalized." The bailiff in Act Nine mimed the gait of his galloping horse and also clucked as the driver and whinnied as the horse. Many scenes in the play cry out for pantomimic action: the chase of the gamblers and masseur through the streets to the temple; the thief creeping through the night and knocking a hole through the wall in order to enter the victim's house; the chase of Vasantasena; the several scenes of bullock and horse carts being driven through the streets. Much of this pantomimic action was accompanied by music, which was performed by a group of Indian and American musicians who sat on a raised platform to one side of the stage. Dances appropriate to the action of the play were created by Narendra Sharma in the *bharata natyam* style of classical dance and were danced by American students.

The Toy Cart

The director aimed at creating a total approach to the play, based on valid Indian traditions—in this case, the traditions of folk theatre—but set within a frame of reference which an American cast and audience could bring to the play. "Music, exaggerated make-up, colors, and rhythms were used to inject poetry, drain off sentiment, and focus attention," the director said of his production. We cannot fail to note that the content of the play is not mentioned; technical, conventional devices were used to achieve artistic and aesthetic ends, including the very non-Western end of reducing emotion.

Characters

CHARUDATTA, *a merchant*
VASANTASENA, *a courtesan*
SANSTHANAKA, *the king's brother-in-law*
MAITREYA, *a Brahmin*
ARYAKA, *a cowherd*
SHARVILAKA, *a thief*
MASSEUR, *later a monk*
COURTIER
CHANDANAKA ⎫
VIRAKA ⎬ *captains of the guard*
MATHURA, *chief gambler*
GAMBLER
RADANIKA ⎫
VARDHAMANAKA ⎬ *Charudatta's servants*
MADANIKA ⎫
PALLAVIKA ⎬ *Vasantasena's maids*
KUMBHILAKA, *Vasantasena's servant*
STHAVARAKA, *Sansthanaka's servant*
STAGE MANAGER
ACTRESS, *the stage manager's wife*
DARDURAKA
JUDGE
BAILIFF
RECORDER
CLERK
VASANTASENA'S MOTHER
FIRST EXECUTIONER
SECOND EXECUTIONER

TOWN-CRIER

OLD MERCHANT

YOUNG GIRL

GRADS, RETAINERS, LAWYERS, PLAINTIFFS, HANGERS-ON, CITIZENS, TWO STAGEHANDS, MUSICIANS, DANCERS

The Toy Cart

An arena stage, with four entrances, one at each corner. A large one-foot-high round platform center represents specific locales —house, temple, garden, prison, etc.—as needed. A passage circling it is the street. Steps lead up to the platform from each entrance. At one side, near an entrance, is a higher raised-platform. MUSICIANS, *who play the horizontal drum, flute, sitar, tamboura, and cymbals, sit on it. They wear traditional Indian dress. Two* STAGEHANDS *sit on either side of the* MUSICIANS' *platform when they are not placing or moving properties. They wear black saris.*

Prologue

The gong strikes three times on a darkened stage. With the last fading sound the MUSICIANS *start chanting a classical raga as a beam of amber light silhouettes them. Incense is burning before the image of Shiva on the raised platform, near the* MUSICIANS. *Slowly the melody rises. The light fades in and reveals six* DANCERS *sitting in meditation in a dance pose on the central platform. The* DANCERS *arise, holding tiny cymbals, and dance a devotional temple dance. At the climax the* STAGE MANAGER *enters.*

STAGE MANAGER Stop! (*The* DANCERS *stop and bow out.*) It bores my audience. I offer homage to you, ladies and gentlemen, and am glad to announce that we are presenting to you

21

The Toy Cart. The author is believed to have been King Shudraka of the fourth century. A brilliant poet, he was expert in stagecraft, statecraft, mathematics, astronomy, sculpture, music, and in the science of courtesans and elephants. He lived for one hundred years and ten days, and after relinquishing his throne to his son and performing the horse sacrifice, walked into fire.

This play tells the story of a poor merchant of the city of Ujjain. His name is Charudatta. He fell in love with the most beautiful courtesan of the city. Her name is Vasantasena. Through these two characters the king-dramatist reveals the ecstasy of dignified love and the dangers involved in it. How people become jealous, how justice is perverted, how crooks and thieves behave, how the wicked succeed, and how finally they are destroyed. (*He walks about the stage and looks around him.*) Why, the stage is empty! Where have the actors gone? (*Thinks.*) Now I have finished my rehearsal and they are gone. I have been rehearsing so long that my eyeballs are cracking like dried seeds. This is all because I'm hungry. I shall call my wife and ask if there is anything to eat. Here I go. (*Cuts a circle.*)

I've reached my home. Let me go in. (*Goes up steps, entering.*) What is going on here? The floor is covered with iron pots and pans and marks of black soot. I'm terribly hungry. Nothing to eat for me this morning, but here they are making preparations of all kinds. Some girls are weaving garlands, some grinding spices, some pounding rice paste. A river of milk. Is it my house? I must know the truth from my wife.

ACTRESS (*enters*) Here I am.

STAGE MANAGER Welcome, welcome, my wife.

ACTRESS What are your orders? Command and I shall do.

STAGE MANAGER My dear, I have been rehearsing so long that I'm hungry. My body is dried up like a lotus stalk. Anything to eat?

ACTRESS Everything.

STAGE MANAGER Everything?

ACTRESS Yes. Honeyed rice, milk pudding, sugar cakes, saffron rice with almonds and raisins. A complete feast.

STAGE MANAGER So much? And in the house of a theatre man? Are you joking?

ACTRESS (*to herself*) Of course I'm joking. (*Aloud.*) Everything, my master, of course; everything is available at the shops in the market.

STAGE MANAGER (*angry*) You slut! May your dreams be destroyed as you have destroyed mine.

ACTRESS Forgive me, my master. Be calm. I was only joking.

STAGE MANAGER Then what are all these preparations here?

ACTRESS I'm observing a fast.

STAGE MANAGER A fast? Why?

ACTRESS So that I may get a good husband in the next life.

STAGE MANAGER Look at her, gentlemen! She is desiring a good husband in her next life, and I have to pay for it!

ACTRESS Come, my dear, don't be angry. I'm observing a fast to find a good husband—that means you! (*She drops to the floor at his feet.*)

STAGE MANAGER (*pleased*) Get up, get up, my dear. Tell me, who is going to preside over this ceremony?

ACTRESS Invite a noble Brahmin so that he comes and has a meal at our house. Only then can we eat.

STAGE MANAGER You ask me to find a noble Brahmin? Well. I go in search of him. (*He walks around the outside passage.*) This city is so rich. But how am I going to find a noble Brahmin? (*Looks around.*) There is Charudatta's friend Maitreya coming here. I will ask him. Master Maitreya, will you come and grace our house and have food?

VOICE OFFSTAGE Sorry, I'm very busy. Better ask someone else.

STAGE MANAGER Sir, be gracious, come and have food.

VOICE OFFSTAGE Why do you ask me again and again? I have told you I'm very busy. I cannot come. Ask someone else.

STAGE MANAGER All right, I shall ask someone else. Let's go, my dear.

They exit. The lights go out center and come up on MAITREYA,
who enters on the outer passage.

MAITREYA   I have told you I am very busy. I cannot come. Ask
someone else. . . .

Act One

Meanwhile, CHARUDATTA *enters from the right and sits on the
low hexagonal stool covered with rough cotton which the two*
STAGEHANDS *have quickly placed in the center of the stage.*
MAITREYA *walks along the passage.*

MAITREYA *(muttering)*   I am sorry, I am very busy; ask some
other Brahmin. . . . *(He looks up.)* What an awful mess you
are in, Maitreya. There was a time—ah, those were the days!
—when Charudatta had money in his pockets, and I could go
to his house and stuff myself with scented sweets. I could sit
by the door and poke my finger into a thousand delicious
cakes . . . shove these aside, touch those, and eat the others,
like a painter dipping his fingers in his colors. If I wished, I
could stand in a corner of the market, like a well-fed bull,
chewing away without a care in the world. But now he is
poor. So I knock about from door to door, picking up whatever crumbs I can find. Here I am bringing a shawl for
Charudatta from his friend—a jasmine-scented shawl that he
has been asked to wear after he finishes his morning prayers.
(He looks around, sees CHARUDATTA.*)* Ah, here he is. *(Approaching the steps near him.)* My greetings to you, sir.
CHARUDATTA   Ah, my friend Maitreya. It's very good to see you,
Maitreya. Sit down.
MAITREYA   Thank you. *(Goes up steps, entering.)* Your friend

sends you this shawl, fragrant with jasmine, and asks you please to wear it after prayers. (*He hands the cloak to* CHARUDATTA, *who takes it absent-mindedly.*) Sir, you look very sad today.

CHARUDATTA Happiness after sorrow is wonderful: a glowing lamp that scatters darkness. But a man who falls from riches to poverty is a spiritless body.

MAITREYA Would you rather be dead than poor?

CHARUDATTA I'd rather be dead, my friend. Death is only an instant of suffering, but being poor drags on and on.

MAITREYA That well may be, but there is more than that. The money you spent on your friends has increased their respect for you in their hearts.

CHARUDATTA You misunderstand me. It is not that I mind the wealth that's lost, but that my friends desert me.

MAITREYA Let's change the subject.

CHARUDATTA My friend Maitreya, I have offered prayer to the gods of my house. Go where the four roads meet and offer better prayers on my behalf.

MAITREYA Not me, sir.

CHARUDATTA No?

MAITREYA If the gods don't favor you here, they won't favor you at the four roads either.

CHARUDATTA Don't refuse, Maitreya. We must do our duty; that is all. I have no doubt that the gods are pleased with whatever is offered to them in humility and piety, in thought and deed. Go.

MAITREYA No, sir, not me. (*Sarcastically.*) I might mess things up. I'm a useless Brahmin and as muddle-headed as a mirror —right side left and left side right. Besides, what's worse, evening is the time when courtesans, thieves, and gamblers stalk the main road. I'm just the man they'd see a prize catch. No, sir, I won't be the mouse that gets gobbled up by the snake who's out frog-hunting!

CHARUDATTA Very well, then, stay here. Let me finish my prayers and then I'll go.

CHARUDATTA *takes on the same worship posture.* MAITREYA *looks around and exits. Lights dim on* CHARUDATTA.

VOICE OFFSTAGE   Vasantasena, stop! Stop, Vasantasena!

VASANTASENA *enters, running in the darkness, pursued by the king's brother-in-law* SANSTHANAKA, *one of his* COURTIERS, *and his* SERVANT. *They circle the passage.*

COURTIER   Stop, Vasantasena, stop! Why do you run so fast? Your feet should dance—dance, not run. Why do you run like a frightened deer, looking at the hunters from the corners of your eyes?

SANSTHANAKA (*wildly groping, as if in the dark*)   Stop, Vasantasena, stop! You need not fear. My heart overflows with love for you. It is burned to a cinder, sweet girl, like meat on blazing coals.

SERVANT   Stop, Vasantasena, stop! My lord can run faster, like a hound chasing a bird in the woods.

COURTIER   Stop, Vasantasena! You are trembling like a plantain tree; the hem of your dress is fluttering in the wind.

SANSTHANAKA   Stop, Vasantasena! Why run away from a love that you create? Sir, I have loved her by ten different names. I called her the whip of the god of love. I called her snake-eyed, flatnose, angel, heavy-lipped, harlot, sweet-throated, the daughter of an elephant. All those wonderful sweet names. But, sir, she won't spare a word to throw at me.

COURTIER   Why run from us, Vasantasena?

SANSTHANAKA   Your jewels jingle as you fly from me. I shall catch you, my sweetheart, and kiss you, my sweetheart.

SERVANT   Do as he says, lady. He's the king's brother-in-law.

COURTIER   A hundred stars flash from your waist; your face is marvelous. O goddess, O guardian of our city!

VASANTASENA   Pallavika! Madanika! O Pallavika!

SANSTHANAKA   Men, eh?

COURTIER   I know how to deal with *them*.

VASANTASENA   Pallavika, Madanika!

COURTIER   Fool! She's calling her servants.

SANSTHANAKA   You mean women?

COURTIER   Yes.

SANSTHANAKA   Women, eh? Who's afraid? I can fight a hundred of them at once.

VASANTASENA (*getting no reply*)   No one to help! I'll have to use my wits.

COURTIER   Keep searching! She's here somewhere.

SANSTHANAKA   Scream away, Vasantasena; scream for your Pallavika and Madanika. Your screams won't help you when I catch you. My sword's out. . . . Slurrp! . . . There goes your head. Call the sun god, call the ten-headed demon! Where can you run, my little pet? Your life's in my hands.

VASANTASENA   Sir, I am a woman, a weak woman.

COURTIER   One reason you're not dead already.

SANSTHANAKA (*laughing*)   Not finished off already!

VASANTASENA (*aside*)   How terribly kind! (*Aloud.*) Sir, why are you chasing me? What do you want? My jewels?

COURTIER   Heavens no! Why pluck the blossoms from a beautiful creeper? No, no, not the jewels.

VASANTASENA   What do you want, then?

SANSTHANAKA   Your love. Vasantasena, love me. I'm a splendid lover, I promise you.

VASANTASENA (*angrily*)   You insult me, sir. Leave me alone. You make me sick.

SANSTHANAKA (*laughing and clapping his hands*)   Now what do you say to that, my courtier? This pretty girl says, "You're sick for me." That's a good one. Yes, my pretty little chick, I'm sick for you. I'm sick for your love. . . . Oh, love me, Vasantasena!

COURTIER (*aside*)   But what she said was, "I'm sick of you." The fool! (*Aloud.*) That's a strange way for a courtesan to talk. You know, Vasantasena, how it is: the doors of a courtesan's house are open to all young men. She gives the same greeting to the man she likes and to the man she loathes. Come,

Vasantasena; the stream gives a cleansing bath to both the genius and the fool, the Brahmin and the outcaste. The crow and the peacock perch on the same glittering tree. The soldier and the merchant and the scholar—the same boat takes them across the river, doesn't it? It's a courtesan's business to be . . . er . . . friendly to all.

VASANTASENA I've never heard of love being forced, sir. It has to be deserved.

SANSTHANAKA Is that so? The real trouble, sir, is that this slut is in love with a wretch by the name of Charudatta, whom she met in the garden of Kama's temple. So she won't give me a second look. His house is near, on our left. See that she doesn't slip out of our fingers into his house.

COURTIER (*aside*) This utter idiot: he has to say the wrong thing every time! So she's in love with Charudatta. (*Aloud.*) Did you say that Charudatta's house is on our left?

SANSTHANAKA Yes, on our left.

VASANTASENA (*moving around passage to steps near* CHARUDATTA) Oh, what a relief! On my left. Just by trying to hurt me, he's helped me. The house of the man I love.

SANSTHANAKA (*following, groping*) It's dark, dark! I can't see a thing. Now you see her, now you don't. It's like hunting for a bottle of ink in a coal mine.

COURTIER (*same business*) The darkness closes down over my eyes so I can't see even the road. It's all over my body, as if it were raining darkness.

SANSTHANAKA I *must* find her.

COURTIER How? Have you anything to go by?

SANSTHANAKA Go by? What do you mean?

COURTIER The tinkling of her jewelry, the perfume of her garland.

SANSTHANAKA (*as* VASANTASENA *moves*) Yes, sir, I hear the tinkling of her garland, but I cannot see the perfume of her jewels.

COURTIER Listen, Vasantasena. Though the darkness hides you, the fragrance of your garland will give you away; the music

of your anklets will give you away. Where are you, Vasantasena?

VASANTASENA (*aside*) Thanks for the warning. (*She takes off
her garland and anklets, and feels for the doorway.*) This is
the way, I think. I can feel it with my fingers. And here's the
back door. (*Mimes trying to open door.*) Oh dear, it's shut!

The lights come up center stage on CHARUDATTA. MAITREYA
enters from the side of the stage opposite from where VASANTA-
SENA *and her pursuers stand frozen in tableau.* RADANIKA, *a
servant to* CHARUDATTA, *follows him. One* STAGEHAND *places a
lighted candle on the floor between* VASANTASENA *and* CHAR-
UDATTA. *The other* STAGEHAND *gives* MAITREYA *a bowl containing offerings.*

CHARUDATTA My prayers are finished. Now, Maitreya, it's time
for yours. Pray for me at the four roads.

MAITREYA Not me!

CHARUDATTA

Ah, who listens to a poor man?
His friends? Once they loved him, now they say good-bye.
His sorrow grows and grows.
The crimes of others are loaded on his shoulders.

MAITREYA All right, I'll go. But I should like Radanika to
come with me.

CHARUDATTA Radanika! Go with him.

RADANIKA Yes, sir.

MAITREYA Do you mind holding this offering a minute,
Radanika, while I open the back door?

MAITREYA *hands the bowl to* RADANIKA. *He turns to the imaginary door beside which* VASANTASENA *is standing. He mimes
lifting the latch and pushes the door open.* MAITREYA *turns back
to* RADANIKA, *and in that instant* VASANTASENA *mimes stepping
over the door threshold and slips into the room unseen.*

VASANTASENA   I'm lucky: the door has opened by itself! (*She starts.*) Oh! a candle! (*She bends and snuffs the candle out with a fold of her dress.*)

CHARUDATTA (*surprised*)   What was that, Maitreya?

MAITREYA   Something blew out the candle—the wind, I think, sir. Never mind. You go first, Radanika. I'll light another candle and follow you.

As MAITREYA *receives another lighted candle from a* STAGEHAND, RADANIKA *feels her way carefully to the door, steps across the threshold, and walks down the steps onto the passage outdoors.* SANSTHANAKA *and his two men come out of the tableau they were holding and begin groping forward toward the door.*

SANSTHANAKA   Where the devil has she disappeared to?

COURTIER   She's here. She can't go far.

In the dark the men lose their sense of direction, and SANSTHANAKA *makes a circle. He bumps into the* COURTIER *and grabs him.*

SANSTHANAKA   I have her! I have her!

COURTIER   You fool, let go of me!

SANSTHANAKA *lets go of the* COURTIER *and continues groping. The* COURTIER *and the* SERVANT *circle each other, changing places.*

SANSTHANAKA   Oh-ho, oh-ho, look around. (*Seizes the* SERVANT.) I have her! I have her!

SERVANT   You have *me*, sir.

SANSTHANAKA   Me, sir? Oh-ho, oh-ho, master and servant, servant and master. (*Lets him go.*) Stay where you are, stay where you are. Don't move! Look about, search! Search! (*He pivots, reaches out blindly, and catches hold of* RADANIKA *by the hair.*) Oh-ho, I caught her. This time I really caught her! I can tell her by the scent of the garland. Oh-ho.

COURTIER A pretty hide-and-seek we played, didn't we, my sweet girl? (*Sniffing, seeking her location.*) That's a nice head of hair, all scented with flowers.

SANSTHANAKA I have her by the hair. Oh-ho, my girl! Scream away, yell, call your friends, curse your God!

RADANIKA (*struggling*) Sir! Sir! What is all this?

COURTIER Hey, that isn't her voice.

SANSTHANAKA I know these cats, sir. When they want milk, they have a different mew. Don't believe her.

COURTIER I'm not sure. . . . Still, why not? She must know the tricks of her trade.

MAITREYA, *carrying a candle in an earthen dish, steps over the threshold, turns back to close the door, and goes down the steps onto the passage.*

MAITREYA How queerly the candle flickers . . . like the fluttering heart of a goat that can't escape. (*He sees* RADANIKA *and the others.*) Radanika!

SANSTHANAKA Ho, sir, sir! A man, a man!

RADANIKA He laid hands on me, Maitreya. He insulted me.

MAITREYA Insulted you? You insult *us*, sir.

RADANIKA He laid hands on me, Maitreya.

MAITREYA Who? This one?

RADANIKA Yes.

MAITREYA Sir, even a worm will turn—and I, I am a Brahmin! (*Clenches and raises his fist, miming a staff.*) This stick of mine is crooked, sir, but it's still good enough to crack a skull or two!

MAITREYA *places the flickering candle on the ground; a* STAGE-HAND *whisks it out of sight. As if holding the staff in both hands,* MAITREYA *turns on the men.*

31

COURTIER   O great Brahmin, please, please . . .

MAITREYA   This can't be the one. (*He turns to* SANSTHANAKA.) You are the man. Ha! The king's own brother-in-law! Ha! Sansthanaka, you coward! You damned sex fiend! Don't you know that Charudatta is the finest citizen of Ujjain? And you break into his house! And you lay hands on his servant! You idiot, don't you know that poverty isn't a crime—not yet, at least—that there are still plenty of rich rascals around?

COURTIER (*embarrassed*)   Sir, we had no idea. . . . We're sorry. It's a case of mistaken identity. We were looking for a girl——

MAITREYA (*angrily*)   And you found her?

COURTIER   Oh, no. No. It was a girl that can take care of herself that we were looking for, and now it seems that we have insulted her in the process. (*He points to* RADANIKA.) We didn't mean to. Believe us, we're terribly sorry. (*He drops his sword and falls at* MAITREYA'S *feet.*)

MAITREYA   I see that you at least have sense. It's all right—you may rise. I did not know you when I abused you. I too am sorry.

SANSTHANAKA   This is intolerable! Why should you slobber in front of this cardboard man and join your palms and fall at his feet?

COURTIER   Fear.

SANSTHANAKA   Of what?

COURTIER   Of Charudatta's virtue.

SANSTHANAKA   Fine virtue, that! Why, you can't find a crumb to eat in his house!

COURTIER   Come, let us go.

SANSTHANAKA   Without Vasantasena?

COURTIER   She isn't here.

SANSTHANAKA   I shall not go without her.

COURTIER   May I remind you of a wise saying? Hold an elephant with a chain, a horse with a bridle, a woman with love. Let's go.

SANSTHANAKA   You may go, but I'm not going.

COURTIER   Very well. (*He leaves.*)

SANSTHANAKA   Good riddance! (*He speaks to* MAITREYA.) Now, you hairless lump of holiness, let's see you bow; let's see you bow to us.

MAITREYA   We are bowed down already.

SANSTHANAKA   And who has been bowing you down?

MAITREYA   Fate.

SANSTHANAKA   All right, then, stand up, stand up.

MAITREYA   We will.

SANSTHANAKA   When?

MAITREYA   When Fate is kind enough.

SANSTHANAKA   What a crybaby!

MAITREYA   We are crying.

SANSTHANAKA   Why?

MAITREYA   We are poor.

SANSTHANAKA   Then laugh, you fool, laugh.

MAITREYA   We will.

SANSTHANAKA   When?

MAITREYA   When Charudatta is rich again.

SANSTHANAKA   In the meantime, then, take this message from me to Charudatta. Tell him: "A common slut, by the name of Vasantasena, saw you in the garden of the temple of Kamadeva and lost her heart to you; that is, she fell in love with you. When we tried to set her right, using a bit of persuasion, she slipped in and took shelter in your house. The point is this: if you give her up unconditionally, then you have my best regards. If you don't, you are my enemy, and God help you!"

See that you break this news to him politely but firmly—and *distinctly*. If you swallow a word or two, I'll chew your head off with my own teeth—like this—like a nut cracked in a door hinge.

MAITREYA   He will get your message.

SANSTHANAKA   (*to the* SERVANT)   Has the courtier really left?

SERVANT   Yes, sir.

SANSTHANAKA   We must be off, too.

SERVANT Your sword, sir.
SANSTHANAKA Oh, yes, my sword. You carry it.
SERVANT Your sword, sir. Take it.
SANSTHANAKA *(taking the sword by the wrong end)* My sword sleeps in its sheath on my shoulder.

They both stride off.

MAITREYA Radanika, there's no need to tell Charudatta about this incident. This will make him feel bad.
RADANIKA I won't say a word to him, sir.
MAITREYA Good.

They move along the passage, circling the stage until they return to the place where CHARUDATTA's *door is imagined to be. The lights come up on center stage.* CHARUDATTA *is standing behind* VASANTASENA, *who keeps her face hidden.*

CHARUDATTA Radanika, it's time you brought the boy in. It gets quite chilly at this hour. Cover him with this shawl. *(He gives her his shawl.)*
VASANTASENA *(aside)* He thinks I'm the servant girl. *(She takes the shawl. Its fragrance strikes her.)* Such sweetness! He isn't a *complete* saint yet. *(She puts the shawl on her shoulders.)*
CHARUDATTA Radanika, bring the boy home.
VASANTASENA *(aside)* If only I had the right to!
CHARUDATTA You don't answer, Radanika?

MAITREYA and RADANIKA reach the steps indicating the door. MAITREYA mimes lifting the latch and opening the door. They step inside.

RADANIKA Did you call, sir?
CHARUDATTA But . . . then who is this lady? How shameful of me to be so familiar. . . . My shawl . . .

34

VASANTASENA (*aside*) How wonderful!

CHARUDATTA She's half in shadow, a slice of moon among autumn clouds. No, I mustn't—how dare I speak like this? She must be someone's wife.

MAITREYA (*recognizing her*) Not someone's wife, sir. She is Vasantasena, who fell in love with you when she saw you in the temple of Kamadeva. (CHARUDATTA *reacts with surprise.*) Sir, the king's brother-in-law sends a message.

CHARUDATTA To me?

MAITREYA He says: "A common slut, by the name of Vasantasena, saw you in the garden of the temple of Kamadeva and lost her heart to you; that is, she fell in love with you. When we tried to set her right, using a bit of persuasion——"

VASANTASENA (*aside*) "Set her right, using a bit of persuasion." Well put!

MAITREYA "——she slipped in and took shelter in your house. The point is this: if you give her up unconditionally, then you have my best regards. If you don't, you are my enemy, and God help you!"

CHARUDATTA What a remarkable woman she must be! Money has no fascination for her. She told him to be off; for me, she has gracious silence. Lady, I am sorry, mistaking you for my servant.

VASANTASENA Oh, sir, it is I who should be sorry, walking into your house, an uninvited guest. (*Aside.*) He is gracious. He is good. But I mustn't take advantage of his goodness—I have no right. Sir, I thank you deeply for your kindness and hope you will not mind if I leave these jewels here. They were trying to rob me when I ran in.

CHARUDATTA This poor house does not deserve such a precious trust.

VASANTASENA Sir, it is not houses we trust, but men.

CHARUDATTA Maitreya, take these jewels.

VASANTASENA Thank you very much. (*She takes off her jewelry and hands it to him.*)

The Toy Cart

MAITREYA (*taking it*) Thank *you.*
CHARUDATTA They aren't for you!
MAITREYA (*aside*) They're for thieves, I suppose.

A STAGEHAND *has placed a small jewel box on the floor of the room a few moments before; into the box* MAITREYA *places the jewels.*

CHARUDATTA (*to* VASANTASENA) You may have them again whenever you want them.
VASANTASENA I should be grateful, sir, if you could send an escort with me.
CHARUDATTA See her safely home, Maitreya.
MAITREYA You are the best man for that, sir: a fine handsome escort for a graceful lady. I'm a miserable Brahmin, and a poor one; they'll yap at me in the market place, as dogs snap at an elephant.
CHARUDATTA Very well, I'll go with her. Have torches lighted; I don't want any trouble on the way.
MAITREYA Hey, Vardhamanaka! (*A* SERVANT *comes quickly to center stage.*) Light the torches.
VARDHAMANAKA Without oil, sir?
MAITREYA You're right. Torches are like courtesans—they don't give you warmth unless you feed them.
CHARUDATTA Never mind; we'll do without the torches. The moonlight will do. (*The* SERVANT *slips away unobtrusively.* MAITREYA *mimes opening the door.* CHARUDATTA *crosses over the threshold and goes down the steps onto the passage, followed first by* VASANTASENA, *then* RADANIKA, *and last* MAITREYA, *who mimes closing the door and latching it. They walk slowly around the passage.*) Look at its crystal light falling like milk on marshes. (*They reach steps representing* VASANTASENA's *door and halt.* CHARUDATTA *turns to* VASANTASENA *and gestures toward the door.*) Here you are, Vasantasena. (*She looks at him tenderly.* RADANIKA *mimes open-*

36

ing the door. The two women go up the steps, over the threshold, and into the room.) Now, Maitreya, shall we turn back? There's not a light on the road now, not a creature stirring. Only the watchman. Let's go home. See that you guard this gold box well at night. Vardhamanaka will keep her eye on it during the day.

MAITREYA   Yes, sir.

They go out of sight down one of the exits. The lights on the passage dim. A STAGEHAND *removes the jewel box and spreads a bright cloth over the stool.* VASANTASENA *sits on it.* RADANIKA *slips offstage.* MADANIKA, *a maid to* VASANTASENA, *enters and sits on the floor beside her mistress.*

Act Two

VASANTASENA's *house. The lights come up on center stage.* VASANTASENA *is painting an imaginary picture. A* MAID, *wearing a sari, enters.*

MAID   Here is a message from your mother. But where is my mistress? (*She looks about her.*) Oh, there! Painting a picture—and lost in her painting.

VASANTASENA   Well, my girl, did you——

MAID   Did I what? Why, mistress, you didn't ask me to do anything.

VASANTASENA   I didn't?

MAID   No. And now you ask, "Well, my girl, did you . . . ?"

VASANTASENA (*confused*)   I did? Yes, I guess I did.

MAID (*approaching*)   Mistress, your mother would like to have you come over today for worship.

VASANTASENA Tell her, my girl, that today I can't. A Brahmin can take my place.

MAID Yes, mistress.

The MAID *exits.* MADANIKA *rises and asks questions drawing out the hidden thoughts of her mistress. She plays this scene mischievously, acting out in exaggerated miming most of her lines as she walks across and around her mistress, at times clasping her breast out of joy and at times feigning ignorance and surprise.*

MADANIKA Please don't be offended—it isn't impertinence but affection that makes me ask—but whatever did you mean just now?

VASANTASENA Madanika, tell me frankly: how do I strike you?

MADANIKA Well, you're certainly very absent-minded. I think you must be in love.

VASANTASENA And so I am. You're a pretty good judge of feelings, I see.

MADANIKA Oh, I'm so happy! The god of love spares no one —and he likes them young! Is it a king you worship? Or a courtier?

VASANTASENA I do not worship, Madanika. I am in love.

MADANIKA Is he a Brahmin—young, pious, brilliant?

VASANTASENA A Brahmin should be worshiped, not loved.

MADANIKA A merchant then—rich, well established, much traveled?

VASANTASENA A merchant is always away, always doing business in foreign lands. Love a merchant? Why, I'd die of loneliness.

MADANIKA Not a king. Not a courtier. Not a Brahmin. Not even a merchant. I give up.

VASANTASENA Oh, Madanika, you went with me to the garden of the temple of Kamadeva.

MADANIKA Yes.

VASANTASENA Then why do you ask? As if you knew nothing!

MADANIKA   I have it! The man who later helped you when you were being pursued.

VASANTASENA   His name?

MADANIKA   Why, he lives just a stone's throw from here!

VASANTASENA   But his name, his name?

MADANIKA   A good name: Charudatta.

VASANTASENA (*happily*)   Yes, you're right, Madanika.

MADANIKA   But they say he's poor.

VASANTASENA   I love him anyway. And now at least no one can say that it was for his money that I ran after him.

MADANIKA   But butterflies don't light on empty flowers, mistress.

VASANTASENA   That's why they're called butterflies.

MADANIKA   If you love him, then why not at least visit him?

VASANTASENA   I will. All in good time. I have a plan. But if something happens . . . It's not easy at all. But we'll see. We'll manage.

MADANIKA   So that's why you left your jewels with him?

VASANTASENA   What a clever girl you are, Madanika!

VASANTASENA *and* MADANIKA *leave. The* STAGEHAND *whisks away the silk embroidered piece from the stool, leaving it a rough wooden hexagon. It now represents the ruined temple for the* MASSEUR *to take shelter in.*

VOICE OFFSTAGE   Hey! Hey! What about my ten pieces of gold, eh? Stop him! That dirty chiseling gambler! Stop, you! Stop!

The MASSEUR *enters running and speaks his lines as he circles around the center platform on the passage.*

MASSEUR   Damn gamblers! And damn gambling! Aces and deuces and pocket flippers! Bastards! But did I give them the slip? The moment the keeper turned his back! (*Stops and looks around.*) Whew? So here I am, running like mad, but now what's the next stop? The keeper and his gambling friend are close behind. (*Runs. Stops by steps.*) Aha, a deserted temple. Perhaps I could become a temple god, yes?

With comic gestures he backs up the steps to center stage. He steps onto the stool as if into the niche reserved for the deity, hands held rigid at the sides, eyes popping. MATHURA *and a* GAMBLER *enter running. They circle the passage, cursing and shouting.*

MATHURA   Ten pieces of gold that massage-man owes us, and he's skedaddled! Stop the bastard! There he goes.

GAMBLER   You may hide yourself in hell, friend, but we'll fish you out, never fear.

MATHURA   You two-timing crook, you double-crosser of honest Mahura! I can hear you, your frightened steps; you're trembling with fear; you're stumbling. Drop dead, you rascal, you blackener of your family's name!

Panting, they stop by the steps where the MASSEUR *entered the temple. They examine the ground.*

GAMBLER   His footprints stop here.

MATHURA   Ha, they turn, they turn back, and—and this temple has no idol. (*He reflects.*) The swine, he walked backward into the temple with his feet facing front.

GAMBLER   After him!

MATHURA   Ha!

They enter the temple and look around, at first using just sign language. Then they speak.

GAMBLER   Would you say this idol was made of wood?

MATHURA   No, stone, I think. (*He gives the "idol" a push; it teeters comically.*) Who cares? Well, the masseur's gone. Say, shall we have a little game?

The GAMBLER *nods. First one, then the other, mimes shaking and rolling dice. They blow on their hands and imitate the sounds of dice clicking.*

MASSEUR (*fascinated, aside*) It's like the sound of a drum to a king without a kingdom, the rattle of dice to a man without a stake. Fascinating. I know it's bad. To gamble is to fall into ruin. But it's fascinating. The rattle of dice—ah, it's a koel's song.

GAMBLER My turn!

MATHURA No, mine!

MASSEUR (*jumping down out of the niche*) No, no, mine!

GAMBLER We have him.

MATHURA (*seizing him*) My little pet! And what about those ten pieces of gold?

MASSEUR I'll pay.

MATHURA Cough up, cough up! Now!

MASSEUR I'll pay. Give me a few days.

MATHURA No! Now!

MASSEUR Let go my head!

He falls to the ground. They beat him up.

MATHURA Ten pieces! Ten solid pieces of gold!

MASSEUR (*getting painfully to his feet*) Sir, sir! (*He speaks worriedly.*) I just haven't got the money. You must give me time. How can I pay this minute?

MATHURA A pledge!

MASSEUR Oh, all right, all right. (*He draws the* GAMBLER *to him.*) Let me off half, and I'll give you half. All right?

GAMBLER Suits me.

MASSEUR (*drawing* MATHURA *to him*) I'll give you my word I'll pay you half. Let me off half, won't you?

MATHURA Suits me.

MASSEUR (*to the* GAMBLER) You let me off five gold pieces?

GAMBLER   That's what I said.

MASSEUR (*to* MATHURA)   And you let me off five?

MATHURA   Suits me.

MASSEUR   Well, that's that. Be seeing you. (*He starts to leave.*)

MATHURA   Hey, not so fast, friend! Where's my ten pieces?

MASSEUR   What's wrong? You let me off half, five pieces; and *you* let me off half, five pieces. That's ten pieces. And that's that.

MATHURA   Ve-ry funny! Look here, friend, my name's Mathura, and no free-and-easy tricks get by with me, see? I want my ten pieces, and I want them *now!*

MASSEUR   I haven't got ten.

MATHURA   Then sell your father for ten pieces.

MASSEUR   I have no father.

MATHURA   Sell your mother, then.

MASSEUR   I have no mother.

MATHURA   Sell yourself.

MASSEUR   Whatever you say. All right, take me to the main street.

MATHURA   You go in front.

The MASSEUR *walks around the passage, hawking his own sale. The others follow.*

MASSEUR   Here we go. Hey! Hey! For sale! A bargain! Ten gold pieces for this excellent masseur! (*A* PASSER-BY *enters. The* MASSEUR *stops him.*) Hey! What can I do? What *can't* I do? I'll keep house for you. (*The* PASSER-BY *brushes on. To the two men.*) No go. (*Another* PASSER-BY *enters. He stops him.*) Hey! Ten gold pieces for me. No? (*The man shrugs and exits.*) No. Bah! Ah, Charudatta is no longer my patron. He's poor, so I'm poor. And no one wants me.

MATHURA   Come on, cough up, cough up.

The MASSEUR *breaks away and runs around the passage, pur-*

*sued by the two men. He rushes into the temple, where they
pull him to the ground.*

MASSEUR But I haven't *got* ten pieces. Help! Murder! Hey,
help! Help! Hey!

*They catch him by the neck, push him down on the wooden
hexagon, and kneel on both sides, pinning him down forcibly
so that his wailing is smothered. The three freeze in this pose
as* DARDURAKA *enters.* DARDURAKA *walks the passage while speaking his lines to the audience, mocking his own state.*

DARDURAKA A gambler is a king without a crown. Nothing to
lose, everything to spend: servants, money, wife, friends—
won, kept, and lost at the gambling table. A throw of three
took my money . . . the deuce took my health . . . the ace
threw me out in the street. . . . (*By steps, sees inside temple.*)
Oh, there's Mathura. Well, this shawl should help to hide me.
(*He examines it.*) No, it's threadbare stuff; too many holes—
big ones. (*He folds it up again and puts it under his arm.*) But
who cares, anyway? What can he do? He can't eat me.
(*Stealthily mounts steps.*)

MATHURA (*still addressing the* MASSEUR) Cough up!

MASSEUR I told you: I haven't got the money.

DARDURAKA (*aside*) What's going on here? (*He addresses an
imaginary spectator.*) What's that you said, sir? "Mathura's
beating up the masseur"? Well, let's see. (*He steps forward.*)
Poor man, he's been beaten black and blue! Poor fellow, what
has he to do with gambling? Oh, hello, Mathura. What do I
see here?

MATHURA You see a swine who owes me ten gold pieces.

DARDURAKA Only ten?

MATHURA (*pulling* DARDURAKA's *tattered shawl from under his
arm*) "Only ten?" Look who's talking! The man with the
threadbare shawl!

43

DARDURAKA   Mathura, my foolish friend, haven't you seen me
risk ten gold pieces a thousand times? If a man has money,
should he lug it around in his pockets? But you, you foolish
wretch, you're ready to knock out this poor fellow's five senses
for ten pieces.

MATHURA   Ten pieces may be "only" ten pieces to you, but to
me they're ten solid-gold coins.

DARDURAKA   Good. Good. So why not give him ten solid-gold
coins, set him free, and let him gamble away?

MATHURA   Are you mad?

DARDURAKA   If he wins, he'll pay you back.

MATHURA   And if he loses?

DARDURAKA   Then he won't pay you back.

MATHURA   Bloody clever, aren't you? Why don't *you* give him
ten pieces? Look, my name is Mathura, and I'm a crook. I
play a crooked game—I play it well—and everyone knows it.
But you don't frighten me, you lily-livered bastard.

DARDURAKA   Who's a bastard?

MATHURA   *You* are!

DARDURAKA   Your father was a bigger bastard!

MATHURA   Why, you son-of-a-dog, aren't you a gambler yourself?

DARDURAKA   Me? A gambler?

MATHURA   (*turning to the* MASSEUR *and starting to drag him by
the hair*)   Come on, cough up.

DARDURAKA   Stop! No one's going to lay hands on him while
I'm here!

MATHURA, *regardless, punches the* MASSEUR *on the nose. The*
MASSEUR *mimes a bleeding nose, then collapses.* DARDURAKA *steps
in and scuffles with* MATHURA.

MATHURA   You damned son-of-a-dog! I'll get you for this!

DARDURAKA   You fool! Suppose I say you beat me up on the
road as I was quietly passing by? You'll see in court tomorrow
if they let you off so easily.

MATHURA All right, we shall see, we shall see.

DARDURAKA You will? And how will you see?

MATHURA (*thrusting his face in* DARDURAKA's *and opening his eyes wide*) Like this. Does that satisfy you?

DARDURAKA *stoops and mimes picking up a handful of dust. He throws it into* MATHURA'S *eyes;* MATHURA *flinches and falls back.* DARDURAKA *makes signs to the* MASSEUR *to escape. The* MASSEUR *scrambles up and runs off.*

DARDURAKA This fellow has a lot of influence around here; I'd better scoot too.

The two GAMBLERS *exit, pursuing the* MASSEUR *around the passage and off.* DARDURAKA *walks off quickly.* VASANTASENA *and* MADANIKA *enter from the direction they exited.* MADANIKA *spreads the embroidered silk piece on the stool, and the courtesan sits.* MADANIKA *sits in her place on the floor, near her. The* MASSEUR *enters running, cuts a circle around the stage on the passage, and stops in front of the steps facing the* COURTESAN.

MASSEUR This house is open. (*He enters, going up the steps, and sees* VASANTASENA.) Please help me. Please help me.

VASANTASENA Don't be afraid—you are safe here. Madanika, shut the door. (*She mimes doing so.*) What are you afraid of?

MASSEUR I owe a man some money.

VASANTASENA Madanika, open the door.

MASSEUR (*aside*) She isn't afraid of creditors. Little does she know. But it's a good proverb that says a man must face the music—meaning that I'll have to face it.

MATHURA *and the* GAMBLER *rush into the passage, on the side of the stage opposite the steps leading to* VASANTASENA's *house.*

MATHURA (*rubbing his eyes*) Cough up, cough up!

GAMBLER He isn't here. While you two were scuffling, the swine scuttled off.

MATHURA I gave him a punch on the nose, though, and he's bleeding. He won't get far. We'll track him down. Look, here's blood.

They follow the imaginary trail of blood around the passage.

GAMBLER He's in here.

They stop at VASANTASENA's *door.*

MATHURA Good-bye, ten pieces. My ten gold pieces, good-bye.
GAMBLER Let's go file a complaint in court.
MATHURA And have the bird fly away while we're gone? Not me! I'm sitting tight till the bastard coughs up.

The lights dim on the passage and the two men freeze. Inside VASANTASENA *makes a sign to* MADANIKA.

MADANIKA Sir, my mistress wishes to know where you come from, who you are, why you are here, and what you are really afraid of.
MASSEUR Well, I was born in Pataliputra, the son of a householder. I'm a masseur.
VASANTASENA A delicate, pleasant art, sir.
MASSEUR I learned it very well, madam, so now it's just routine work.
MADANIKA I see. Go on.
MASSEUR While with my father, madam, I used to hear visitors tell stories of other lands, and I wanted to see things for myself. So I came to the city and became masseur to a first-class gentleman, a model of good manners and handsomer than I can say. He was quick to give away money and bore insults in silence, forgiving his worst enemy—in short, such a fine man that he seemed to be caring for the whole world.

MADANIKA Is there such a man in Ujjain?
VASANTASENA I know him. My heart tells me.
MADANIKA Go on.
MASSEUR He gave so freely, so liberally, that——
VASANTASENA ——he hasn't anything left.
MASSEUR How did you guess? Did I——
VASANTASENA I only had to put two and two together. Goodness and money go together very seldom. But you can't call a good man *poor*; such a man is richer than anyone else.
MADANIKA And his name?
MASSEUR Who hasn't heard of him? Who hasn't heard of the moon? His name is Charudatta. He lives very near here.
VASANTASENA (*standing up, looking very happy*) A fan, Madanika. Can't you see he's tired? Sit down, sir. There's no need to be formal.
MASSEUR (*aside*) All this at the mere mention of his name! God bless you, Charudatta! You really live; others merely pass time in the world. (*He falls at* VASANTASENA's *feet.*) Thank you, madam. Please sit down. I'm all right like this.
VASANTASENA But go on with your story.
MASSEUR Well, as I said, I was his masseur; but when he had no more money left, I took to gambling. And my luck was against me and I lost ten gold pieces.

The lights come up on the passage. MATHURA *pounds on the door.*

MATHURA I've been cheated! I've been robbed!
MASSEUR That's him, madam. Him and the other one. What shall I do?
VASANTASENA (*removing her bracelet and giving it to* MADANIKA) Give them this, Madanika, and say this gentleman sends it.
MADANIKA Yes, mistress.
MATHURA (*still shouting*) I've been robbed!

MADANIKA *goes down steps representing a side door, so that she comes onto the passage at the rear of the two men. She observes them and speaks to herself.*

MADANIKA   Such shouting and crying! Such muttering and anxiety! And the way their eyes are pinned to the front door! These must be the ones. (*Aloud.*) Good morning, sir.

They turn, surprised.

MATHURA   And good morning to you.

MADANIKA   Which of you gentlemen is the chief gambler?

MATHURA   Me, my pretty one. But it won't do. No pouting lips at me, no sweet words. Don't give me the come-hither, my girl. I have no money.

MADANIKA   Gamblers don't talk like that. Is there someone who owes you money?

MATHURA   Yes, ten gold pieces. Why?

MADANIKA   My mistress sends this—no, *he* sends this, by way of payment.

MATHURA   (*grabbing the bracelet*)   Aha! Tell him we're quits. And tell him to drop in again whenever he wants some fun.

The men walk off. MADANIKA *goes back in and closes the door. The lights dim on the passage.*

MADANIKA   They've gone, looking very pleased.

VASANTASENA   Now, sir, you may go safely.

MASSEUR   If I can be of any help to you, madam . . .

VASANTASENA   You can be of more help to the man for whom you were working and thanks to whom you learned your art.

MASSEUR   (*aside*)   A neat way of saying, "No, thanks." (*Aloud.*) Madam, my work brings me only disgrace. I'm going to become a Buddhist monk.

VASANTASENA   Don't do anything rash.

MASSEUR   My mind's made up. (*He starts to leave.*) When I gambled, everyone looked down on me. Now I can hold my head high and walk freely in the streets. (*Loud shouts are heard offstage.*) What's up now? (*He listens again.*) What! The royal hunting-elephant has broken loose? Ha! What fun! I must go see the mad beast! Oops!—I nearly forgot. I'd decided to become a monk. It won't do. (*Lights come up on the passage as he exits chanting a Buddhist hymn.*)

> *Bhuddam Sharanam Gachhami . . .*
> *Dharmam Sharanam Gachhami . . .*
> *Sharanam Gachhami. . . .*

VASANTASENA Quick, Madanika, to the balcony! Perhaps we'll catch a glimpse of the scene! Quick!

They go off in the same direction as the MASSEUR. *The lights dim slightly center stage. A* STAGEHAND *removes the stool.*

Act Three

VARDHAMANAKA, CHARUDATTA's *servant, enters with grass mats under his arm. He goes to center stage as the lights come up and spreads the mats on the floor. A* STAGEHAND *places a lighted candle on the floor.*

VARDHAMANAKA A good, kind master is the man for me. Who cares if he is poor? My master is still at the concert, and it's not quite midnight yet, so there's still time before he returns. I think I'll take a little snooze. (*He lies on the mats and sleeps.*)

CHARUDATTA *and* MAITREYA *enter and walk around the passage toward the house.*

49

MAITREYA   Yes, yes, yes. It is time we were home.

CHARUDATTA   Oh, Rebhila sang exquisitely, didn't he?

MAITREYA   Well, if you must know, there are two things I can't stand: one is a woman reading Sanskrit aloud, and the other is a man trying to sing in a soft key. When a woman reads Sanskrit, all you get is "moosh, moosh, moosh," as if a cow were sneezing. And when a man tries singing softly, he's like a priest chanting through his nose. I tell you, it's not pleasant at all.

CHARUDATTA   You are hard to please. But Rebhila sang exquisitely this evening. . . .
>   It seemed that my own love was singing.
>   I can hear it even as I walk with you now—
>   I'll never forget it.

MAITREYA   Fine, fine. But let's get home. Even the street dogs are fast asleep. The moon has set, leaving the world to pitch-darkness. (*They stop by the steps.*) Well, here we are. Vardhamanaka, wake up! Open the door!

VARDHAMANAKA   (*wakes up*)   That's Maitreya's voice! They're back. (*He mimes lifting the latch and opening the door.*) Sir, the couch is ready.

MAITREYA   (*entering*)   Call Radanika; we need water for our feet.

CHARUDATTA   (*entering*)   Let her sleep. Why disturb her now?

VARDHAMANAKA   I'll get the water, Maitreya, and you can wash his feet.

MAITREYA   (*losing his temper*)   The impertinent slave! He will bring the water, and I—a Brahmin—must wash the feet!

CHARUDATTA   Oh, come, Maitreya, you get the water and he'll wash my feet if that suits you better.

VARDHAMANAKA   Gladly. Yes, Maitreya, you bring the water.

MAITREYA *circles the stage, bends over, picks up an imaginary pot of water, and brings it to* VARDHAMANAKA, *who washes* CHARUDATTA's *feet and then starts to move away. A* STAGEHAND *places the jewel box beside* VARDHAMANAKA.

CHARUDATTA And now, Vardhamanaka, what about washing the Brahmin's feet?

MAITREYA Don't bother. It's water wasted, because I shall be going out again, trudging along like a dirty donkey.

VARDHAMANAKA But you are a Brahmin, Maitreya.

MAITREYA Yes, sir. I am a Brahmin. I am a Brahmin among Brahmins, like a boa constrictor among snakes.

VARDHAMANAKA Then I must wash your feet. (*He mimes washing his feet.*) And here's the golden box, which I look after during the day. It's night now, so it's your turn.

He picks up the box, gives it to MAITREYA, *and leaves. Lights dim on the passage.*

MAITREYA The golden box! Let me just put it away inside. (*Starts to go.*)

CHARUDATTA Of course not. It has been left in our care. Look after it, as a good Brahmin should. It must be returned safely to its owner. (*He lies down on a mat.*) Such sweetness!

MAITREYA Going off to sleep?

CHARUDATTA Yes, I hope so. Let us sleep.

MAITREYA *wraps the box carefully in a cloth and tucks it under his arm. He lies down with his back to* CHARUDATTA. *Both go to sleep and begin to snore gently.* SHARVILAKA *creeps silently along the dimly lighted passage. He is the lover of* MADANIKA. *He walks as if parting shrubs of the garden outside the house.*

SHARVILAKA I've managed to slip through. (*He looks up.*) The moon has set. Night's a good mother to people like me, who work in the dark. I've scaled the garden wall all right and got in; now for the house. They call it a crime, this slinking in under cover of darkness. We're crooks, they say. All right, I'd sooner be a crook than an exploited slave. But now, how do I get in? (*Mimes feeling a wall.*) On which side is the wall dampest—that will make the least noise. Where can I make a hole that I can cover up later? (*Feels his way along the wall, moving along the passage.*) Where is the brickwork old and crumbling? How do I get in so that no woman spots me? And where's the swag? That's what the textbook says. (*Pokes at the bricks about waist high.*) This spot seems a bit weak. It's been exposed to the sun and rotted away. And here's a convenient rathole. (*Puts his arm clear through.*) Wonderful! O god of thieves, blessed sir! A thousand thanks! Sir, you advise four ways of breaking in. First for baked bricks—pull them out. Second for unbaked bricks—cut through them. Third for clay—soften it up by wetting. Fourth for wood— saw through it. Here we have baked bricks. So pull them out. Next, what shape shall I make the hole? Lotus, lake, half-moon, sun? Swastika, waterpot? The book says take your choice. The waterpot: that will look nice in this wall. Last night they complained I wasn't artistic: the hole, they said, should have been made with better taste. O god of thieves, blessed sir, thanks again. Thanks to my teacher, who taught me the whole bag of tricks. No one sees me, no sword finds me—damn, I've forgotten my tape. I hope this will do instead. (*He unties the cord from around his neck.*) The sacred thread's a useful thing to a Brahmin. It's just the thing to measure walls; it's handy to pull up jewelry, to pick locks; and if a snake bites, it's first-class for first aid. But let's get going. First, measure the wall. Then, out with the bricks. (*He mimes removing bricks and stacking them.*) One still left. Here it goes. (*He peeps through the hole.*) I see a light, a candle. The light floods the darkness like pure gold. (*He takes out and stacks more bricks.*) Now in I go. No, wait; first, the "feeler." That's what the book says. (*He puts his hand through and gropes about.*) All clear. A thousand thanks, blessed sir. (*He crawls through, making a scraping sound as his clothes catch. He stands and looks.*) Two men sleeping. I'd better open the front door: it helps in an emergency. (*He tiptoes over and mimes opening the door. He imitates the squeak of rusty hinges.*) How it creaks! Everything's rusty here. A little water. (*He sees the jug and mimes picking it up. He sprinkles water on the door hinges.*) Not too much—it might make a splash on the floor. (*He puts his back against the door and carefully eases it open.*) That's done. Now, are these two really out or just faking? (*He takes the candle and passes it close over their faces.*) Fast asleep. (*He looks around.*) What's this? A drum . . . a lute . . . pipes . . . (*He makes the sound of each instrument as he mentions its name.*) Books . . . Hell, have I got into the house of a poet? A dancer? I thought he was a big shot. I don't steal from beggars. Is he really poor or is he just hiding his money? Poor fellow. What am I doing here, then?

MAITREYA (*in his sleep, rolls over in the direction the* THIEF *entered*) I see a hole in the wall. I see a thief. Here, you'd better keep the golden box. (*Pushes box toward* CHARU-DATTA.)

SHARVILAKA Has he seen me? Is he making fun of me? Then he dies, the swine! (*He comes close to* MAITREYA *and studies him.*) No, he's just babbling in his sleep. What's this? Something wrapped in a towel. How about taking it? No, it wouldn't be right. He's a poor man; why make him even poorer? (*He starts to move away.*)

MAITREYA Take it, take it away, for the sake of a sacred cow, for the sake of a Brahmin!

SHARVILAKA Well, if it's come to cows and Brahmins, then it's all right for me to take it. Thanks, Brahmin, I'll take the box. (*Grasps box.*)

MAITREYA (*pulls box back*) Oh, how cold your fingers are!

SHARVILAKA Idiot of a thief that I am! The water chilled them. I'll warm them. (*He rubs them on his thigh, then takes the box.*)

MAITREYA You have it safe?

SHARVILAKA Yes, Brahmin, I have it.

MAITREYA Good. Now, like a merchant who's sold all his horses, I can sleep in peace. (*Rolls over again.*)

SHARVILAKA Sleep, sir, sleep a thousand years. Oh, what a shameful thing to do—and all for the sake of love. To ruin this good Brahmin for the sake of Madanika! I hate it, but I do it. And now to Vasantasena's house to buy Madanika's freedom! (*He listens.*) Footsteps! (RADANIKA *enters and goes around the passage during the following lines.*) Who can it be? Shall I stand motionless and let him pass? Bah, what do I care about watchmen? I crawl like a cat, run like a deer, pounce like a hawk, twist like a snake, and yowl like a dog! I'm a lamp, a house, a boat, a snake, a rock.

SHARVILAKA *sidles up beside the door, holding himself ready to leap on the intruder.* RADANIKA *lifts the latch, opens the door, and enters.*

RADANIKA Where is Vardhamanaka? He was sleeping outside, I know, but he isn't there now. I must find Maitreya.

SHARVILAKA (*starts to stab her, then stops*) Just a girl! I'm safe.

He mimes tucking the knife away and boldly makes for the door. As he slips out and off down the passage, RADANIKA *sees him and raises the alarm.*

RADANIKA Help! A thief! Stop, thief! He's cut through the wall. There he goes! Maitreya, wake up! (*Shakes him. Runs to the door.*) Where are you? A thief! There he goes, out the door!

MAITREYA What thief? What's all this nonsense?

RADANIKA Don't be silly. Help! Thief! Can't you see? There!

MAITREYA What? The door's open! Help! (*Calls out. Goes to* CHARUDATTA.) Charudatta, wake up! A thief broke in and he's escaped! Wake up!

CHARUDATTA I'm in no mood for jokes, Maitreya.

MAITREYA This is no joke. Look! (*Points to wall.*)

CHARUDATTA   Where? How did he get in?

MAITREYA   There.

CHARUDATTA   (*seeing the breach in the wall, goes over to it*)   But that's well done! A very neat bit of work. Just look: a few bricks from the top, more below. Why, this fellow is a genius.

MAITREYA   Either the man's new to this city and doesn't know how poor we are—for everyone in Ujjain knows there's nothing to steal in this house—or else he was a beginner just practicing.

CHARUDATTA   Very likely a stranger to this city. He probably didn't know about my poverty and thought that the house looked promising from the outside. How disappointed he must have been when he ran away. Poor fellow! He'll have to go round admitting to his friends, "I broke into a merchant's house—and found nothing!"

MAITREYA   Yes, he must have entered with high hopes—for a jewel box at least. (*He remembers his dream.*) A golden box! Thank goodness! You always call me a fool, don't you? "Maitreya, you know nothing!" "Maitreya, you're a baby!" Well, wasn't it brilliant of me to hand the golden box over to you in the middle of the night? If not, the thief would have walked off with it.

CHARUDATTA   The box? What are you talking about?

MAITREYA   No, no, I'm serious. I may be a fool, but I know when to joke and when not to.

CHARUDATTA   When did you give me the box?

MAITREYA   Don't you remember? When I said your fingers were cold?

CHARUDATTA   I don't know. You might have. (*He searches; then speaks in a cheerful tone.*) Well, thank you, Maitreya.

MAITREYA   Whatever for?

CHARUDATTA   The box *has* been stolen. At least, it isn't here.

MAITREYA   But why should I be thanked?

CHARUDATTA   Because at least the poor fellow didn't go away empty-handed.

MAITREYA But it's the box that we were supposed to keep in safe custody.

CHARUDATTA *That* box!

MAITREYA Oh, I'm sorry. But it is not *your* fault that a thief ran off with it.

CHARUDATTA (*recovering*) Maitreya, who will believe us? The poor man is always suspected—that's the way it is. Till now Fate was unkind only to my riches; now she is unkind to my good name.

MAITREYA What's to prevent us from saying that she never gave us the box? She never gave it; we never took it. There was no witness.

CHARUDATTA Tell a lie like that? Never. I will beg in the streets and pay off the entire amount of the box. It's a blot on my soul. (*Takes off his necklace.*) Thank goodness I have a few precious things left. Take this necklace to Vasantasena, Maitreya. Tell her we gambled away the golden box, forgetting it was hers, and that I send this necklace instead.

MAITREYA No, I can't. Are we going to give away this priceless sacred ornament for a silly box that a thief has decamped with? What did we get out of the box?

CHARUDATTA What does that matter? The box was left in our trust. You shall not return till you have given this necklace into her hands. Radanika, put those bricks back in place again.

CHARUDATTA, *followed by* MAITREYA, *goes through the door, down the passage, and off.* RADANIKA *rolls up the mats and follows them. The lights dim center stage. A* STAGEHAND *places the brightly covered stool center.* VASANTASENA *re-enters, sits;* MADANIKA *re-enters and sits on the floor near her.*

Act Four

VASANTASENA's *house. The lights come up.* VASANTASENA *mimes painting.*

VASANTASENA You think this resembles Charudatta? You really do?

MADANIKA Oh, yes.

VASANTASENA How can you tell?

MADANIKA From the way you look at it with so much love in your eyes.

VASANTASENA You're just being polite, as all we courtesans are.

MADANIKA But politeness can be true too, sometimes.

VASANTASENA Not with us, I'm afraid. We meet so many kinds of men that mostly we're reduced just to saying pretty things.

MADANIKA But you needn't have asked. The way you looked at the picture, it was obvious——

VASANTASENA Tell me, Madanika, do I behave strangely these days?

MADANIKA You're all right, mistress. Women understand one another pretty well.

A MAID *enters on the passage.*

MAID Another message from her mother. (*She looks toward the platform.*) Ah, there is my mistress, looking at a picture and talking to Madanika. (*Goes up steps to center stage.*) A carriage is waiting for you at the side door, mistress; and your mother wishes you would come.

VASANTASENA Is it Charudatta who sent the carriage?

MAID No, mistress. But the man who sent it has sent ten thousand gold pieces with it.

VASANTASENA   Who is it?

MAID   Sansthanaka, the king's brother-in-law.

VASANTASENA (*angrily*)   No. Go tell him I'm busy. And don't bother me again!

MAID   Forgive me, mistress. I was only bringing the message.

VASANTASENA   I'm not angry with you; I'm angry with the message.

MAID   But what news shall I take back to your mother?

VASANTASENA   Tell her, if she doesn't want me dead, to stop sending such messages.

VASANTASENA *walks in a small circle to the other side of the center platform, indicating she has gone into another room.* MADANIKA *follows.*

MAID   Yes, mistress. (*She leaves.*)

SHARVILAKA (*entering on passage in the opposite direction*)   Last night I worked wonders. But this morning I'm just a bundle of nerves. Who was that following me out there? Why was he chasing me? I didn't like the looks of him. Damn, a man's worst enemy is his own conscience. At least I did it for Madanika—that's some consolation. I made it a point to talk to no servants, and *no* women; and when the guards passed by, I stood as still as a doorpost. I had a busy time last night—a hundred little tricks.

VASANTASENA   Put this painting on the couch, and bring me my fan.

VASANTASENA *passes the imaginary painting to* MADANIKA, *who retraces her steps, carrying it into the previous room.*

SHARVILAKA   Vasantasena's house! (*Sees* MADANIKA *and calls.*) Madanika!

MADANIKA (*turning, startled*)   Oh, it's you, Sharvilaka! How nice to see you. Where have you been all this time?

SHARVILAKA   I'll tell you later.

He looks nervously about. She places the picture on the stool and goes out on the passage with him.

VASANTASENA Where has she gone? She *does* take her time. (*She mimes opening a window and looks out.*) There she is talking to a man. She looks completely lost in him. That must be the man who wants to buy her freedom.

MADANIKA Why do you look like that, Sharvilaka? What's wrong?

SHARVILAKA Can you keep a secret? Are you sure we're alone?

MADANIKA Absolutely alone.

VASANTASENA (*aside*) A secret? I shouldn't be listening.

SHARVILAKA Tell me, Madanika, if I ask Vasantasena to set you free, what price will she demand?

VASANTASENA (*aside*) If it concerns me, there's no harm in listening.

MADANIKA She's often said that if she had her way, she'd free all of us without asking anything. But where have you managed to lay hands on so much money that you can buy my freedom?

SHARVILAKA I am poor. I am in love. So last night I did something I shouldn't have done.

VASANTASENA (*aside*) He looks too happy to have a crime on his conscience.

MADANIKA Sharvilaka, you did it for *me*? You risked both for *me*?

SHARVILAKA Both what?

MADANIKA Your life and your good name.

SHARVILAKA Oh, it was nothing. Fortune favors the brave.

MADANIKA I know you couldn't have done anything very bad —even for my sake—could you?

SHARVILAKA Well, I didn't steal from a woman. I may be a thief, but I know the difference between right and wrong. Tell Vasantasena these jewels are for her.

MADANIKA Jewels? And not to be worn by women? Let me see them.

SHARVILAKA   Here. (*He brings them out and shows them uneasily.*)

MADANIKA   Haven't I seen these before somewhere? Where did you get them?

SHARVILAKA   That's my business. Don't ask me questions.

MADANIKA (*angrily*)   If you love me, why are you afraid to tell me?

SHARVILAKA   All right, if you must know. . . . Last night, in the business quarter of the city, a man called Charudatta—— (VASANTASENA *and* MADANIKA *both faint.*) Madanika! What's the matter? Can't you hear me? Have I done wrong?

MADANIKA (*recovering*)   You fool! Tell me, did you hurt anyone? Did you kill anyone in the house where you stole these?

SHARVILAKA   I don't kill sleeping men. I harmed no one.

MADANIKA   Is that true?

SHARVILAKA   Of course.

MADANIKA (*recovering*)   Thank God!

SHARVILAKA (*jealously*)   What's going on here anyway, Madanika? I did it because I love you. You know my family commands respect: my virtue is of some worth. Is this all I get for the love and devotion I've shown for you—that you should love another man? Oh, I know all the tricks: a good man duped by a cunning courtesan. We're fools, fools, all of us who believe in women. A woman's a snake—don't trust her. Never love a woman. A woman will laugh and cry for money, and makes use of a man's trust as long as it suits her. Run, young man, if you value your purse and your good name. Oh, what a fool I've been! Charudatta, this time you shall die! (*Starts to rush off.*)

MADANIKA (*catching hold of him*)   What's come over you? You're behaving like a fool! (*She moves away from him, looking at the jewels.*)

SHARVILAKA   Who's a fool?

MADANIKA   These jewels belong to Vasantasena.

SHARVILAKA   They do?

MADANIKA   And she had left them with Charudatta.

SHARVILAKA   She had?

MADANIKA   And here's why. (*She whispers in his ear.*)

SHARVILAKA (*looking silly*)   Damn it, I didn't mean to rob *him* in order to free you.

VASANTASENA (*aside*)   I'm glad he's sorry.

SHARVILAKA   So what now, Madanika?

MADANIKA   You should know.

SHARVILAKA   I wish I did. Man learns only from books, but a woman is born with common sense.

MADANIKA   Well, I think you should give these jewels back to Charudatta.

SHARVILAKA   And go to jail?

MADANIKA   Did you ever hear of heat coming from the moon?

VASANTASENA (*aside*)   Thank you, Madanika.

SHARVILAKA   I'm not so much afraid of him, Madanika, as of myself. What made me do such a shameful thing? I'd feel so small having to face him. Can't you think of anything else?

MADANIKA   Well . . .

VASANTASENA (*aside*)   I should like to know, too.

MADANIKA   You can always say to my mistress that you're Charudatta's servant and return the jewels to her.

SHARVILAKA   How will that help?

MADANIKA   Then you're not a thief. Charudatta has lost nothing, for my mistress has her jewels.

SHARVILAKA   What! You rob me, a robber?

MADANIKA   And if you don't do as I say, you'll be a real robber.

VASANTASENA (*aside*)   I do admire you, Madanika. You're a good friend.

SHARVILAKA   Thanks for that advice. I was lost in darkness, and you came like the moon.

MADANIKA   Wait here. I'll go tell my mistress.

SHARVILAKA   Right.

MADANIKA (*enters the house and speaks to* VASANTASENA)   A Brahmin from Charudatta has come to see you.

VASANTASENA   How do you know he comes from Charudatta?
MADANIKA   I have my own ways of knowing, mistress.
VASANTASENA (*smiling*)   Naturally. Let him come in.
MADANIKA   Come in, Sharvilaka.

She escorts him in to VASANTASENA.

SHARVILAKA (*embarrassed*)   Charudatta sends greetings.
VASANTASENA   I am glad to receive them. You may sit.
SHARVILAKA   He says his house is insecure. So he returns this
box and hopes you will not mind. (*He gives it to* MADANIKA
and starts to leave.)
VASANTASENA   That was very thoughtful of him. Wait; I have
something for him.
SHARVILAKA (*aside*)   I didn't think of that. (*Aloud.*) What mes-
sage shall I take?
VASANTASENA   No message. Take Madanika.
SHARVILAKA   I don't understand.
VASANTASENA   You see, we had an agreement that the person
who returned the box would get Madanika as a present from
me on Charudatta's behalf. So take her, and thank Charudatta
for his kindness.
SHARVILAKA (*aside*)   She's seen through the game. Thank you,
Charudatta. (*Aloud.*) Thank you.
VASANTASENA (*calling*)   Is my carriage here?

A SERVANT *enters.*

SERVANT   Your carriage is ready, mistress.
VASANTASENA   You may go, Madanika. Use my carriage. Look
at me, my girl—and smile. That's better. And think of me
now and then.
MADANIKA (*sobbing*)   What shall I do? (*She falls at* VASANTA-
SENA's *feet.*)
VASANTASENA   Don't be silly, my girl. Stand up. *I* should honor
you now. Go. Everything's ready. But think of me.

SHARVILAKA How can I thank you, sweet lady? Bow to her, Madanika. She has given you the dignity of a wife.

SHARVILAKA *and* MADANIKA *bow to* VASANTASENA.

VOICE OFFSTAGE A proclamation by the governor! A proclamation by the governor! "To all citizens." Hear ye! "An astrologer has declared that the son of a cowherd, by the name of Aryaka, will be king. Therefore, King Palaka has thought fit to arrest him and put him in solitary confinement. There is nothing to fear. There is nothing to fear. This is a warning."

SHARVILAKA Aryaka, my friend, arrested! And I about to be married and to live happily ever after! No. A friend is in trouble. I must go to his aid.

MADANIKA Don't leave me now, my lord. At least take me first to the house of one of your friends, where I can stay safely.

VASANTASENA Leave her with me until you come back. She will live with me, waiting for you to return.

SHARVILAKA And so I will, my love.

MADANIKA Take care of yourself. I'll be waiting for you.

SHARVILAKA (*aside*) Now to work. First I must get in touch with Aryaka's friends—all of us who have suffered at the hands of this king and are ready to fight back. This is most illegal, most treacherous—the act of a spineless king. But we'll have you out, Aryaka, in no time!

He crosses swiftly out of the house and off. A MAID *enters, followed by* MAITREYA.

MAID (*seeing* VASANTASENA) Oh, what a lucky morning! A Brahmin from Charudatta brings you a message, mistress.

VASANTASENA Yes, isn't it lucky? Receive him respectfully, Madanika, and show him in to me.

VASANTASENA *turns and unobtrusively exits, leaving the center stage empty, as* MADANIKA *and the* MAID *go down the steps. They bow to* MAITREYA *and ceremoniously gesture for him to mount the steps.*

MAITREYA   I am a simple Brahmin and I don't pray much, but I go around with the prettiest ladies in town.
MAID *and* MADANIKA   This is the front door, sir.

They lead the way up the steps and he follows. He looks about, admiring the beauty of the first courtyard. As he speaks, the girls pantomime in graceful gestures the objects he describes.

MAITREYA   All spick and span, flowers on the threshold, the jasmine creeper swaying in the winds. The arch is of ivory. Beautiful? Lead on, girls.
MAID *and* MADANIKA   This is the second court, sir.

They move forward a few paces and indicate another gateway. He enters.

MAITREYA   Balconies white as seashells; golden stairs, dotted with gems; the stairs lead up to pearly windows. Lead on, girls.
MAID *and* MADANIKA   This is the third court, sir.

They move forward several steps.

MAITREYA   There are horses being groomed, and there's a monkey tied to a post like a thief, and over there an elephant breakfasting on huge balls of rice. Lead on, girls.
MAID *and* MADANIKA   This is the fourth court, sir.

They usher him ahead a few steps more.

MAITREYA   The gate is of gold and diamonds, the rest of sapphires; it sparkles like a rainbow. Jewelers at work, I see, with pearls, topazes, sapphires, emeralds, rubies, coral, and lapis lazuli. Some are setting rubies in gold; some are stringing pearls; some are polishing lapis lazuli, some coral. Betel leaves are served to courtesans and their lovers—flirting and laughter and drinking and merriment. Lead on, girls. (*They move ahead.*) Who is that, that overdressed man in silk, stumbling as he wanders about, his body covered with superfluous ornaments?

MAID The brother of my mistress, sir.

MAITREYA He must have done a lot of penance in his last birth to be so lucky in this! Yet he's not too happy, after all, poor fellow. And who is that lady with shoes on her oiled feet and wearing expensive silks?

MAID My mistress' mother.

MAITREYA I can hardly believe my eyes. Is this the house of a courtesan or the palace of the god of wealth? Lead on, girls.

MAID *and* MADANIKA This is the final court, sir.

MAITREYA Here is a girl plucking the vina; drums, cymbals, flutes. And here come the dancers. (*They have almost circled the stage. Six* DANCERS *come into the passage. They mount the platform and dance in classical* bharata natyam *style, their dazzling grace revealing the elegance of a courtesan's life.* MAITREYA *squats on a cushioned seat, happily watching the spectacle. When it is finished, he gets up and blesses them. The* DANCERS *leave.* MAID *and* MADANIKA *lead* MAITREYA *around the stage.* VASANTASENA *has re-entered and taken a seat on the stool.* MAITREYA *admires the scene.*) The asoka tree laden with fiery blossoms. Trees bent under the fruit. Perfect! Where is your mistress?

MADANIKA If you lowered your head, you would see her!

MAITREYA Ah, there! (*He approaches* VASANTASENA.) I bring you greetings, lady.

VASANTASENA Ah, Maitreya. Please make yourself comfortable. You are very welcome here.

MAITREYA Thank you.

The Toy Cart

VASANTASENA   I hope Charudatta is well.

MAITREYA   Very well, thank you.

VASANTASENA   Maitreya, do birds still find shelter under the gentle boughs of that excellent tree, whose leaves are virtues, whose roots are courage, whose flowers are honor, and whose fruit is goodness?

MAITREYA (*aside*)   A pretty sentence, that! (*Aloud.*) They do.

VASANTASENA   And what brings you here, Maitreya?

MAITREYA   This: Charudatta sends his greetings—(*He joins his palms.*)—and wishes——

VASANTASENA (*joining her palms*)   ——commands——

MAITREYA   He wishes me to report that he has lost the golden box in gambling, and the keeper has gone away on royal business.

VASANTASENA (*aside*)   He is too proud to admit that a thief stole it. I love him all the more.

MAITREYA   And he asks you to accept this pearl necklace in lieu of the lost box.

VASANTASENA (*aside*)   Shall I tell him the truth? (*She reflects, then speaks half aloud.*) No. Not now.

MAITREYA (*hopefully, thinking she has spoken to him*)   You will not accept the necklace?

VASANTASENA   Why not, Maitreya? (*She takes it and presses it to her heart, speaking aside.*) The mango tree is dry, yet drops of honey fall from its branches. (*Aloud.*) Sir, tell Charudatta, who is a noble gambler, that I shall call on him this evening.

MAITREYA (*aside*)   What for? What more does she want? (*Aloud.*) I will, my lady. (*Aside.*) And I hope that will be the end of our acquaintance! (*He swiftly strides off.*)

VASANTASENA   Take this necklace, and come with me to Charudatta's.

MAID   But a storm is coming up; look how dark the sky is.

VASANTASENA   Let it come. Let it rain till the world ends. How does it touch me? I am going to meet the man I love. Take this necklace, and come with me!

66

In a state of rapturous anticipation VASANTASENA *decorates herself with jewels and flowers, while her two maids perform a peacock dance, expressing her inner yearnings. At its conclusion they go through the door, down the passage, and off,* MADANIKA *holding an imaginary umbrella over her mistress' head. A* STAGEHAND *removes the bright cloth from the stool and replaces it with the plain cotton cloth. Lights dim.*

Act Five

CHARUDATTA's *garden. Lights come up on* CHARUDATTA *sitting on the floor beside the stool, which is a shelter in the garden.*

CHARUDATTA (*looking up*) It is going to storm. The peacocks and the swans are disturbed; so is the lover far from home. As the clouds climb, the lightning flashes briefly, and the rain spatters down. (*Reflects.*) Maitreya should be back by now.

MAITREYA (*entering*) Scheming, selfish woman! Not a word, not one civil word; she just pockets the necklace. And she isn't exactly so poor. She could have said, "Maitreya, my good friend Maitreya, sit down; here are sweets for you and a cool drink." But no, not even a miserly glass of water. Damn her! What they say is right: "there's no such thing as a lotus without a root, a goldsmith without a swindle, a village meeting without a quarrel, or a courtesan without selfishness." I must tell Charudatta to keep a safe distance away from such women. (*Standing on the passage, he sees* CHARUDATTA.) Ah, he's out here in the garden. (*He goes up the steps.*) Looks like a storm blowing up.

CHARUDATTA (*rising and coming forward to greet him*) So it

67

The Toy Cart

does. It is good to see you back, Maitreya. Come in here and sit down.

MAITREYA Thanks.

They sit on the floor.

CHARUDATTA What news, my friend?

MAITREYA It's over, finished.

CHARUDATTA Why—did she refuse to take the necklace?

MAITREYA No such luck! She greeted me with her lotus-soft palms joined very respectfully—and took the necklace.

CHARUDATTA Then what did you mean by saying, "It's over, finished"?

MAITREYA A damned pretty bargain, wasn't it? Giving away a fabulous necklace for a shiny gold box that a thief ran off with. What did we get out of it?

CHARUDATTA Don't be silly. She trusted us. That's reward enough.

MAITREYA That isn't all. She'd tipped off her maids, and they were giggling behind my back, veiling their faces. Giggling at a Brahmin! Please, I beg of you, keep away from her. She will destroy you. A courtesan's like a thorn in the foot: you'll have a hell of a painful time getting it out. (*He hops about, imitating the situation.*) It's a good warning that says, "Keep away from a courtesan, an elephant, an accountant, a begging monk, a snooper, a swindler, and an ass. If you don't, you're asking for trouble."

CHARUDATTA What nonsense, Maitreya! I am poor—isn't that protection enough? What can she want of me? I have nothing to give her. Such women are gold diggers: no money, no love.

MAITREYA (*aside*) You can't argue with a man in love. I warned him to keep clear, but from the way he sighs and moans, that seems only to encourage him. (*Aloud.*) She said she would drop in this evening. She's probably looking for more than a necklace.

CHARUDATTA Let her come. She will not go away unsatisfied.

68

VASANTASENA'S SERVANT *enters and comes to the steps, huddling in the rain.*

SERVANT What a downpour! The more it rains, the wetter I get; the wetter I get, the more I shiver. Brrr, it's a cold night outside. (*He laughs suddenly.*) A nice day for a genius like me, who plays the flute and sings like a god! All I do is carry messages from her to him. (*Sees* CHARUDATTA.) He's here in the garden, and that blithering fool Maitreya is with him. The garden gate's closed. I'll prod him. (*He mimes picking up mud pellets and throwing them at* MAITREYA.)

MAITREYA What's this? Lumps of mud? What am I, a man or an apple tree?

CHARUDATTA Oh, it's very likely the pigeons.

MAITREYA Dirty-minded pigeons! This stick will show you! I'll bring you down, nests and all. (*Raises his fist to the sky, miming the staff.*)

CHARUDATTA (*holding him back by the sacred thread*) Calm down, Maitreya. Poor little pigeons. Leave them alone.

SERVANT The blithering fool! He sees the pigeons but can't see me. Here goes another. (*Throws another mud pellet.*)

MAITREYA (*looking up*) Another! (*Seeing no pigeon overhead, he looks around him.*) Oh, it's you, Kumbhilaka. Wait. (*He goes and opens the garden gate.*) Come in, come in. What brings you here?

SERVANT (*entering, going onto the center platform*) Thank you, sir.

MAITREYA Well, what brings you here, in spite of the wind and rain?

SERVANT She sent me.

MAITREYA She? Who? Who?

SERVANT She. See? She.

MAITREYA What's all this she-she-she-ing about, you clod, you wheezy beggar? Who? Who? Who?

SERVANT What's all this who-who-who-ing about, you frightened owl of a fool?

MAITREYA   Come, man, let's talk sense.

SERVANT   First, a riddle for you.

MAITREYA   And a box on the ears for you.

SERVANT   If you solve it. Here it is. In what season does the mango tree blossom?

MAITREYA   That's easy. In summer.

SERVANT *(grinning)*   Wrong.

MAITREYA *(reflecting)*   Wait. I'll ask Charudatta. *(He goes over to* CHARUDATTA.*)* Sir, when does the mango tree blossom? *(Mimes the tree.)*

CHARUDATTA   In spring, of course, in *vasanta*.

MAITREYA *(returning to* KUMBHILAKA*)*   In spring, of course, in *vasanta*.

SERVANT   That's it. Now another. Who protects the cities?

MAITREYA   The town guard, of course.

SERVANT *(grinning)*   Wrong.

MAITREYA *(calling to* CHARUDATTA*)*   Sir, who guards the cities?

CHARUDATTA   The army, of course, the *sena*.

MAITREYA   The army, of course, the *sena*. *(Mimes soldiers.)*

SERVANT   That's it. Now, quick, quick, put the two together.

MAITREYA   *Sena,* army. *Vasanta,* spring. Sena-vasanta!

SERVANT   No, no, the other way round.

MAITREYA *(pivoting around)*   Sena-vasanta.

SERVANT   Idiot! Clod! Moron! Turn the stems around!

MAITREYA *(turning his feet in)*   Sena-vasanta!

SERVANT   No! The words! Turn the *words* around!

MAITREYA *(after deep reflection)*   Vasanta-sena.

SERVANT   Right. She's here.

MAITREYA   I must tell Charudatta. *(He goes to* CHARUDATTA.*)* Sir, a creditor's here.

CHARUDATTA   A creditor? In my house?

MAITREYA   Not in the house—at the door. Vasantasena is here.

CHARUDATTA   No!

MAITREYA   Kumbhilaka says so. Hey, Kumbhilaka! Come here.

SERVANT *(approaching)*   Sir, I bring you greetings.

CHARUDATTA   Is Vasantasena really here?

SERVANT Yes, sir.

CHARUDATTA (*joyfully*) You are a bringer of good news. Take this: it's my gift to you. (*He gives him his shawl.*)

SERVANT Yes, sir. (*He goes off to inform* VASANTASENA.)

MAITREYA There you are. There's only one reason why she comes out on a foul night like this.

CHARUDATTA What's that?

MAITREYA Oh, I can tell. She thinks the necklace isn't worth the price of the box, and she wants more. Take my word for it.

CHARUDATTA (*aside*) She will get what she comes for. (VASANTASENA *enters gracefully, followed by* MADANIKA, *holding an imaginary umbrella, and a* COURTIER. *They walk completely around the stage on the passage and stop where they entered, by the steps leading to* CHARUDATTA'*s garden.* VASANTASENA *shakes the raindrops out of her sari, smooths her hair, and stands hesitant, suddenly overcome by shyness. Though a courtesan, she is as weak as any woman near her lover. She looks to* MADANIKA *for support. At that moment* CHARUDATTA *sees her at the gate.*) Welcome her in.

MAITREYA (*goes onto the passage, approaching* VASANTASENA *respectfully*) We are honored to receive you.

VASANTASENA You flatter me. Thank you. (*To the* COURTIER.) Sir, the maid will attend you with the umbrella.

COURTIER (*aside*) I can take a hint. (*Aloud.*) No, thank you. (*He leaves.*)

VASANTASENA Now, Maitreya, where is the good gambler?

MAITREYA (*aside*) "Good gambler!" A nice way to begin. (*Aloud.*) Over there, madam, in the dry garden.

VASANTASENA Dry? How is that?

MAITREYA Nothing to eat or drink. (*He mimes hunger and thirst.* VASANTASENA *smiles.*) Please come in.

VASANTASENA (*shyly, aside to* MADANIKA) What shall I say? How shall I begin?

MADANIKA (*aside to* VASANTASENA) "Good evening, Sir Gambler."

71

VASANTASENA (*aside*) I can't. I shouldn't dare.

MADANIKA (*aside*) Don't worry. You will at the right time.

MAITREYA Please come in. This way.

MAITREYA *gestures for* VASANTASENA *to enter. Gathering her courage, she goes up the steps and crosses directly to* CHARU-DATTA, *the others following. Playfully she throws him a flower.*

VASANTASENA Good evening, Sir Gambler.

CHARUDATTA (*rising*) Vasantasena! It is so good to see you. Believe me, I have been most unhappy. Please sit down. (*She moves to sit away from him.*) No, here.

MAITREYA Here.

VASANTASENA *sits near* CHARUDATTA. *The others sit around her.*

CHARUDATTA But you are dripping wet, Vasantasena. I can see the drops trickling down from the flower in your ear. Maitreya, bring her a new dress; she should change into something dry.

MADANIKA No, wait, Maitreya. I'll go. (*She turns to go.*)

MAITREYA (*aside to* CHARUDATTA) May I ask her a question?

CHARUDATTA Of course.

MAITREYA (*stopping her at the steps*) Why do you come here, madam, at this time of night—a night so dark, moonless, windy, and raining?

MADANIKA (*aside*) The cheek of him!

VASANTASENA (*aside*) No, he's just being careful.

MADANIKA My mistress has come to inquire the value of the pearl neaklace given to her.

MAITREYA (*aside to* CHARUDATTA) Didn't I say so? She wants something better.

MADANIKA You see, she gambled it away. And now the keeper of the gambling house has left on royal business, so she can't find out what it's really worth.

MAITREYA (*aside*)   Tit for tat. I've heard that before.

MADANIKA   In the meantime, while we're searching for him, my mistress asks you please to accept this gold box. (*She shows the box.* MAITREYA *looks at it sharply.*) Sir, you are examining it very closely. Have you seen it before?

MAITREYA   No, but it's a real work of art. Very pretty.

MADANIKA   You aren't very sharp. It's the same gold box.

MAITREYA (*joyfully*)   It is! Charudatta, here's the gold box that the thief carried away from our house.

CHARUDATTA   The trick we played on her is now being played back on us. I can't believe it. The box may look the same, but it can't be.

MAITREYA   But it is. As I am a Brahmin, it is the very same box.

CHARUDATTA   If true, this is splendid news.

MAITREYA (*aside to* CHARUDATTA)   Shall I ask where they found it?

CHARUDATTA (*aside to* MAITREYA)   A reasonable question. Do.

MAITREYA (*whispering in* MADANIKA's *ear*)   So . . . pss . . . pss . . .

MADANIKA (*whispering in* MAITREYA's *ear*)   So . . . pss . . . pss . . .

CHARUDATTA   What is it? Why not tell us?

MAITREYA (*whispering in* CHARUDATTA's *ear*)   So . . . pss . . . pss . . .

CHARUDATTA (*to* MADANIKA)   So this is the same gold box.

MADANIKA   Yes, sir.

CHARUDATTA   That is good news. Here, take this ring from me; it's for you. (*He feels his finger, finds there is no ring, and is extremely embarrassed.*)

VASANTASENA (*aside*)   How lovable he is.

CHARUDATTA (*aside to* MAITREYA)   What's the use of living, Maitreya, if a man has no money at all? His anger is futile; his love is futile. Birds without wings, pools without water, trees without leaves, snakes without venom—such are the poor. (MAITREYA *mimes the objects.*)

MAITREYA (*aside to* CHARUDATTA) But you mustn't take it so seriously. (*Aloud, laughingly.*) And I should like, madam, to get back my towel in which the box was wrapped when the thief took it.

VASANTASENA (*ignoring him*) It was not right of you, Charudatta, to send this pearl necklace in place of the stolen box. You think very poorly of me to have done so.

CHARUDATTA Who would have believed the truth? The world is merciless to the poor.

MAITREYA (*to* MADANIKA) And you—are you going to spend the night here?

MADANIKA That's not very polite, sir.

MAITREYA (*to* CHARUDATTA) The storm has started again, and the rain is simply tumbling down.

CHARUDATTA How well you put it.
The rains pierce through the clouds, as lotus roots
Pierce the soil, softly, as if
Weeping for the absent moon.
My dearest, look at the sky, black-haired, scented with wind.
The lightning scoops her into his arms.
Tenderly but fiercely, as lover does lover.

VASANTASENA *embraces him.* CHARUDATTA *puts his arms around her. Lights fade to black.*

Act Six

The lights come up center stage. VASANTASENA *is seen asleep, lying on a bed of cushions.* MADANIKA *enters.*

MADANIKA Not awake yet? It's time she was up. I must wake

her. (*Waking her.*) It's morning, mistress! Wake up, it's morning!

VASANTASENA (*stretches blissfully*)   So soon? Is the sun up?

MADANIKA   It's certainly up for us.

VASANTASENA   And where is our excellent gambler?

MADANIKA   He rose, gave Vardhamanaka his orders, and went to the Pushpakaranda flower garden.

VASANTASENA   Did he leave any message?

MADANIKA   He told Vardhamanaka to have the carriage ready before dawn. He said to take you——

VASANTASENA   Where?

MADANIKA   To join him in the garden.

VASANTASENA (*embracing her*)   Last night I hardly got a good look at his face. Now I shall see him to my heart's content. Tell me, did I enter the inner chamber last night?

MADANIKA   Not only the inner chamber, but everyone's heart.

VARDHAMANAKA *enters as though driving a bullock cart. He mimes reins held in one hand and whip cracking in the other. His body jolts rhythmically as if riding in the cart. He shouts at the oxen as he moves around the passage.* RADANIKA *enters and he sees her.*

VARDHAMANAKA   Radanika, tell her the carriage is ready.

RADANIKA (*goes up steps into the house*)   Vardhamanaka is here and says the carriage is ready.

VASANTASENA   Tell him I'll be coming in a minute.

RADANIKA (*shouting to* VARDHAMANAKA)   Wait a little, Vardhamanaka. (*She goes off.*)

VARDHAMANAKA (*looking into the back of the cart*)   Damn, I've left the cushions behind! I'll have to go back and get them. But these beasts are too jumpy to be left alone. Oh, I'll be back soon. (*He drives away, cracking his whip and shouting.*)

VASANTASENA (*to her own* MAID)   Get me my shawl; I'll put it on myself.

STHAVARAKA, SANSTHANAKA's *servant, drives a horse carriage into the passage, now the square outside. He clucks the horses along, his body bouncing briskly.*

STHAVARAKA What a jam! And Sansthanaka has ordered me to take the carriage to the flower garden and to be quick about it! Giddap! Giddap! (*The carriage advances a little, and he stands up to look around.*) A real traffic jam; village carts everywhere. (*He shouts and slowly edges the horses on.*) Hey, you! Make room! Move over, move over! Who am *I*? Me? Sir, it may interest you to know that I am the driver of Sansthanaka, the king's own brother-in-law. (*Cracking his whip.*) Move over, move! Make room there! Pull to the left, you! (*He looks up ahead.*) Hey, you village louts, get a move on! I don't care if you're bogged down. What, give you a hand? *Me,* give you a hand? The driver of Sansthanaka give *you* a hand? All right, all right, just one little push. I'll stop here, in front of Charudatta's garden gate. (*He jumps down and goes off to help, leaving the "carriage" at the door.*)
MADANIKA That must have been the carriage driving up: I heard the wheels.
VASANTASENA I feel nervous. See me to the gate.
MADANIKA This way, mistress.

They go to the steps.

VASANTASENA That will do. Now go and rest.
MADANIKA Thank you.

She goes across the platform and off the other side of the stage. VASANTASENA *goes out the gate and mimes getting into* SANSTHANAKA's *carriage.*

VASANTASENA Why should my right eye twitch? It's a bad omen. But what does it matter? Meeting Charudatta will cancel all bad omens.

STHAVARAKA (*returning*) There, the road's clear now. Off I go. (*He climbs up and drives off. The two move in unison, re-acting to the same bounces.*) Why does the carriage feel heavier? Or am I just tired from helping them with the bogged wheels? (*Cracks whip.*) Giddap! Giddap! Move on, my beauties!

VOICE OFFSTAGE Police! Police! The traitor is loose! The jailer is killed! All guards at their posts! The traitor is loose!

STHAVARAKA There's going to be trouble here. I'd better clear out while there's time.

He lashes the horses. They go off just as ARYAKA *dashes in, dragging the chains on his feet, on the opposite side of the passage.*

ARYAKA It's behind me, that terrible sea of jail and suffering —all on account of the tyrannous Palaka. Thank God. It's worth it, even if I must drag these broken ankle chains along wherever I go. Thanks, Sharvilaka; you're the one who got me out. What shame! Snatched away from my house, shoved into a dingy cell, left to die—all because a trembling king is afraid of an astrologer's words! (*Raises his voice.*) And what did I do? What did I do to deserve this, to be treated as a wild beast? If the stars said something, is that my fault? Can I fight Fate? Can I change Fate? (*By the steps.*) Here's a gate left ajar. Some kind man doesn't believe in locks. The hinges are rusted; Fate's not been kind to this man either. I'll slip in. (*Pushes gate open and goes up onto platform.*)

VARDHAMANAKA (*off*) Giddap! Giddap!

ARYAKA (*pausing inside gate*) A carriage! If it's a rich man's carriage returning empty from town, or some noble lady's, or even a bunch of villagers—this is the thing for me!

VARDHAMANAKA *re-enters, driving* CHARUDATTA's *oxcart.*

VARDHAMANAKA There, now I have the cushions. (*He calls.*)

Radanika, tell Vasantasena the cart is waiting to take her to the Pushpakaranda flower garden. (*He turns cart around, so his back is to the gate.*)

ARYAKA   A courtesan's carriage going out of the city! I'm lucky. (*He looks out carefully.*)

VARDHAMANAKA (*hearing the sound of* ARYAKA's *broken ankle chains*)   The tinkling of anklets! That must be her. I have to manage these oxen, mistress; please get in at the back. (ARYAKA *climbs in.*) There, the carriage slumps to the right with more weight. (*His body slumps right.*) Giddap, you lazy lumps, giddap!

He cracks his whip and drives off. VIRAKA, *a captain of the guard, enters with* GUARDS.

VIRAKA   Here, all of you! Jump to it, my fine fellows; there's no time to waste. The traitor cowherd is loose; the king can't sleep any more. You, take the east gate; you, the west; you, the south; you, the north. I'll climb this old wall here and look around. (GUARDS *move to all parts of the passage.* VIRAKA *goes up onto the platform.*) Chandanaka, follow me!

CHANDANAKA, *another captain, enters with more* GUARDS.

CHANDANAKA   Come on! Hop to it!—or the old king will be out and a new king in. Search the streets, the roads, the gardens, the houses, the markets, the shops—leave not one stone unturned! Where will he escape as long as Chandanaka lives?

GUARDS *dash in all directions.*

VIRAKA   Well, the bird's been flown since dawn. And he has many friends outside.

VARDHAMANAKA, *with* ARYAKA *behind him, comes on bouncing along in the imaginary oxcart.*

VARDHAMANAKA Giddap! Giddap!

CHANDANAKA What's this doing here? A covered cart—mighty suspicious! (*To* GUARDS.) Search it.

VIRAKA (*blocking cart on passage*) Stop, you! Whose cart is this? Who's inside? Where are you going?

VARDHAMANAKA Charudatta's cart, sir. I am taking Mistress Vasantasena, who is inside, to meet Charudatta in the flower garden.

VIRAKA (*to* CHANDANAKA) He says it belongs to Charudatta, Vasantasena is inside it, and he's taking her to Pushpakaranda.

CHANDANAKA He may pass.

VIRAKA You mean without a search?

CHANDANAKA Without a search.

VIRAKA Why?

CHANDANAKA It's Charudatta's.

VIRAKA And who is Charudattta, who is Vasantasena, that this carriage shall pass without being searched?

CHANDANAKA You haven't heard of Charudatta? Not even of Vasantasena? My poor man, they are the finest citizens in our noble city.

VIRAKA That's all very well, but I have my duty to do. My own father can't pass here without a proper search.

CHANDANAKA If that's the way you feel, go ahead.

VIRAKA Oh, you look in.

CHANDANAKA *mimes climbing into the back of the cart. He peers in and finds* ARYAKA.

ARYAKA Please, don't give me away.

CHANDANAKA You have my word, Aryaka. (*Aside.*) Trapped like a poor bird. But I know he isn't guilty. Besides, he's Sharvilaka's friend, and Sharvilaka saved my life once. I'll die for them—and happily too—if I have to. (*He gets down, then speaks to* VIRAKA.) I'm afraid that he—I mean she, Vasantasena—thinks it highly improper to insult her in this fashion on the royal road.

79

VIRAKA   He—she—does, eh?

CHANDANAKA   That's what I said.

VIRAKA   I don't like this he-she shuffling, my friend.

CHANDANAKA   Are you mad? Can't a man make a slip of the tongue, like any honest person?

VIRAKA   Can't a second honest person take a look too? The king has ordered it. I obey the king.

CHANDANAKA   You mean I don't obey the king?

VIRAKA   The king has ordered a general search.

CHANDANAKA   (*aside*)   If the king is told that Aryaka was hiding in Charudatta's cart, Charudatta will have quite a job of explaining to do. I'll give Viraka a dose of South Indian rhetoric. (*Aloud.*) Viraka, I have searched the carriage, and now you tell me you're going to search it again? As my name is Chandanaka, and as I stand here, what the devil does this mean? Who are you, sir, to challenge my competence?

VIRAKA   Damn and blast! And who are *you*, sir, may I ask?

CHANDANAKA   A person of eminence, worthy of your respect. You are low-caste.

VIRAKA   Low-caste? *My* family, low-caste!

CHANDANAKA   The less said about it, the better.

VIRAKA   Say it!

CHANDANAKA   Oh, what's the use? It wouldn't help. You can't restore a rotten apple.

VIRAKA   Go on, say it!

CHANDANAKA *makes a gesture to show that* VIRAKA *is a leather-stitcher.*

CHANDANAKA   Didn't you deal in dead skins? Stitch flesh and bones? Cut tough skins—(*He gestures.*)—like this, and this, and this? And now you're a captain of the king!

VIRAKA   A nice caste you come from, Chandanaka! Or have you forgotten?

CHANDANAKA   Forgotten what?

VIRAKA Let's forget such things.

CHANDANAKA Go on, say it! What?

VIRAKA Your father was a drum, your mother was a kettle-drum, your brother is a tambourine. You—tanner!

CHANDANAKA (*losing his temper*) I, a tanner? Chandanaka, a tanner? All right, go and search the carriage!

VIRAKA Hey, you! Driver! Wait! I *will* search it! (*As* VIRAKA *moves to climb into the cart,* CHANDANAKA *grabs him by the hair, pulls him down, and kicks him.* VIRAKA *rises, speaking violently.*) You bloody swine! What does this mean? I was only doing my duty. Why, I'll have you dragged into court and whipped. You'll see.

He leaves with the GUARDS.

CHANDANAKA (*shouting after him*) Run to the palace! (*Kicks.*) Run to the court. (*Kicks.*) You dog. Run with your tail between your legs. (*Kicks.*) Who cares? (*To* VARDHAMANAKA.) Drive on, quick. If anyone stops you, say that Viraka and Chandanaka have already searched the carriage. (*To* ARYAKA.) My lady Vasantasena, a passport for you. (*He hands over his sword to* ARYAKA.)

ARYAKA Thanks, friend. This brings my courage back. I'm safe now.

CHANDANAKA Remember me, sir—my name is Chandanaka. I speak from love, not selfishness.

ARYAKA I shall indeed. Fate sent you to me, my friend. If everything turns out right, I'll remember you very specially.

CHANDANAKA God give you courage and luck, sir. (VARDHA-MANAKA *and* ARYAKA *ride off.* CHANDANAKA *stands gazing after them.*) I see my friend Sharvilaka following at a discreet distance. Good! I had better tell my family to join him, too. Viraka is no doubt up to mischief behind my back.

He goes off. The lights dim.

Act Seven

Lights come up on center stage. CHARUDATTA *and* MAITREYA *are seen walking in the Pushpakaranda flower garden.*

MAITREYA Such a lovely garden.

CHARUDATTA Yes, pretty as a market; here are the trees, small shopkeepers with glittering things; and the bees, like the king's officers, busily collecting taxes.

A STAGEHAND *places a stone seat on stage.*

MAITREYA This is a nice stone seat. (*He motions to* CHARU-DATTA *to sit on it.*)

CHARUDATTA (*sitting down*) Vardhamanaka takes his own time, doesn't he?

MAITREYA I told him to hurry.

CHARUDATTA Why does he take so long, then? Is the carriage too heavy for the oxen? Did a wheel break? A tree fall across the road? Did he lose his way?

VARDHAMANAKA *enters driving the cart, with* ARYAKA *hiding, bent low behind him.*

VARDHAMANAKA Giddap, you! (*He cracks his whip and circles the passage.*)

ARYAKA (*aside*) Safe for the time being. But what next? Here I am in a stranger's carriage, like a koel's eggs in a crow's nest. But the chains are still on my legs, and the king's spies are everywhere. At least I'm far outside the city. (*Sees the garden as they pass.*) Shall I hide here in this garden? Or shall I wait till the owner of the carriage comes and appeal to him? They say Charudatta is a fine man and always ready to help. I'll wait till he comes. It will help me to meet him and talk to him.

VARDHAMANAKA (*stops by steps*)   Here we are. Ho, Maitreya!

MAITREYA   That's the voice of our friend Vardhamanaka. Vasantasena is here.

CHARUDATTA   Welcome her to the garden.

MAITREYA (*going to the gate*)   And why are you so late, Vardhamanaka?

VARDHAMANAKA   Now don't lose your temper, Maitreya. I had to go back for the cushions that I'd left behind.

CHARUDATTA   It's all right, Maitreya; help her down.

MAITREYA (*aside*)   Does she have chains on her feet so that she can't get down by herself? (*Goes behind cart and mimes lifting the curtain off the cart door.*) This isn't Mistress Vasantasena! It's Mister Vasantasena!

CHARUDATTA   What a time to choose for joking, Maitreya. Here, let me help her. (*He rises and approaches.*)

ARYAKA (*aside*)   That's the man. He not only is noble, he looks every inch a good man. I'm safe.

CHARUDATTA (*on the passage, seeing* ARYAKA)   A man! Strong, brawny, fierce-eyed. Why that chain on his feet? Sir, who are you?

ARYAKA   Aryaka, a herdsman. I need your help.

CHARUDATTA   The same Aryaka whom the king arrested out of fear?

ARYAKA   Yes.

CHARUDATTA   You are welcome to my help. Fate has brought you here, so I cannot refuse you. Vardhamanaka, remove that chain.

VARDHAMANAKA (*doing so*)   It's quickly done, sir.

ARYAKA   Now I am bound to you by a stronger chain. Charudatta, you must forgive me: I made use of your carriage without your permission. I thank you for your kindness, and with your permission, I should like to leave.

CHARUDATTA You have my permission. (*He watches* ARYAKA *get down from the cart.*) But you can't go on foot, sir; you're cramped and tired. Besides, if you go in the carriage, you need not fear: no one will suspect you. You had better keep the cart.

ARYAKA Thank you.

CHARUDATTA And you have my best wishes for the journey to your friends.

ARYAKA I am leaving a good friend behind.

CHARUDATTA If you need me again, you are welcome.

ARYAKA I'll keep that in mind.

CHARUDATTA And God be with you.

ARYAKA As you were with me.

CHARUDATTA Don't waste time. There are spies and soldiers everywhere. You must hurry to your friends.

ARYAKA (*getting in again*) We shall meet again. Until then, good-bye.

VARDHAMANAKA *drives him off in the cart.*

CHARUDATTA Now I'm not safe from the king's anger, either. Even walls have eyes. Throw this chain in the well, Maitreya. (MAITREYA *goes to do so;* CHARUDATTA'*s left eye twitches; he speaks aside.*) A twitching eye's a bad omen. I did want to see her. But it won't be today, I fear. (*To* MAITREYA, *returning.*) Let's go, Maitreya. (*Begins to walk along passage, then stops.*) Oh, a Buddhist monk coming this way. Another bad omen! (*He turns to* MAITREYA.) Let's take this other path; I want to avoid him.

They reverse their steps and go off out of sight.

Act Eight

A Buddhist MONK, *formerly the* MASSEUR, *enters the garden, carrying a wet robe.*

MONK (*chanting*)
> Buddham Sharanam Gachhami
> Dharmam Sharanam Gachhami
> Sangham Sharanam Gachhami. . . .

I have dyed this robe saffron. Now to rinse it in the pool. It's the garden of the king's brother-in-law, but I shan't take long. (*He begins to rinse the robe in mime.*)

VOICE OFFSTAGE   Stop, you rascal! What are you doing there?

MONK (*fearfully*) Here he comes—Sansthanaka himself! God help me! He hates all monks. What shall I do? The Lord Buddha is my refuge.

A COURTIER *enters, followed by* SANSTHANAKA.

SANSTHANAKA   You bastardly monk, stop it! Stop it before I make radish jelly out of you! (*He strikes the* MONK.)

COURTIER   Don't be a fool. Can't you see his yellow robe? He's a monk. Forget him. Look at the garden: it opens out like a feast before your eyes.

MONK   Oh, thank you, my Lord, my savior.

SANSTHANAKA   The rascal! He's insulting me.

COURTIER   Why, what has he done?

SANSTHANAKA   He called me a shaver.

COURTIER   No, he was praising you. He said "savior."

SANSTHANAKA   Praise me more, Monk, praise me more. But why are you here?

MONK I was rinsing this robe, sir.

SANSTHANAKA Was this pool meant for washing clothes, you rascal? My sister's husband gave it to me. But who comes here? Just dogs and jackals and monks! I don't even dare to have a bath here. One good clout should finish you off.

COURTIER Leave him alone. He seems to be a neophyte: he seems to have recently joined the monks.

SANSTHANAKA I don't think so.

COURTIER Look at his head: it's freshly shaven. He's hardly worn that rough robe: no scars on his body. It fits him loosely, too; you can see he doesn't feel at home in it.

MONK Yes, I have only recently joined.

SANSTHANAKA And why? Why not all your life, you fraud? You rascal! (*He strikes the* MONK.)

MONK Glory to the Buddha!

COURTIER Stop it. Let him go. (*The* MONK *hurries off. The* COURTIER *speaks quickly.*) Just look at the lovely garden, now. Those creepers around those trees, like a wife meeting her husband. Sit here on this stone seat.

SANSTHANAKA I will. (*They sit down and relax.*) You know something? I can't forget Vasantasena. It's like when a man abuses you; you can't forget it, can you?

COURTIER *You* can't, of course.

SANSTHANAKA Why does that devil of a driver of mine take so long? I told him to get here in record time. The sun's up. It is noon. I can't walk in this heat.

COURTIER It *is* hot.

SANSTHANAKA The sun here is roasting me brown. Well, how about a song to make the time pass? (*He sings.*) Wasn't that brilliant?

COURTIER You sing like an angel.

SANSTHANAKA Naturally. Pepper and chili and curry powder and coconut oil—recipe for a good voice. Damn it, the man's still not here!

COURTIER He'll be here soon.

STHAVARAKA *drives the carriage containing* VASANTASENA *up before the steps marking the gate.*

STHAVARAKA   Giddap, you two! I'm late; it's past noon. I hope he doesn't blow up.

VASANTASENA   That isn't his driver's voice. Did Charudatta send another driver? My right eye twitches. I suddenly feel faint. Where am I?

SANSTHANAKA (*approaching*)   So, you are here at last!

COURTIER (*approaching*)   About time, too!

SANSTHANAKA   I heard the wheels squeal. Have you arrived, Sthavaraka, my boy, my slave? Good to see you.

STHAVARAKA   Yes, sir.

SANSTHANAKA   And the carriage, too.

STHAVARAKA   Yes, sir.

SANSTHANAKA   And the horses, too.

STHAVARAKA   Yes, sir.

SANSTHANAKA   And you, too.

STHAVARAKA   Yes, sir.

SANSTHANAKA   Drive in, man, drive in!

STHAVARAKA   Sir?

SANSTHANAKA   This way, you fool, where the wall's broken down.

STHAVARAKA   But, master, the opening's too narrow. That will wreck the carriage, kill the horses, and break my neck.

SANSTHANAKA   If the carriage is wrecked, I'll get another. If the horses are killed, I'll buy two more. And if your neck breaks, I shall get it fixed.

STHAVARAKA   But I shall be dead, sir.

SANSTHANAKA   No back talk, you idiot! Drive! Drive! Let the whole thing crash!

STHAVARAKA   As you say, sir. Here go the horses! Here goes the carriage! Here go the wheels! And here go I! (*He drives through the gate, up onto center stage.*) I made it! I am lucky, sir.

SANSTHANAKA Nothing wrong? The horses not killed? The carriage was not wrecked? And your neck was not smashed?

STHAVARAKA No, sir.

SANSTHANAKA Good! I like you. You are my dearest friend. You must be honored as though you were my blood brother. (*To the* COURTIER.) Let's get in and see if the inside of the carriage is all right, too.

COURTIER Yes. (*He starts to get in.*)

SANSTHANAKA (*pulling him back*) Me first, my friend. This isn't your father's carriage. I am the owner. I get in first.

COURTIER But you asked me to do so.

SANSTHANAKA So what? Haven't you the politeness to say, "Sir, after you"?

COURTIER After you, sir.

SANSTHANAKA That's a good boy. (*He looks in, backs away in great fright, and falls on the* COURTIER.) Help, thief! Help! A robber in the carriage! A demon in the carriage!

COURTIER Don't be silly. What would a demon be doing in a carriage?

SANSTHANAKA If there is a demon in the carriage, we both will be robbed; and if there is a robber in the carriage, we both will be gobbled up! Help! Sthavaraka, my slave, are you still alive?

STHAVARAKA Yes, sir.

SANSTHANAKA Take a look in the carriage. I tell you, if it is not a demon, then it is a woman inside!

COURTIER A woman!

VASANTASENA (*frightened, to herself*) It's Sansthanaka. What shall I do? Fate has deceived me.

SANSTHANAKA Hey, you rascal, didn't I tell you to look in? (*To the* COURTIER.) Come.

COURTIER A woman can do no harm. (*He puts his head inside the carriage.*) Vasantasena? No! That you should do this, I should never have believed it!

VASANTASENA (*shaking her head violently*) No!

COURTIER   A courtesan, after all!

VASANTASENA   It's all a mistake. A wrong carriage. Please help me, please . . .

COURTIER   Since you ask me. Leave everything to me. (*He withdraws his head and turns to* SANSTHANAKA.) Yes, there's a demon inside.

SANSTHANAKA   Why didn't she eat you up?

COURTIER   Thank God, she spared me. How about a nice pleasant walk back to Ujjain under the shady roadside trees?

SANSTHANAKA   Let's go. Wait, let's see. . . . I go on foot only before gods and Brahmins. The carriage suits me best. People will see me from afar and say, "There he is, the king's brother-in-law, in his royal carriage!"

COURTIER   (*aside*)   Ah, the devil. What now? I hope this helps. (*Aloud.*) There wasn't any demon; I was joking. It's Vasantasena. She has come to see you.

VASANTASENA   (*to herself*)   Oh, no!

SANSTHANAKA   And why shouldn't she? I'm a first-class nobleman, am I not?

COURTIER   Yes.

SANSTHANAKA   What luck! What wonderful luck! The last time, I made her angry. This time, I'll fall down before her and ask her forgiveness.

COURTIER   An excellent idea.

SANSTHANAKA   Watch me. (*He approaches and kneels before* VASANTASENA.) Listen to me, my dear. My lotus hands supplicate you in prayer. Please forgive the mistakes I made in the past. Yours sincerely, your lover, your slave.

VASANTASENA   (*angrily*)   Go away. You insult me. (*She spurns him with her foot.*)

SANSTHANAKA   (*rising*)   What! Kick this head? Sansthanaka's head, that does not bow even to gods? And you kick it the way jackals kick rotting flesh? Hey, Sthavaraka, where did you pick this woman up?

STHAVARAKA   The road was blocked, sir. I stopped near Charudatta's garden gate while the traffic cleared. I was helping to get a villager's cart unmired. I think she must have got in then, thinking it was her carriage.

SANSTHANAKA I see! She *wasn't* coming to meet me. Get out, you! This is my carriage. You were going to meet that beggar Brahmin, weren't you? Not in my carriage. Get out, get out!

VASANTASENA Yes, I was going to meet Charudatta. And I am proud of it.

SANSTHANAKA How I always wanted to lay hands on your lovely body. Now I'll drag you down by the hair, my sweet beauty.

COURTIER This is no time to insult a lady. (*He helps her down.*)

SANSTHANAKA (*aside*) First she refused me. Now she kicks me. She'll die for this. (*Aloud to the* COURTIER.) Do me a favor.

COURTIER I'll do anything for you—within reason.

SANSTHANAKA Oh, wonderfully reasonable, most wonderfully reasonable. I promise you I'll give you a gold mantle with a hundred tassels, and a taste of the most delicious bird's meat. Do as I tell you.

COURTIER What?

SANSTHANAKA Kill Vasantasena.

COURTIER (*shocked*) The finest lady in Ujjain, a most blameless courtesan—kill her? My soul would forever rot in hell.

SANSTHANAKA I'll take care of your soul. If you kill her in this lonely garden, who will ever know?

COURTIER The sky, the gods, the wind, the moon, the big-eyed sun, my heart, my conscience. The whole world will know.

SANSTHANAKA That's too bad. Hide her, then, and kill her.

COURTIER You mad fool!

SANSTHANAKA You're afraid of the gods. You're a poor jackal. Sthavaraka will do it. (*He calls him over.*) Sthavaraka, my boy, my slave, do you want gold bracelets?

STHAVARAKA I'll wear gold bracelets.

SANSTHANAKA Do you want a golden couch?

STHAVARAKA I'll sit on a golden couch.

SANSTHANAKA   Do you want delicious dishes?

STHAVARAKA   I'll eat delicious dishes.

SANSTHANAKA   Do you want to boss over my slaves?

STHAVARAKA   I'll boss over the slaves.

SANSTHANAKA   But first, you'll have to do as I say.

STHAVARAKA   Say it, and it shall be done.

SANSTHANAKA   It's a small thing, a very small thing.

STHAVARAKA   Say it.

SANSTHANAKA   Kill Vasantasena.

STHAVARAKA   Please, master, I didn't mean anything. I only brought her here. She got into the wrong carriage.

SANSTHANAKA   Why, you're my slave, aren't you? What are you afraid of?

STHAVARAKA   Of the future.

SANSTHANAKA   What is this future? Bah!

STHAVARAKA   It brings good and bad.

SANSTHANAKA   What good, damn you?

STHAVARAKA   Well, master, if I'm a good man now, later I'll be rich and powerful like you.

SANSTHANAKA   And what bad, damn you?

STHAVARAKA   If I do evil, I'll remain as I am, a slave. I won't do evil, master.

SANSTHANAKA   You mean you won't kill her? (*He knocks him down.*)

STHAVARAKA   Beat me, kill me. But I won't do evil. I was born a slave; I'll die a slave. But I don't want to be born a slave again.

VASANTASENA   I throw myself on your mercy. Let him alone.

COURTIER   He's had enough; let him go. That was brave of you, Sthavaraka!

SANSTHANAKA   (*aside*) The first is a fool: he's afraid of his conscience. The second is a bigger fool: he's afraid of the future. But I'm afraid of nothing, for I am the king's brother-in-law. (*To* STHAVARAKA.) Very well, you may go. Go, and never show your face to me again.

STHAVARAKA   Yes, sir. (*To* VASANTASENA.) I had no hand in this, lady. (*He leaves.*)

SANSTHANAKA   Look, why don't you leave us alone? She can't make up her mind so long as you stay here. I am sure Sthavaraka has taken to his heels. Catch him and bring him back. In the meantime this proud lady will say yes to me.

COURTIER (*aside*)   Perhaps he'll come to his senses when she pleads with him in private. (*Aloud.*) All right, I'll go.

VASANTASENA (*clutching at his garments*)   Please don't leave me with him. Please!

COURTIER   It's all right, Vasantasena. (*To* SANSTHANAKA.) It is as a pledge that I leave her in your hands, and I will come back for her.

SANSTHANAKA   Very good—as long as you leave her in my hands.

COURTIER   I want your word of honor.

SANSTHANAKA   You have my word.

COURTIER (*aside*)   He might trick me. I know him well. I'll hide myself here for a minute and see what he does. (*He crosses away on the passage, then circles back around and drops to his knees, watching.*)

SANSTHANAKA (*aside*)   Now to kill her. No, wait! Who knows? That fox may have slipped in somewhere to see what I do. But he won't catch me. (*He picks flowers and adorns himself. Moves onto center stage and addresses* VASANTASENA.) Vasantasena, my dearest, sweet of my heart, come to me!

COURTIER (*aside*)   I see that he just wants to make love to her, as he said. Fine. (*He exits.*)

SANSTHANAKA   You'll have gold, jewels, my head, my turban at your feet. Love me, my dearest. Take me to your heart.

VASANTASENA   Gold? Take it away! Do the bees leave the lotus because it grows in filthy ponds? I am in love with a good man. His love has given me honor. Shall I leave the mango tree and love a withered thornbush?

SANSTHANAKA   Charudatta a mango tree? And I just a thorn-

bush! I'll cut him apart, and you too. You filthy mistress of
Charudatta! (*Grabs her.*) Call him! Call his name! See if he
saves you now.

VASANTASENA He would help me if only he knew.

SANSTHANAKA Help you? What is he? The monkey god? The
chief of gods? The god of wind? The god of rain? A vulture?
A demon? Let him be all these, and he cannot help you now.
You are going to die!

VASANTASENA Help me, Mother! Help me, Charudatta! Help!

SANSTHANAKA That bastard's name again! (*He strangles her.*)
Say his name again, say his name again! And you, Vasantasena, die, Vasantasena. (*She collapses to the ground.*) That's
done. She is dead. (*He laughs.*) A lovely way she died. I did
nothing; she just fell like a wet rag. I must hide her; the fox
will be back soon. Is she dead? Or must I kill her again? (*He
looks at* VASANTASENA's *body.*) Stone dead. This mantle
should cover her. No, it has my name on it. These dry leaves
are better; they'll hide her. (*He scoops leaves over her.*) Now
to the court, where I'll file a charge against Charudatta for
the murder of Vasantasena. Let's say he lured her into the
Pushpakaranda flower garden and killed her for her money.
That sounds good. Trapping Charudatta is the next step. But
I must go about it cleverly. Too many puritans in this city;
even the killing of a cow pinches their conscience. (*He starts
to leave but suddenly halts.*) Damn! Here's that fool monk
again, with his yellow robe, coming my way. He hates me.
(*He looks around.*) Over the wall for me. Run, fly, like the
monkey to Lanka—off I go, off I fly!

*He scales the wall in mime, drops down onto the passage, and
runs off. The* MONK *appears from the other direction.*

MONK My robe is rinsed. Shall I hang it to dry on this branch?
No, too many monkeys here. And the ground's much too
dusty. (*He looks around and goes up steps to center stage.*)

93

This should do: a heap of leaves blown up here by the wind. (*He spreads the wet robe over* VASANTASENA, *chanting to himself.*) *Buddham Sharanam Gachhami* . . . Heaven is mine, but not until I have thanked Vasantasena. She put me on the right path by paying those ten gold pieces to the chief gambler. I am her slave forever. What's that? A sigh among the leaves? Maybe the heat and the wet robe are making the leaves curl up and crackle. (VASANTASENA, *recovering consciousness, slowly stretches out a hand from under the robe.*) A hand from among the leaves! A woman's hand, with lovely pearl rings. (*Her other hand appears.*) Another hand! (*He examines it carefully.*) I know this hand. Of course. It's the hand that saved me. Let's look. (*He throws the wet robe aside and recognizes* VASANTASENA.) Vasantasena! Disciple of the Lord Buddha! (VASANTASENA *gasps.*) She needs water, but the pool's far away. I'll wring this wet robe over her. (*He does so, passing the robe over her face and body.*)

VASANTASENA (*sitting up*) Who are you, sir?

MONK Don't you remember? You paid ten gold pieces to buy me my freedom.

VASANTASENA I remember you. I can't remember anything else. Oh, I could die. I have suffered.

MONK What happened, good lady?

VASANTASENA I deserved it.

MONK Try to get up. Hold on to this creeper and pull yourself up. (*He mimes bending down the creeper; she grasps it and pulls herself to her feet.*) There is a hermitage nearby, where a holy sister lives. She'll nurse you till you are well. No, slowly, walk slowly. (*He moves onto the passage.*) This way, good lady, this way.

Slowly she follows. He leads her off. Lights center dim. The STAGEHANDS *place the stool, richly covered, to one side of the center platform. They lay a ramp connecting the* MUSICIANS' *platform with the center stage area.*

Act Nine

A court of justice. Lights come up. From offstage come shouts of many people. Above the tumult can be heard, "Make way for the Judge! His Honor the Judge!" The JUDGE's procession comes into view, led by a BAILIFF wearing a richly made turban. He is riding a spirited horse—a dummy horse, within which the BAILIFF stands and prances. He is followed by a RECORDER and a CLERK, dressed in dark clothing. Both walk with superior air, in the knowledge of their important positions. The RECORDER carries flags indicating the JUDGE's rank, and the CLERK carries a large book and files of papers. Next comes the JUDGE, sitting on cushions in a richly decorated palanquin carried by four RETAINERS. Flowing robes of bright-hued cotton cover his fat body. Well-fed and corrupt, he arrogantly accepts the flattering homage of the crowds lining the route; that is, the audience. HANGERS-ON, PLAINTIFFS, and LAWYERS crowd on after the great man. GUARDS bring up the rear. The lively procession travels the full circle of the passage. The JUDGE heaves himself up from the palanquin with the solicitous help of all who wish his favorable judgment. The JUDGE takes his place on the stool; CLERK and RECORDER sit cross-legged on either side, attending to the business of the court. The CLERK mimes passing a summons to the BAILIFF, who prances down the steps onto the passage, calls out the name, and escorts a PLAINTIFF. In mime the man pleads, is summarily dismissed, and a GUARD takes him away. This happens quickly several times. A dissolute old MERCHANT with a lovely young GIRL he has purchased for his bride are brought before the JUDGE. In mime she pleads for release, he to retain his possession. The JUDGE, torn between the beauty of the GIRL and the large bribe of gold slipped to him by the MERCHANT, *finally decides in favor of the old man. The court laughs as the* MERCHANT *drags the protesting* GIRL *away.* SANSTHANAKA *enters unseen on the passage.*

SANSTHANAKA   I've had a real bath, in cool, cool water. And a rest under shady trees in the company of soft, lovely girls— angels, every one of them. They played with my hair—such soft fingers!—now a curl, now a knot, now a twist, now a braid. Oh, I'm a perfect gentleman. But there's a fear inside me. Well, here's the courtroom. (*Stands by the entrance but does not go in.*)

JUDGE   Recorder.

RECORDER   Your Honor?

JUDGE   Note this down. (RECORDER *mimes writing* JUDGE's *words.*) "The most difficult part of a trial is to discover the motives of those involved in it. A judge is the worst suffered; no one has a good word for him. This is natural, for he must be learned, sagacious, eloquent, impartial, and cool-headed; he must reserve judgment until all the evidence is presented and sifted; nothing may corrupt him; he must protect the innocent and punish the guilty, and be in all things honest and truth-loving. And he has to do all this without incurring the displeasure of the king."

SANSTHANAKA (*stepping forward*)   I demand justice; I have a case. Note also that I'm a famous man, I come of a noble family. I am the king's own brother-in-law.

CLERK   The king's brother-in-law. Please wait a minute, sir; I'll inform the judge. (*He approaches the* JUDGE.) Your Honor, the king's brother-in-law has come with a case.

JUDGE (*fearfully*)   The court is very busy today. Tell him, Clerk, that the court will admit his case tomorrow.

The CLERK *goes to* SANSTHANAKA.

CLERK Sir, the judge says the court is very busy today; the court will admit your case tomorrow.

SANSTHANAKA (*angrily*) Is that so? And why not today? Tell the court that if my case is not heard today, I'll go to the king, who is my sister's husband and hence my brother-in-law, and have the judge dismissed.

CLERK (*returning to the* JUDGE) Your Honor, the king's brother-in-law says: (*He repeats* SANSTHANAKA's *words.*)

JUDGE He is a fool, but he has all the connections. Well, bring him before us; we'll hear him today.

CLERK (*going to* SANSTHANAKA) Please come before the court, sir. Your case will be heard today.

SANSTHANAKA It will, ha? And a minute ago it wasn't going to be, ha? (*Steps up to the* JUDGE.) I am very happy to see you, Judge. I hope you are happy to see me, for I have the power to make people sad or happy, as I like.

JUDGE You may be seated.

SANSTHANAKA You bet I will. This place belongs to me, and I'll sit where I like and when I like. (*To the* RECORDER.) Here? (*To the* CLERK.) You think this is better? Well, let's try this. (*He sits.*)

JUDGE You wish to present a case?

SANSTHANAKA You bet I do.

JUDGE The court is ready to hear it. Proceed with your complaint.

SANSTHANAKA There's no hurry. *I'm* not guilty. Well, you see, it is a habit of mine to go to the Pushpakaranda garden daily to see that it is watered and weeded and the pretty flowers kept flowering. And this morning when I went there, I saw—I couldn't believe my eyes!—the body of a woman on the ground!

JUDGE Do you know her?

SANSTHANAKA Know her? Who doesn't know her? It was Vasantasena, the courtesan. Some rascal must have lured her into the garden and strangled her—for her jewels. I didn't— (*He stops abruptly, putting his hand over his mouth.*)

JUDGE Recorder, make a note of that: the complainant said, "I didn't."

RECORDER Yes, your Honor.

SANSTHANAKA (*aloud*) What's all the fuss about, Judge? I was only saying, "I didn't . . . see it happen." (*He mimes wiping out the record with his foot.*)

JUDGE How can you tell that she was strangled and that it was for her jewels?

SANSTHANAKA Her neck was exposed and swollen, and there were no ornaments left on the body.

CLERK We can believe that.

SANSTHANAKA (*aside*) I've convinced them. Good!

CLERK What next is necessary, your Honor, in the conduct of this case?

JUDGE Clerk, see that Vasantasena's mother is brought here, but do not upset her unduly.

CLERK Yes, your Honor.

He gestures to BAILIFF, *who goes out and returns on the passage almost immediately, leading* VASANTASENA'S MOTHER.

MOTHER My daughter went to a friend's house. Now suddenly this news, and no sooner do I reach the courthouse than I am summoned into the court. I don't like any of this; I feel faint. Sir, where do I go?

BAILIFF Come this way, please.

He leads her to the JUDGE.

MOTHER My blessings on you, good sirs.

JUDGE You are very welcome. Please sit down.

MOTHER Thank you. (*She sits.*)

SANSTHANAKA Ah, you mother of a common slut, so you are hers!

JUDGE Ignore him. You are the mother of Vasantasena?

MOTHER   Yes, sir.

JUDGE   Do you know where Vasantasena is now?

MOTHER   I thought she was at a friend's house.

JUDGE   Could you tell the court his name?

MOTHER   (*aside*) This is so embarrassing. (*Aloud.*) Must I answer that question, sir?

JUDGE   I am sorry, but the court asks it, so you must answer it.

CLERK   You should answer it; it has to do with the conduct of the case.

MOTHER   Well, in that case, my daughter went to the house of a very proper man, the son of a nobleman. His name is Charudatta. He lives in the merchants' quarter.

SANSTHANAKA   That's him! Charudatta! I accuse him of the murder.

CLERK   He might be her friend, but that doesn't make him a murderer.

JUDGE   In that case, the court must have the evidence of Charudatta.

CLERK   Yes, your Honor.

JUDGE   Recorder, put this down: "Vasantasena went to meet Charudatta at his residence." His presence is therefore required. Clerk, bring him here; say that the court summons him.

CLERK   Yes, your Honor.

He gestures to BAILIFF, *who goes out and returns quickly with* CHARUDATTA.

CHARUDATTA   (*aside*) The king knows me well, yet I am summoned into the court. Perhaps his spies have told him that it was in my carriage that Aryaka escaped; perhaps he thinks I am involved in the conspiracy.

BAILIFF   This way, sir.

He ushers CHARUDATTA *onto center stage.*

CHARUDATTA My greetings to the court, and to you, your Honor.

JUDGE (*disturbed*) You are welcome, sir. Clerk, see that he has a comfortable seat.

A STAGEHAND *gives the* CLERK *a small stool, which the* CLERK places for CHARUDATTA.

CLERK Sir.

CHARUDATTA *sits.*

SANSTHANAKA Bah, call this a trial, where seats are given to women-killers?

JUDGE Could you tell the court, Charudatta, if at any time there was attachment, affection, or friendship of any kind between you and the daughter of this lady?

CHARUDATTA Which lady?

JUDGE This lady. (*He indicates* VASANTASENA'S MOTHER.)

CHARUDATTA (*rising*) My most respectful greetings.

MOTHER May you live long, my son. (*Aside.*) So this is Charudatta.

JUDGE Charudatta, how long have you known Vasantasena?

CHARUDATTA *is unable to conceal his embarrassment.*

SANSTHANAKA He's shamming, you can see; it's a guilty mind that does that. He strangled her, and he stole her jewels, and I shall prove it.

CLERK Speak up, Charudatta. The court asks you a question. You need not be afraid.

CHARUDATTA (*confusedly*) What can I say? How can I confess that a courtesan was my friend?

JUDGE I must ask you to be truthful. This is a court, and nothing must be hidden. There is a charge against you.

CHARUDATTA Who has accused me?

SANSTHANAKA I have. You woman-strangler! You kill a fine woman like Vasantasena for the sake of stealing her jewels, and now you try to cover it up by pretty lies!

CHARUDATTA You must be mad.

JUDGE Answer the question: was she your friend?

CHARUDATTA Yes.

JUDGE And can you tell us where she is now?

CHARUDATTA I know only that she left my house.

CLERK Where did she go? Did anyone go with her? Speak, sir.

CHARUDATTA She left my home. That's all I know for certain.

SANSTHANAKA Is that all? What about the way you lured her into my garden, strangled her, and stole her jewels? What about that?

CHARUDATTA Liar!

JUDGE Whatever made you think that Charudatta strangled her? He gave away his whole wealth to charities, and do you think he would steal Vasantasena's jewels—and murder her on that account?

SANSTHANAKA I repeat: it is not your business to speak in his defense. I want a fair trial.

MOTHER It is false; the whole charge is false! I know she left a gold box in his care, and when a thief stole it, he replaced it with a much more valuable necklace. How could such a man kill her for her jewels? Never! Oh, my daughter, my child, if only you were here! (*She weeps, bows down, and goes out.*)

JUDGE Could you tell us, Charudatta, if she left on foot or in a carriage?

CHARUDATTA I did not see her leave. I cannot say.

VIRAKA *dashes in.*

VIRAKA I'll go to the court. He abused me, he kicked me— *me*, a captain! For doing my duty, as was proper. Sirs, I greet you respectfully.

101

JUDGE Ah, Viraka, a captain of the guard. What brings you here, Viraka?

VIRAKA It's a long story, your Honor. I was only doing my duty, as is proper, searching for Aryaka, who had broken out of jail. Well, your Honor, I didn't like the looks of a carriage, so I stopped it.

JUDGE Do you know who the owner of the carriage is?

VIRAKA The driver said it was this gentleman here, your Honor—Charudatta—and that Vasantasena was in it, going to meet him in the flower garden.

SANSTHANAKA Didn't I say so?

JUDGE A bad day for Charudatta. We shall look into your complaint later, Viraka. In the meantime, tell us if you saw anything in the garden.

VIRAKA Yes, your Honor. There is a woman's body in the garden. The animals had been at it.

CLERK Are you sure it was a woman's body?

VIRAKA Yes, to judge from the long hair and the size of the hands and feet.

JUDGE The more we investigate, the greater is my confusion. Charudatta, you must tell the court the whole truth.

CHARUDATTA This is the truth. But no one believes me. This too is the truth. A crazy man plants a crime on me, and he is believed.

SANSTHANAKA What nonsense is this! Why should this killer remain seated?

JUDGE Clerk, take his seat away.

The CLERK *removes* CHARUDATTA'*s seat. A* STAGEHAND *takes it away.*

CHARUDATTA I shall obey, your Honor, but I am innocent. (*He squats on the floor.*)

SANSTHANAKA (*aside*) Ha-ha! My sin is now on his head. I'll sit near him. (*He edges closer to* CHARUDATTA.) Come, Charudatta, admit your crime and say: "I killed Vasantasena."

MAITREYA *enters with jewels in his girdle.*

MAITREYA (*aside*) Charudatta asked me to return these jewels
to her, but I heard on my way that Charudatta had been
summoned into the court. So I didn't go to Vasantasena's,
but hurried here. (*He comes forward.*) I humbly greet the
court. Where is my friend?

JUDGE Charudatta? There.

MAITREYA My friend Charudatta, may happiness——

CHARUDATTA Happiness later; sorrow now.

MAITREYA Be patient.

CHARUDATTA I am.

MAITREYA Why were you summoned?

CHARUDATTA It seems I am a murderer. . . . No hope for me.
. . . Woman's love . . . Instead, I killed her. . . . They'll
tell you the rest.

MAITREYA What!

CHARUDATTA (*whispering in his ear*) That's the story.

MAITREYA Who says so?

CHARUDATTA (*indicating* SANSTHANAKA) He is the man chosen
by Fate to accuse me.

MAITREYA (*aside to* CHARUDATTA) Why not tell them that we
did not wait for her and she must have gone home alone?

CHARUDATTA No one believes me.

MAITREYA Gentlemen, what is this? A man who gave all his
money to decorate this city with gardens, temples, wells,
and fountains—would he kill a woman for a few measly
jewels? (*He speaks more and more angrily.*) And you, you
bastard, Sansthanaka, you king's brother-in-law, you stuffed
monkey, you foul dunghill, say it! Say it in front of *me!* Say
it and I'll crack your skull wide open with this crooked stick!
(*Raises fist.*)

SANSTHANAKA Listen to that, gentlemen! I have accused Charudatta. My business is with Charudatta. And this swine, whom
I've hardly met, wants to crack my skull. Go ahead, try it!

MAITREYA *lifts his fist.* SANSTHANAKA *leaps and hits him first.*
A scuffle ensues, and the jewels slip out of MAITREYA'S *girdle.*
SANSTHANAKA *picks them up and displays them triumphantly.*

SANSTHANAKA Look, gentlemen, look! The woman's jewels!
The reason he strangled her.

The JUDGE *and others favoring* CHARUDATTA *hang their heads.*

CHARUDATTA (*aside to* MAITREYA) My fate plays terrible tricks
on me. With the falling jewels, I fall too.
JUDGE Examine them, Clerk.
CLERK Are these jewels your property, Charudatta?
CHARUDATTA No.
CLERK Whose are they?
CHARUDATTA They belong to Vasantasena.
CLERK How did she lose them?
CHARUDATTA It is true she lost them once.
SANSTHANAKA Liar! You lured her into the garden, killed her,
and stole them.
JUDGE Charudatta, speak the truth.
SANSTHANAKA Why don't you admit it? Say: "I killed her."
CHARUDATTA You have said it.
SANSTHANAKA There! There! He confessed! He says he killed
her! Sentence him!
JUDGE The court has no other alternative. Clerk, arrest Charu-
datta.

At the CLERK'S *gesture,* GUARDS *move to each side of* CHARUDATTA.

SANSTHANAKA (*aside*) A tidy bit of work I've done today. (*He
struts off.*)
JUDGE Charudatta, our task is to sift the evidence. Recorder,
write down the sentence. (RECORDER *mimes writing.*) "Since
he killed Vasantasena for such a trifle, let the same jewels
be hung from his neck, let him be led to the southern burial

ground, and there let him be executed." Take the prisoner away! Let the executioners receive their orders.

Two EXECUTIONERS *enter and stand on either side of* CHARU- DATTA, *who sits with his head hung low as the* CLERK *puts the plaque of death around his neck. Tableau. Blackout.*

Act Ten

The execution ground near the prison. The lights come up on an empty stage. To slow drumbeats and offstage shouts of a crowd, the two EXECUTIONERS *lead* CHARUDATTA *through city gates to the execution ground.* CITIZENS *come on from the four entrances to watch and call their disapproval, always carefully keeping their distance, however.*

FIRST EXECUTIONER Don't worry, sir. It only takes a second. We'll have your head off in no time. We're pretty good at it. (*To* CITIZENS.) Hey, make way, you! This is the noble Charudatta, going to have his head chopped off.

SECOND EXECUTIONER What's the big idea, there? Move on, move on! It isn't a pretty sight. He was a good tree once— that's what some birds tell me. But now it's the ax for him.

CHARUDATTA Who can escape Fate? A Brahmin dragged like a beast to the sacrifice!

They stop at the first steps, as if they were the first city gate.

FIRST EXECUTIONER Beat the drum and I'll announce the sen- tence. (*Drumbeats.*) Gentlemen of the city! The king is pleased to proclaim that Charudatta, son of Sagaradatta and grandson of the merchant Vinayadatta, having seduced the

courtesan Vasantasena into the lonely flower garden, and
there having strangled her and robbed her of her jewels, and
having confessed his guilt in a court of law, is hereby sentenced to be executed! Let this serve as a warning to all who
contemplate crimes heinous both to this world and the next!
(*They move around the passage to the next set of steps.*) Out
of the way, gentlemen, out of the way! Let's announce the
sentence again.

They stop. The drum sounds. A STAGEHAND *places center a tall
stool with black bars painted on it, representing a prison tower.*
STHAVARAKA *mounts the stool. His speech and the* EXECUTIONER'S
*announcement at the second, third, and fourth gates continue
simultaneously.*

STHAVARAKA (*as if looking down from a high window*) Charudatta sentenced to death? And me thrown in jail? Sirs, sirs,
listen to me! I am the man who took Vasantasena to the
flower garden; she entered my carriage by mistake. I swear
it. There my lord Sansthanaka strangled her with his bare
hands because she refused to love him. Listen! Can't you
hear me? No, they're too far away. My voice doesn't reach
them. Shall I jump down? That might save Charudatta. This
window is so high that it's not barred; I can slip out of it.
But shall I die? Oh, then let me die; let Charudatta live—
that's all I want. Heaven is mine if I die so nobly. (*He
makes the leap.*) Not hurt! And the jump snapped my ankle
chains. Oh, where are you? Where are you? It's me, Sthavaraka! (*A* STAGEHAND *whisks away the stool.* STHAVARAKA
*rushes onto the passage, and shouting frantically, tries to
push his way through the* CITIZENS *following the execution
procession. The* EXECUTIONERS *have led* CHARUDATTA *through
the fourth gate, up the steps, and to the execution ground on
the center platform. Pushing his way through the throng,*
STHAVARAKA *throws himself on his knees before the* EXECU-
TIONERS, *one of whom is holding* CHARUDATTA *while the other*

mimes holding a heavy ax in two hands.) Stop! Listen to me!
It's important. It was I who took Vasantasena to the flower
garden, where Sansthanaka strangled her because she refused
to love him, and——

CHARUDATTA   Thank God, I am saved.

FIRST EXECUTIONER   Is all that true?

STHAVARAKA   Of course it is. And Sansthanaka threw me in
jail and put me in chains so that no one would know.

Unsure, the EXECUTIONERS *mime conversing. Then* SANSTHANAKA
appears on the passage, and all action center stage freezes.

SANSTHANAKA (*picking his teeth and chuckling*)   What a dinner
I've had—meat, fish, sauce, and vegetables. Hm, I hear
voices. . . . The drums and kettledrums that announce an
execution. It's that swine Charudatta. What fun to watch an
enemy's head chopped off! I must see the execution. They
tell me that if a man watches his enemy die, he gets better
eyesight in his next birth. I'll climb to the first window in
this palace tower. (*A* STAGEHAND *places a stool in the entrance
aisle farthest from the tableau.* SANSTHANAKA *stands on it and
peers out, as if from a window.*) Oh, what a crowd to watch
the fun! But when *I* die, I'll draw even bigger crowds. I'm
a great man, the brother-in-law of the king. Well, there he
is, dressed up like a prize cow. But why have they stopped
so near the palace jail? And what is that rascal slave of mine
doing there? Has he broken out of jail? This is getting serious! I must go down and see for myself. (*He steps down. The
stool is taken away. He wades into the crowd.*) Make way for
a lord!

FIRST EXECUTIONER   Make room, please make room.

SANSTHANAKA   Sthavaraka, you'd better come along with me.

STHAVARAKA   No! Leave me alone! Isn't it enough that you
strangled Vasantasena? Why do you want to murder Charudatta too?

SANSTHANAKA What do you mean? I'm as honest as gold. I killed no woman.

CITIZENS He says you killed her. Charudatta did not kill her.

SANSTHANAKA Who says that? Tell me, who says that? (*Members of the crowd point out* STHAVARAKA. SANSTHANAKA, *frightened, aside.*) The devil! I should have had him better chained. He's a witness to the crime. (*Aloud.*) A pack of lies, my friends. He's a no-good lout. I caught him red-handed stealing gold and had him put in chains. He's got a grudge against me; oh, yes, he has. He's invented this story. Isn't that so, you rascal? (*He edges up to* STHAVARAKA *and slips him a gold bracelet.*) Here, take this, and keep your mouth shut.

STHAVARAKA (*taking the bracelet and showing it*) Sirs, sirs! He's trying to bribe me with this!

SANSTHANAKA (*snatching the bracelet from him*) That's it! That's the bracelet I caught him stealing! (*To the* EXECUTIONERS.) Look here, you! I caught him red-handed and had him whipped. Look at his back if you don't believe me.

FIRST EXECUTIONER (*examining the lashes*) Yes, sir, that's true; he has been whipped. No wonder he's making up stories.

STHAVARAKA Oh, no one believes a slave. (*He speaks sadly.*) Charudatta, I did what I could. (*He falls at* CHARADATTA's *feet.*)

CHARUDATTA Rise, Sthavaraka. It's not your fault. My fate is against me.

SANSTHANAKA Run off, you! (*He pushes* STHAVARAKA *away.*) And now what's the delay? Kill him.

FIRST EXECUTIONER Kill him yourself, sir, if you think we're too slow.

MAITREYA (*entering, embraces* CHARUDATTA) Do you think I can live without you?

CHARUDATTA Your life is your life, Maitreya. You have no right to treat it so lightly.

MAITREYA (*aside*) Yes, but I cannot live without you. I'll go and then I'll follow my friend's road to death. (*Aloud.*)

I'll do as you say. (*He embraces* CHARUDATTA *and falls at his feet.*)

FIRST EXECUTIONER Go away. (*They push him to one side.*) Beat the drums and announce the sentence.

Drum sounds.

SANSTHANAKA (*aside*) This won't do. No one is listening. (*Aloud.*) Charudatta, open your mouth and speak the truth: "I killed Vasantasena." (CHARUDATTA *is silent.*) The swine won't speak. Make him speak! Give him a taste of cane!

FIRST EXECUTIONER Speak up, Charudatta.

CHARUDATTA I am afraid of nothing any more, save only this: that men should say I killed the thing I loved.

SANSTHANAKA Speak up!

CHARUDATTA Friends, citizens of Ujjain, my city——

SANSTHANAKA Say: "I killed her."

CHARUDATTA You have said it.

An execution block is placed beside CHARUDATTA *by a* STAGE-HAND. CHARUDATTA *kneels and places his head on the block.*

FIRST EXECUTIONER It's your turn today, Ahinta.

SECOND EXECUTIONER No, it's yours, Geha.

FIRST EXECUTIONER Let's see. . . . Ah, yes. (*Tosses a coin. Both stare at the coin to see if it is heads or tails.*) Well, there is no hurry. My father once said to me, "Geha, my son, you never know. Some kind man might come along and buy his freedom. A son might be born to the king, and a general pardon proclaimed. An elephant might break loose, and the lucky beggar might escape. You never know. There might even be a new king come to the throne, and all the prisoners set free." That's what he said.

SANSTHANAKA A new king? What!

FIRST EXECUTIONER That's why I never hurry.

SANSTHANAKA Come on, come on, kill him. Finish it off.

FIRST EXECUTIONER Forgive us, noble Charudatta. We are only carrying out the king's orders. Say your prayers.

VASANTASENA, *very agitated, enters on the passage at the other side of the crowd, accompanied by the* MONK.

MONK It does look a little odd—me, a monk, in the company of a courtesan. Lady, where shall I take you?

VASANTASENA Please, to Charudatta's house. When I see him, I know I shall live again.

MONK We'll go by this royal road. Come, follow me. (*Sees the crowd.*) But what are they shouting there?

VASANTASENA What a great crowd of people! The whole city of Ujjain seems to have turned out here. What does it mean?

FIRST EXECUTIONER It won't be long now, Charudatta.

The execution announcement is proclaimed once more to the flourish of drums. SANSTHANAKA, *content, moves to the edge of the crowd.*

CHARUDATTA I am ready.

MONK (*fearfully*) Lady, the noble Charudatta is going to be executed for murdering *you!*

VASANTASENA (*in terror*) Take me there. Quickly!

MONK Make room for us, please. Room for us, please.

VASANTASENA Please, sirs. Please . . .

As they push their way through the resisting crowd, one EXE-CUTIONER *holds* CHARUDATTA *while the other mimes raising the heavy ax over his head.*

FIRST EXECUTIONER Noble Charudatta, do not move. A single stroke will do it.

As he is about to strike, VASANTASENA *breaks through the crowd.*

VASANTASENA Stop it! Stop it! I am Vasantasena. Oh, Charu-datta! Charudatta, my love! (*She falls on his breast.*)

FIRST EXECUTIONER (*worried*) Vasantasena! And we nearly killed an innocent man!

MONK Charudatta is alive. Glory to the Buddha!

VASANTASENA And I, too, am alive at last.

FIRST EXECUTIONER Let's go to the king with the news. He is at the place of sacrifice.

SANSTHANAKA (*seeing* VASANTASENA) A ghost? No, still alive! I'm ruined. I must run; I must fly! (*He runs off.*)

FIRST EXECUTIONER Our orders were to behead the man who killed Vasantasena. Let's go after the king's brother-in-law; he must be the man.

Both EXECUTIONERS *run off after him.*

CHARUDATTA Saved from death, from eternal shame. Are you Vasantasena? Or a goddess from heaven?

VASANTASENA I am Vasantasena, my love, the cause of all your troubles.

CITIZENS Vasantasena is alive!

CHARUDATTA (*seeing the* MONK) And who is he?

VASANTASENA A kind monk to whom I owe my life.

MONK You may not remember me, sir. I was the man you engaged to be your masseur. But when I left you, I fell among gamblers and got into debt; then this good lady bought me my freedom with her jewels. I renounced gam-bling and became a Buddhist monk. And then many things happened. She got into the wrong carriage by mistake. I found her in the flower garden, where she had been left for dead by Sansthanaka.

VOICES (*shouting offstage*) Aryaka has won! Glory to Aryaka!

SHARVILAKA *enters.*

SHARVILAKA Yes, I killed Palaka. This hand of mine slew the king and anointed Aryaka the Shepherd as the new king. Now to free Charudatta. Make way, you! (*He sees* CHARU- DATTA.) Charudatta living? And Vasantasena! My king will be please to hear this. Noble Charudatta, greetings!

CHARUDATTA Who are you, sir?

SHARVILAKA I am the thief who stole the gold box from your house. I throw myself on your mercy.

CHARUDATTA (*embracing him*) It has been a blessing in dis- guise, my friend.

SHARVILAKA And also bring the news that I killed King Palaka at the place of sacrifice and that Aryaka is the new king.

CHARUDATTA Aryaka!

SHARVILAKA Yes; your carriage saved him, and now he is king.

CHARUDATTA And you are the man who helped Aryaka escape from the palace prison?

SHARVILAKA Yes, sir. A small thing, sir.

CHARUDATTA I am happy to hear it.

SHARVILAKA His Majesty King Aryaka bestows on you, as a token of gratitude and affection, the Kingdom of Kushavati, and hopes you will honor him by accepting it. (*He turns.*) And now bring that swine.

SANSTHANAKA, *his hands tied behind his back, is dragged in by the* EXECUTIONERS.

SANSTHANAKA Well, I'm caught now; bound and dragged like an ass or a dog. But I still have a trick or two about me. (*He appeals to* CHARUDATTA.) Noble Charudatta, help me, help me.

CITIZENS Don't, Charudatta. We'll teach the swine. Leave him to us.

People rush forward and beat up SANSTHANAKA.

SANSTHANAKA Help me. Please help me.

CHARUDATTA Yes, whoever seeks help shall not go without it.

SHARVILAKA Take him away from here. (*To* CHARUDATTA.)

What shall we do to him, sir? Drag him till his flesh is torn off? Throw him to the dogs? Cut him up with a saw?

CHARUDATTA Listen to me.

SHARVILAKA Sir.

SANSTHANAKA (*on the ground*) Charudatta, help me! Please help me!

CITIZENS Kill him! Kill the swine!

VASANTASENA *takes the plaque of death from* CHARUDATTA'*s neck and throws it around* SANSTHANAKA'*s.*

SANSTHANAKA Please help me now, good courtesan. Have pity. I promise I'll never kill you again.

SHARVILAKA Drag him away. Noble Charudatta, what punishment shall we give him?

CHARUDATTA You will do as I say?

SHARVILAKA I promise.

CHARUDATTA Thank you. In that case——

SHARVILAKA Kill him. But how?

CHARUDATTA No, set him free.

SHARVILAKA What!

CHARUDATTA It is said that the sword should never be used on a man who begs for mercy.

SHARVILAKA We won't use the sword; we'll throw him to the dogs.

CHARUDATTA No. Just untie him; let him go.

SHARVILAKA *does so.*

SANSTHANAKA Ha-ha! I'm free! Free! (*He runs out.*)

SHARVILAKA His Majesty has asked me, madam, to confer on you the title of Lady of the Court.

VASANTASENA Please thank him for me.

SHARVILAKA (*placing a veil of honor on* VASANTASENA'*s head, then turning to* CHARUDATTA) Sir, what does the monk desire?

The Toy Cart

CHARUDATTA   What do you want, holy sir?

MONK   All things pass. And nothing remains. I want nothing.

CHARUDATTA   In that case, you shall be the spiritual head of all Buddhist monasteries in the kingdom.

The MONK *blesses* CHARUDATTA *and* VASANTASENA. *The* CITIZENS *embrace each other with joy, and to lively music they dance several times around the passage as the others pose in tableau. The lights fade to black.*

Thai Lakon Jatri

Lakon jatri is a folk art, sprung from Thai village life. This means it has no detailed written history, as arts of the court or the urban merchant class so often have. The general outlines of its development, however, seem reasonably clear. It is almost certainly a theatre form which is part of a very old, native tradition of communicating with spirits through the medium of dance. Village performers of *lakon jatri* even today are considered to have special powers of communication. *Lakon* means play and *jatri* is related to invincibility or supernatural power, so *lakon jatri* is literally a play of supernatural power. Animistic belief was overlaid by Brahmanism and Buddhism in later centuries but did not disappear. When Therevada Buddhism was adopted by the Thai, between the fifth and tenth centuries, the *Jataka*, or Buddhist birth stories, became an important part of popular and village culture (in contrast to the Brahmanic *Ramayana* epic, knowledge of which was almost entirely restricted to the court). Buddhist monks could not perform or even watch plays, but lay troupes were encouraged to stage *Jataka* plays to spread Buddhism among the people. Plays about Sang Thong, the heroic prince of the golden seashell, Prince Rothasen, who learned the secrets of magic from ogres, Manohra, the celestial *kinnaree* princess—half bird and half human—from the *Panyasa Jataka*, or *Collection of Fifty Jataka*, became the most widely performed of Thai traditional dramas. Unlike the five hundred and seven *Jataka* tales in the sacred *Pra Tripitaka* collection, which is part of the Buddhist canon, the *Panyasa Jataka* are not originally Buddhist or Indian. They are local Thai legends and tales that were adapted to Buddhist teaching by portraying Sang Thong, Rothasen, or Suton (the prince who loves Manohra) as incarnations of the Buddha in previous lives. Indian dance was introduced to Thailand (when, where, and how, we can only speculate), and *lakon jatri* troupes borrowed at least some elements of it. Troupes may have performed over broad areas of Thailand in the past; the long narrow strip of southern Thailand that leads down to Malaysia is now *lakon jatri*'s homeland and has been for several centuries. So completely do *Manohra* plays dominate the repertory of these folk troupes in southern Thailand that the troupes are commonly called *nora jatri*, *nora* being a southern contraction for *Manohra*. Probably by the seventeenth century *lakon jatri* had assumed its traditional form: a folk performance linked to animistic beliefs, primarily staging the *Jataka* legend about Princess Manohra and Prince Suton in a dance style somewhat influenced by Indian dance.

A traditional *lakon jatri* performance reflects its village origin in its simplicity. A troupe could consist of as few as three performers: male lead (*nai rong*), female lead (*tua nang*), and a clown (*jumouad*) who also played demons, beasts, menials, and other roles as required. A troupe could be made larger by adding musicians and offstage singers. In small troupes performers doubled as musicians and singers. The small musical ensemble consisted of one or two single-faced, pear-shaped *jatri* drums (*thon jatri*), a small stick drum (*klong jatri*), a double gong (*kong khu*), a small bell cymbal (*ching*) used to mark time, and an oboe (*pi*). While the large musicial ensembles for Thai court music were heavy and difficult to move, the *lakon jatri* instruments were light and easily packed away, a necessity since the typical *lakon jatri* troupe was itinerant. Costumes were standardized for each role-type. Crown, necklace, trousers, and sash were basic. To the costume could be added wings to identify a *kinnaree* bird-maiden, a scarf to indicate a woman, a red half-mask for the forester Bun, and so on. *Lakon jatri* was performed on a mat spread on the bare earth, so no scenery was needed or used. At most, a single bench placed along one side of the playing area served as throne, cave, mountain, or whatever special locale was to be indicated.

Because the physical aspects of traditional *lakon jatri* were simple, the attention of the audience was focused upon the performers and their skill in song, dialogue, dance, and mime. Using the most basic of elements, three performers of a provincial, illiterate troupe managed to entertain village audiences, evoke the ancient spirits of local fields, streams, and mountains, and tell tales of the beloved Buddha's previous lives in this world, in performances given on the most important religious occasions in the community. We may ask how this was possible when the performers were illiterate villagers and when the scripts of their plays were not even written down. The plays of *lakon jatri* were transmitted from generation to generation as part of an oral tradition. Within the framework of a general story line, the actors of *lakon jatri* improvised dialogue and lyrics. They were famous for this. (*Lakon jatri* may be linked with the very ancient tradition in Thailand of song competition, *len plaeng*, in which men and women extemporized verses poking ribald fun at the other sex.) Improvisation took place within well-understood conventions. Music was confined to nine melodies, appropriate for love, for sadness, for slow or rapid actions. Songs were chanted or sung without melodic accompaniment, the stanzas being alternately sung by the performer on stage and a chorus offstage, in a special technique called *rai*. The danced entry, exit, or other essentially technical dance sequence (*ram phleng*) accompanied by instrumental music, was distinguished from dance that expressed the words of a song and was therefore emotive and mimetic in function (*ram chai bot*). Dance was based on a vocabulary of twelve basic postures, a limited number when compared with the sixty-four movements of Thai court dance or the one hundred and eight described for Indian dance in the *Natyasastra*. Several of the twelve, however, are unique in Thailand to *lakon jatri*.

Lakon jatri is still performed in folk style by troupes in southern Thailand. I visited one troupe in a tiny village near Songkhla: all the old traditions, including the one limiting performers to males, were faithfully observed at the insistence of the elderly troupe leader and teacher (*kru*). But most *lakon jatri* performances reflect the influence of other Thai theatre arts. *Manohra* is performed in Bangkok by the finest classical dancers in an eclectic Thai national style, which is the product of the intermingling of all major performing styles. A full account of how *khon* masked pantomime, *lakon nai* female court dance-drama, *lakon nok* urban commercial theatre, and *lakon jatri* mutually influenced each other is beyond the scope of these few pages. But a few illustrations may suggest how far-ranging that interchange has been. Originally, perhaps as much as five hundred years ago, all-male *khon* pantomime performances of *Ramayana* episodes were staged only for the king, then later for aristocrats, and finally for the public on special occasions. By then they were influenced by the professionally organized *lakon nok* (*nok* means outside the court). When young women in the king's service performed for him their elegant dance versions of the Javanese tale about Prince Inao Panji as *lakon nai* (*nai* means inside the palace), they were strictly forbidden to mingle with male performers—this kept *lakon nai* isolated from *lakon nok,* and even from court *khon*. But in time this social barrier was broken, and *lakon nai* actresses began to play roles with *khon* troupes. Now they play not only the role of Sita, but usually the refined heroes Rama and Laksmana as well, and they dance in the delicate style of female *lakon nai*. The sumptuous costuming of *lakon nai* came to be used for *lakon jatri* performances of *Manohra,* and in turn the *lakon jatri rai* style of singing was adapted to *lakon nai* performances of *Inao*. As Ubol Bhukkanasut, the translator of *Manohra,* suggests, after several centuries of artistic elbow-rubbing, "the distinctions between types [are] gone . . . a modern style of presentation was gradually adopted by all types of classical dance-drama." At the National Theatre of Bangkok today an audience will attend a performance of *Manohra* that represents a fusion of *lakon jatri* traditional folk simplicity with the beauty of classic court dance and music.

Suggested Reading

There are few accounts of *lakon jatri* in English. The most accessible is in James R. Brandon, *Theatre in Southeast Asia* (Cambridge: Harvard University Press, 1967). Dhanit Yupho's *The Khon and Lakon* (Bangkok: Department of Fine Arts, 1963) contains synopses of thirty-two classical dance-dramas, including *lakon jatri* that have been performed at the Silpakorn Theatre in Bangkok.

Manohra
A Thai Lakon Jatri Play

Translated by Ubol Bhukkanasut

The legend of a celestial bird-maiden, whose feathers are taken from her and who is forced to dwell among mortals, is known in different versions throughout Asia, Europe, the Near East, and among the Eskimos and American Indians. It is one of the universal myths, and a most beguiling one. The Thai legend is as follows. The Kingdom of Pancala has been blessed by the serpent god of the ocean in response to the prayers of the people. But famine strikes and an evil minister of Pancala plots against the ocean god. Though the minister fails, the god assumes the form of a Brahman seer who lives by the water's edge. A forester, Bun, kills the minister and for a while lives in the ocean god's kingdom as a guest, but in time he returns to the forest. He learns from the seer Kassop the secret of capturing a *kinnaree* bird-maiden, whom he plans to present to Prince Suton of Pancala. The secret is to lasso the *kinnaree* with a serpent, and Bun is given one by his friend the serpent god. The seven daughters of the *kinnaree* king come to frolic in a forest pool and Bun uses the serpent as a lasso to snare the youngest and most beautiful of the princesses, Manohra. He takes her wings and her tail feathers so she cannot fly away and marches her to the Pancala palace. Suton and Manohra immediately fall in love and are married. But when Suton is maneuvered into leaving for the battlefield, the crafty advisor to the King, Purohit, orders Manohra burned in a sacrificial fire. Manohra asks for her feathers so that she can perform a final dance. When she receives them, she flies into the heavens and to the home of the *kinnaree* on the top of Mount Krailas. Suton returns from the wars victorious and immediately sets out after Manohra. After seven years, seven months, and seven days of trials, he reaches Krailas, the mountain of immortals, where the two lovers are happily reunited.

The long sequence of events which comprises the complete *Jataka* tale of *Manohra* cannot be compressed into a single play. At the Burmese court *Manohra* was performed in a cycle of three plays, three evenings in succession. Folk troupes in southern Thailand may divide the story into twelve parts, which are staged over as many nights. Today, in Bangkok, just the last part of the legend—from the capture of Manohra by Bun to the reunion of Manohra and Suton—is usually staged as an independent play. The version here, translated by Ubol Bhukkanasut, is based on the script prepared by the Department of Fine Arts for a performance at the Silpakorn Theatre, Bangkok, in 1955. It contains the main episodes of the Suton-Manohra love story.

The play is charmingly simple and direct. The few complications of the plot—the frontier mutiny fomented by the villain Purohit, the King's dream, the sacrifice of Manohra—are sufficient to maintain interest without clamoring for attention. A delightful spirit of innocent humor pervades most scenes: the villains are not villains at all, but mere black-hearted bunglers (how secure we feel, laughing at their slapstick incompetence); Manohra jousts verbally with Bun even when in danger of being captured; Queen Chan-Devi twits the king incessantly; Manohra's father teases her moments after their seven-year separation is over. This good-natured humor is a legacy of *lakon jatri* folk origins, as is the clown character Bun.

A number of characteristics typical of Southeast Asian drama are found in *Manohra*. Suton and Manohra are portrayed as ideal royal figures. He is just, generous, brave, and handsome; she is gentle, respectful, graceful, and beautiful. These are attributes a royal figure was expected to possess. Loyalty and self-sacrifice are important virtues: Suton endures great hardships to fulfill his vow to Manohra; the Queen and even common people offer to exchange their lives for Manohra's; Suton orders

Chaiyut to protect Manohra with his life, and then Manohra insists that he help Suton, each prompted by devotion to the other. (The episode in the *Ramayana* when Rama commands Laksmana to guard Sita, who then countermands the order insisting that Laksmana help Rama, is strikingly similar.) Suton's visit to the magically powerful seer Kassop at a hermitage in the forest is typical of hermitage scenes in a score of other theatre forms: a hero receives some divine knowledge or gift that enables him to overcome the dramatic obstacle of the play. This scene is very different from our Western *deus ex machina* scene in which, at the very end of a play, the hero is rescued from certain defeat by forces beyond his control. Suton receives the seer's help because Suton is righteous, and having received magic powers, he still must struggle heroically to achieve his goal. Far from being fatalistically Buddhist, as one might expect, *Manohra* is unambiguous in showing man as an active agent who, because he functions righteously within a morally directed universe, is fully successful in his efforts. Indeed, the Western concept of *deus ex machina* is much more fatalistic: the hero's struggles have already failed and only an unearned, fortuitous quirk of fate saves him.

In the worldview of *Manohra*, Suton is Buddha reincarnate and a temporal ruler through whom political and spiritual harmony on earth are established. Harmony is the natural state of the universe, which is one reason for portraying the villains comically. To show them as serious opponents of the hero would dignify evil. While conflict is present, it is not the subject of the drama. We see no direct confrontation between Suton and Purohit, other than the subtle maneuvering between them when Suton goes to battle. And the resolution of their conflict, presumably Purohit's downfall when Suton returns to Pancala, is of so little interest it is not even dramatized.

Manohra was translated and performed at the John F. Kennedy Theatre at the University of Hawaii in 1965. A major aim of the translation was to retain the simplicity and rough humor of traditional folk *lakon jatri* while conveying a sense of the elegance and beauty of *lakon nai,* especially in the scenes of court dance. The resulting blend of folk and court theatre is apparent throughout the play. The three basic roles in *lakon jatri*—prince, princess, and clown—are readily identifiable as Suton, Manohra, and Bun, but the cast has been increased by a *corps de ballet,* maidservants, attendants, animals, and a group of secondary clowns. The crude and uneducated Bun speaks ungrammatical English; Suton, Manohra, and the King and Queen speak more formal English. The translator wrote the English text in prose suitable for the stage, working "in the spirit of *lakon jatri,* which allows great freedom of interpretation." In Thailand everyone knows the whole of the *Manohra* legend and even the incidents preceding it (in the *Rothasen Jataka,* Suton's pursuit of Manohra is prophesied), but it was necessary to add exposition to help the American audience understand the background of the play.

The play was directed by Wallace Chappell. Four months were devoted to rehearsing the classical Thai dance. A dancer from Thailand performed the difficult offertory dance and choreographed dance scenes. Traditional music was played by an ensemble of five Thai and American musicians. The actors in the clown roles, Bun, Purohit and his minions, and Purohit Junior, played their scenes broadly in the earthy tradition of folk humor. Costumes, make-up, and properties were modeled on those of productions at the National Theatre in Bangkok. Major characters wore shining silks; Bun, Kassop, and the animals wore plain-colored cottons. A single bench was placed center and used to suggest a number of locales, as in Thailand. Broad silk banners were hung at the rear of the stage to suggest, by changing the color of the banners and the lighting, a palace, a forest, a pool, or a mountain. This technique is not used in Thai theatre, but it was felt to be consistent with the requirements of the play and in harmony with the other aspects of the staging. As in Thailand, the playing area of the stage was kept as open as possible to facilitate fluid stage movement.

Characters

MANOHRA, *a bird-maiden*
SUTON, *Prince of Pancala*
BUN, *a forester*
PUROHIT, *advisor to King Adhitavongse*
PUROHIT JUNIOR, *his son*
CHAIYUT, *Suton's friend*
KASSOP MUNI, *a seer*
KING ADHITAVONGSE, *Suton's father*
QUEEN CHAN-DEVI, *Suton's mother*
KING TUMARAJA, *Manohra's father*
QUEEN CHANKINNAREE, *Manohra's mother*
SIX KINNAREE, *Manohra's sisters*
MAIDS
GUARDS *and* SOLDIERS
CHIEF WORKMAN
WORKERS
MESSENGER
FLAG-CARRIER
ANIMALS
STAGEHANDS
MUSICIANS
DANCERS

Manohra

Prologue

*The rising curtain reveals a backdrop, which remains through-
out the play. It depicts a forest of dark greens and browns, with
branches and leaves swirling together in the shape of the roof
of a Thai temple, characterized by wavy flamelike curves cul-
minating in a sharp point. The locale for the Prologue and the
first scene is Lake Bokkharani, deep in Himmaphan Forest.*
SERVANT GIRLS *hold strips of blue-and-green translucent cloth
at each end, representing a lake. When the strips of cloth are
waved, the surface of the lake ripples. Several trees are placed
at the edge of the lake. The light is predominantly green and
blue, with much of the stage in shadow, as if a full moon were
shining over the dense forest. The traditional Thai stage piece,
the long red bench, is in front of the lake, down right. The*
MUSICIANS *are on the side stage, down left. They wear white
shirts and Thai wrap-around skirts* (panungs). *The five-piece
orchestra* (piphat) *includes a small wooden xylophone* (ranad
ek), *a set of finger cymbals* (ching), *a hand drum* (tone), *a small
gong* (khawng), *and a bamboo flute* (khlui). *At times the rhythm
sticks* (grap khu) *are used. The* MUSICIANS' *area is separated from
the forestage by a low railing made of a repeated Thai crown
motif. The Prologue, or offertory dance, is performed in the
midst of the forest by a barefoot* DANCER *garbed in traditional
royal dress: sharply curved epaulets, shimmering gold-and-silver
headdress, and costume of bright gold, red, and green silk. The
long-sleeved top fits tightly. The elaborately folded panung
which encases the legs is quite loose, allowing freedom of movement as the dance requires. Shiny brass fingernails emphasize*

the curve of the fingers when they are bent backward, a movement typical of Thai dance. The DANCER invokes the gods, asking their blessings for a perfect performance. He honors all
teachers of the arts and all dancers before him. He begins by
sitting on his heels, hands together in front of his chest in the
traditional Thai salutation (wai). Slowly he comes to his feet,
guided by the ringing beat of the small cymbals. His body rises
and falls in a fluid motion. The movement of the shoulders
gracefully emphasizes this pattern. Other instruments join in
the music, which begins softly and builds gradually throughout
the dance to a swift, ringing climax. Arched hands reach out to
the fullest extension of the arm and then curl back toward the
chest. The arms wave above the head and back to the chest, then
from side to side. This basic pattern becomes more complex as
the dance becomes faster. When the dance is completed, the
performer bows low to the audience, his hands in the wai position, then leaves the stage. The forest lights come up for the
opening scene of the play.

Act One

Scene 1

As the dance ends, noises of the forest are heard. ANIMALS appear; they are played by actors wearing masks and appropriate
tunics and tights. Two rabbits enter down right, hop around
a tree, and drink from the lake as a small chicken pecks its way
across the stage. From upstage center a mother and a baby bear
enter and scare the smaller animals away. A water buffalo is
unimpressed by the bears' growling. An elephant frightens the
buffalo and the bears away and greets a small monkey with his
trunk. The movements of the monkey are from khon masked

dance-drama. He scratches his ribs with short, straight-fingered strokes. His hands wave toward his mouth, telling us he is laughing. As the monkey and the elephant go off paw-in-trunk, BUN, *a forester, enters.* BUN *wears a red half-mask with exaggerated eyebrows. He wears a white shirt and dark-green panung and carries a large green shoulder bag.* BUN *is a country bumpkin, whose loud bark is worse than his bite. He is ugly but lovable.*

BUN   Bird-people not here yet! Hermit told me every full moon they come from Mount Krailas to swim and play. Bun don't think he lies. Almost midnight and not here yet. (BUN *pulls a long red and green snake, a naga, from his shoulder bag; he wiggles the snake as if it were alive.*) No kinnaree ever escape this beautiful naga. Kinnaree and naga like poison to each other. Hah! I'll take a gift to Prince Suton that no one else can get. My Prince needs wife real bad. Gods, help me get him one. (*Looks around the stage.*) Where is good hiding-place? (*Finds a spot, circles it three times in dog fashion, sits, and immediately jumps up.*) Damn ants! All right, Bun moving. (BUN *finds a satisfactory place and settles himself; scratching and yawning, he immediately goes to sleep curled up in the naga. Seven* KINNAREE, *half bird and half maiden, enter from up left, making flying motions with the arms. Each wears a short-sleeved blouse and panung of shiny blue-and-green satin trimmed with gold sequins. Wings of the same material are attached to shoulders and wrists. The* KINNAREE *pantomime flying to the lake. They take off their wings and begin to splash each other in the pond, playing such games as crack the whip and blindman's buff. The* KINNAREE *giggle merrily as they wash their faces with stylized gestures. Their happy noises wake* BUN. *He sees the* KINNAREE *and laughs.*) A kinnaree is so beautiful, fit only for royalty; Prince Suton be very pleased.

BUN *sneaks up to the bench and stands on it. He whispers magic incantations to his snake and hurls it at* MANOHRA, *the most at-*

*tractive of the bird-maidens. She screams shrilly. So do the
other* KINNAREE, *and putting on their wings, they circle around*
BUN *and* MANOHRA. BUN *wisely stuffs* MANOHRA's *wings into his
shoulder bag. In spite of their terror the* KINNAREE *repeatedly
attempt to save* MANOHRA. *One by one they try to pull the snake
from her waist, but either the snake's bite or its master frightens
them away. The snake wraps its coils around its victim ever
tighter. Her sisters' attempts to rescue her become more frantic.*
BUN *stamps his foot, roars like a lion, and jumps at the harmless
creatures. Finally, the six* KINNAREE *circle the stage five times
while* BUN *zealously guards his captive in the center of the circle.
The* KINNAREE *cry, alternately wiping the tears from each eye
with a waving motion of the flat of the hand. The* KINNAREE,
circling, begin to make flying movements and exit up center.
MANOHRA *cries plaintively. She wipes her eyes with the same
hand movements as her sisters. However, she does not give up
the fight so easily.*

MANOHRA Help me, Sisters; don't fly away! Sisters! Help! Dear
Sisters, help me. Don't go! Ooooh please, come back, help!

BUN Bun got you! Thank the gods, naga does its work well.
Prince Suton will like this pretty present.

MANOHRA (*sweetly, trying to charm him*) Kind sir, let me have
my wings. Please take this thing off, please!

BUN (*laughing delightedly*) Me help you! Bun help you all
right! Come here and I take that nasty naga off you.

MANOHRA But I cannot move, good sir. Besides, you have my
wings. Please, sir, I cannot breathe. This snake hurts so much
I will die. Ooooooh!

BUN No, you won't die. Bun take off naga if you promise not
to escape.

MANOHRA How can I escape without my wings? Oh, I promise.

BUN All right, no tricks, eh?

BUN *rubs his hands together, chants the magic words, and the
naga flies into his hands, thrown by* MANOHRA *to give the im-*

pression of control by a higher power. MANOHRA *sinks to the ground in relief and struggles not to faint. Head bowed, hands in the wai position,* MANOHRA *begs* BUN *to let her go.*

MANOHRA Thank you very much, good sir. May I have my wings now?

BUN All right! (*Charmed by her words,* BUN *brings* MANOHRA'S *wings out of his bag and begins to help her into them. He then remembers that she can fly away, and stops, slapping his head.*) You stupid Bun! Kinnaree think faster than Bun, eh! Trick Bun, eh! (*He roughly ties her hands together with a long green rope produced from his shoulder bag.*) That'll teach you to be smart with Bun the forester.

MANOHRA Ow! Bun, I did not mean to trick you. Please untie my hands.

BUN No, kinnaree try to trick Bun again.

MANOHRA (*flirting*) No! You saved me from the naga; why should I try to trick you?

BUN Why? Ha! All right, Bun let your hand free, but no tricks, eh, kinnaree?

MANOHRA (*with her most sincere smile*) I promise.

BUN Bun take you to beautiful palace to meet Prince Suton. Prince is handsome, strong—you like him.

MANOHRA (*pleading*) But I want to go home to Mount Krailas; I don't want to meet this Suton. Did he order you to take me to him?

BUN No! But Bun do it for Prince Suton.

MANOHRA (*angrily*) Oh, how I hate this Prince and you, you —son of a three-legged baboon.

BUN (*dragging her*) Ha! We go to Pancala. Kinnaree, walk now!

MANOHRA No! (*She pulls* BUN *to the ground with a sharp jerk of the rope and tries to escape up right.* BUN *jumps up angrily and chases* MANOHRA *through the forest. Down left he pulls her to her knees.* MANOHRA *cries and waves good-bye to her sisters in dance gestures. She gets to her feet and pulls* him *down again.* BUN *chases her down right, sputtering furiously, snapping his end of the rope like a whip.* BUN *gets tangled in the rope and takes a pratfall.*) Please! Bun, let me go, please!

BUN *laughs as he untangles himself. He stands determinedly, unbothered by* MANOHRA's *sobs.*

BUN   Come, kinnaree! To Pancala and Suton!

They exit up left, walking to the strong rhythm of the music. The scene change is made by STAGEHANDS *in full view of the audience. All of the scene changes are made in this fashion, accompanied by musical interludes. The trees are lifted up into the area above the stage, and the lake is carried off by the* SERVANT GIRLS.

Scene 2

In the chamber of PRINCE SUTON *in Pancala Palace. Long silk banners are lowered, confining the acting area to the forestage. The banners are royal blue with gold designs. The bench used in the previous scene is now down left. On it is a traditional Thai stage-prop: a triangular pillow of red velvet with flame-like designs painted in black and gold at either end. The lighting is bright and warm.* SUTON *and his good friend* CHAIYUT *are seated down left playing* ska, *a Thai board-game.* SUTON's *costume is of red silk. He wears gold epaulets. Costume and tall crown are trimmed with gold as well.* CHAIYUT *wears a royal-blue tunic and black panung.* PUROHIT JUNIOR, *son of the* ADVISOR TO THE KING, *is clad in a white robe; he is pretending to be asleep. As the scene begins,* SUTON *throws the dice, makes his piece return to the original position, and wins. Both players laugh good-naturedly.*

CHAIYUT It is amazing, my Prince. I am the ska champion of Pancala, but I am a mere beginner in competition with your Highness.

SUTON The crown prince has the advantage of always winning.

CHAIYUT Yes, you win in everything—except the game of love.

SUTON Chaiyut, I'm too young to get married. (SUTON *crosses right, annoyed by his friend.*)

CHAIYUT But the people are most anxious for you to choose your princess.

SUTON Chaiyut, there are traitors in the country, grasping for the power of the throne. (SUTON *notices* PUROHIT JUNIOR *listening.*) You may go now. Tell your father, the jurisconsult, that I wish to speak with him.

PUROHIT JR. (*lisping*) I shall do so, my Prince. (PUROHIT JUNIOR *bows from the waist, his hands together in front of his face in the wai gesture. He moves off with a prissy walk, then sneaks back and listens through the hanging banners.*)

SUTON (*irritated*) What have you been able to discover about that moron's father, Purohit, who has the King under his treacherous thumb?

CHAIYUT I can prove nothing, but I'm certain the jurisconsult is responsible in some way for the recent bandit raids.

SUTON How can we convict him without evidence?

CHAIYUT I don't know, but his power grows daily, my Prince.

SUTON My father's dependence on his magic power is unshakable. That charlatan has my father so bewitched, he no longer listens to me. I am not afraid for myself, but for the welfare of the people of Pancala.

CHAIYUT The people know that, my Prince.

SUTON Purohit and his band are still raiding villages and desecrating shrines. Why, even our royal supply-wagons are stolen in broad daylight, while the crown prince of Pancala can do nothing.

A GUARD *and a* MESSENGER *enter from down right. Both are clad*

133

Manohra

in red panungs and white cotton vests painted with protective magic symbols.

MESSENGER (*making wai gesture*) My Prince, I bring greetings from the commander of the third border-garrison. (*Hands* SUTON *a scroll.*)
SUTON Chaiyut, look at this. The bandit raids must be the work of a single man.
MESSENGER Begging your royal permission, there are rumors the leader of the bandits lives in Pancala.
SUTON Thank you, my friend. It is a long ride from the border; you must be tired. Guard, take him to the guest chambers and attend his needs.
MESSENGER My Prince.

The GUARD *and* MESSENGER *make the wai gesture and exit.*

SUTON My father must send reinforcements to the border immediately. Chaiyut, we must find their leader!

There is a loud sound of scuffling off down right. MANOHRA *is heard protesting and* BUN *scolding. The* GUARD *enters from down right.*

GUARD (*making the wai gesture*) Your Highness, there is a man, a forester, who insists on seeing you. Shall I tell the guards to remove him?
SUTON No! My chambers are open to any Pancala citizen at any time. Let him come in.
CHAIYUT A forester! Sire, he may have news of the bandits.

The GUARD *exits and brings on* BUN, *who falls to his knees in homage. He bows deeply, but in comic fashion, squatting rather than bowing from the waist.* BUN *holds the rope in one hand; it trails offstage.*

SUTON   Rise, Forester, and tell me what you want.

BUN   My Prince, Bun want nothing. Bun bring gift for Prince Suton.

CHAIYUT (*incredulous*)   A gift for his Highness? Is that the reason for this intrusion?

BUN   Bun bring special gift for Prince Suton. Bun come from Himmaphan Forest. Prince Suton like this gift—Bun sure! (BUN *laughs knowingly, winking at* SUTON.)

CHAIYUT   Where is this wonderful gift?

SUTON   Bun, I thank you for your kindness, but you need not give me anything. I do not want gifts, only friends.

BUN   Bun take long time to bring this kinnaree for Prince. Bun no can take all the way back to Himmaphan Forest. Bun kill her first!

SUTON   You brought a what?

CHAIYUT   I think he said a kinnaree, sire.

BUN   Bun bring kinnaree. If Prince no want, then Bun kill her.

SUTON (*laughing in disbelief*)   Bring in this present; I should like to see it for myself. Kinnaree! They're supposed to be very beautiful. I've always thought they were mythical creatures.

BUN *drags in* MANOHRA, *who is pouting. She sits on her heels, refusing to look at anyone.*

BUN   The kinnaree princess Manohra. Prince Suton like Bun's gift?

SUTON *does not answer. He can only stare astonished at her beauty.*

SUTON   I have never seen such a beautiful creature. And what a lovely name—Manohra. Bun, I must reward you for bringing Princess Manohra to me.

BUN   As long as Prince Suton happy, Bun happy. Now Bun go.

135

SUTON   Wait! (BUN *exits quickly to avoid the embarrassment of further gratitude.*) How beautiful you are, Princess Manohra.

SUTON *dances shyly toward* MANOHRA, *and they begin a gentle dance of first encounter, accompanied by the soft music of the piphat.* MANOHRA *is still on her heels as* SUTON *dances around her, repeatedly forcing her to look at him. He attempts to bring her into his dance. He stands behind her, arms outstretched, fingers curled back, gently tempting her to begin. She refuses.* SUTON *again dances around her, knees bent, arms moving in graceful swimming motions.* MANOHRA *is obviously interested but makes a show of not admitting it. She turns her head away from* SUTON *again and again.* SUTON *coyly traps her into following his lead.* MANOHRA *hides her face as her pride melts and she shyly blushes. She rises and tentatively begins to dance with* SUTON. *He stands behind her, his head close to her.* MANOHRA *still refuses to look at him, but now their movements blend together in unison.* SUTON *raises his hand and* MANOHRA *lowers hers, and they repeat this contrapuntal movement to an increased tempo of the music.* MANOHRA *leads* SUTON *in small circles around the stage. They dance as one, and* SUTON *leads* MANOHRA *off down left.* CHAIYUT *gazes happily after them.*

CHAIYUT   Bachelorhood? Ha!

The lights dim on the down left and center areas of the stage.

Scene 3

Another part of the palace, indicated by the dimly lit down right area. PUROHIT *is center. He wears a white robe and a shiny bald wig.* PUROHIT JUNIOR *is seated in front of his father. Two* SOLDIERS *squat on either side of* PUROHIT. *They wear black tunics. Each time a* SOLDIER *speaks in this scene, he springs up from his squatting position. When his line is finished, he re-turns to the floor. This action resembles a jack-in-the-box.*

FIRST SOLDIER (*jumps up*)   I propose we move against the out-posts as soon as possible.

SECOND SOLDIER (*jumps up*)   Before the reinforcements can ar-rive. Those garrisons cannot stand against us long.

PUROHIT JR.   Suton suspects us already, Father, but he can find no proof. He can only guess that you are the leader of the bandit group. But if Chaiyut does any more snooping around, he is bound to find some evidence.

PUROHIT (*menacing*)   Suton's suspicions are coming too close. That princeling brat is a constant pain in my neck. I'll have to take care of him—and soon.

FIRST SOLDIER (*jumps up*)   And the garrisons?

SECOND SOLDIER (*jumps up*)   I'm ready!

PUROHIT   Fools, dolts, idiots! (PUROHIT *pushes the two* SOLDIERS *to the floor.*) Now, listen to me. Nobody, nobody—you under-stand?—is going to move against those garrisons until I am good and ready. If you three were to head this rebellion, we would have been headless long before now. As long as Suton and Chaiyut do not know for certain that I am the leader of the bandits, we are safe. My influence over that doddering old fool of a king is complete.

PUROHIT JR.   We must act now, Father, before it is too late.

PUROHIT JUNIOR *is slapped to the floor.*

PUROHIT   Pea-brained idiot! Who are you to tell me what to do?

PUROHIT JR.   But, Father, I was only trying to help——

PUROHIT   How many men do we have in the capital? (*As they begin to conspire,* PUROHIT *breaks out of the formal grouping and paces rapidly in front of the others.*)

FIRST SOLDIER (*jumps up*)   Sire, enough to capture the palace and defend it from any attack.

SECOND SOLDIER (*jumps up*) But we will need reinforcements from our troops outside Pancala to subdue the city.

PUROHIT But we must be careful. If Suton——

FIRST SOLDIER Dies?

PUROHIT We die with him. He distrusts us, and whomever Suton suspects, the people will also suspect. Would you like to face hysterical peasants? No, of course not; you are too much of a coward for that. Let him suspect us all he wants. He will find no evidence whatsoever.

PUROHIT JR. Father, can't we do something about Suton?

FIRST SOLDIER A knife in the back some dark night?

SECOND SOLDIER (*cringing*) Are you going to do it? Suton is the best swordsman in Pancala. Chaiyut has a quick sword, too.

PUROHIT (*shouting*) Enough of this wrangling! I have greater problems on my mind than your petty quarrels.

PUROHIT JR. (*shouting*) Yes, shame on you!

PUROHIT You shut up, too! (PUROHIT *slaps his son to the ground and puts his foot on* PUROHIT JUNIOR's *head, an act of extreme debasement.*)

FIRST SOLDIER Begging your pardon, sire, our troops are ready to go. The only stumbling block is Suton; it would be easy to do away with him.

SECOND SOLDIER I disagree! We can never defeat Suton until the people of Pancala give us their support.

PUROHIT Right! But we must first destroy him in the eyes of the people. His strength and virtue are well known. And me, the most powerful man in Pancala, nobody speaks of me in civil terms. I'll show them!

PUROHIT JR. They're all laughing at you now, Father, but remember the time they were all laughing at Suton. When he told the King to depose you. Heh! I liked that.

PUROHIT *slaps him down again.*

PUROHIT You fool! You have more of your mother's blood in you than mine. She was such an asinine chatterbox, I tried to escape to a hermitage, but then you appeared—a squirm-ing, idiotic mess.

PUROHIT JR.   Mother always said that I was more like you than her. She always said, "Like father, like son."

PUROHIT   My son, I wish I were not your father.

PUROHIT JR. (*attempting to gain his father's favor*)   Father, I have news for you.

PUROHIT JUNIOR *follows his father on his knees. He tugs on his father's robe, and has his hand slapped.*

PUROHIT   What is it?

PUROHIT JR.   Suton has a **kinnaree.**

ALL (*incredulous*)   What?

PUROHIT JR.   A forester captured one in Himmaphan Forest and brought it to Suton as a gift.

FIRST SOLDIER (*jumps up*)   You must have seen dreaming.

SECOND SOLDIER (*jumps up*)   No one can ever catch a kinnaree.

PUROHIT JR.   It is a kinnaree. I even saw the wings. (*Shyly.*) She is very beautiful, Daddy, big eyes, round face, beautiful lips, beautiful—all over.

PUROHIT   I must decide what this means. (*Paces three steps and stops, as if thunderstruck.*) Ah, yes, a great event will take place in Pancala. Yes! Of course, Suton's marriage. I told the Queen that Suton could not marry a mere mortal. Now, my prediction is true. (*Laughs in anticipation of foul play to come.*) Suton and a kinnaree, eh?

PUROHIT JR.   She's a princess, too—Princess Manohra.

FIRST SOLDIER (*jumps up*)   The people will love him all the more for this.

SECOND SOLDIER (*jumps up*)   They talk about nothing but his marriage.

PUROHIT   Oh, but they will! They will! Enjoy it while you can, Suton. I, Purohit, wish you great happiness. Until the day . . .

PUROHIT, *his* SOLDIERS, *and his son all laugh heartily.* CHAIYUT *enters from stage left.* PUROHIT *goes to him, and his still-giggling henchmen line up behind him.*

CHAIYUT Honorable Jurisconsult, the King bids me command you to appear at the throne hall immediately.

PUROHIT Now? (*Aside.*) Whatever for?

FIRST SOLDIER (*aside*) Maybe Suton knows something.

SECOND SOLDIER (*whispers to* PUROHIT) What shall we do, sire?

PUROHIT What is his Majesty's wish?

CHAIYUT The Prince would like to speak with you.

PUROHIT (*sarcastically*) The Prince is in good health, I presume.

CHAIYUT (*unruffled*) Excellent health, honorable Jurisconsult. Purohit, why are you so worried? Prince Suton only wants you to consult the stars for an auspicious day for the wedding ceremony.

PUROHIT Wedding? How nice! (PUROHIT *turns to the audience, smirking.*)

CHAIYUT Yes, the Prince is most anxious for an early wedding, even though he feels that a wedding after certain changes in the palace would be more appropriate.

PUROHIT I am much honored by this unexpected visit, Chaiyut. You visit me so seldom. It has not been long ago since you were only this high. (PUROHIT *gestures six inches from the floor.*)

CHAIYUT Very long ago, my friend. But, come with me.

All exit up center, the henchmen still in a tight line behind PUROHIT. *The lights dim on the down right area.*

Act Two

Scene 1

Lights come up on SUTON's *chamber, down left.* MANOHRA *is seated on the bench with her legs under her in Thai fashion.* SUTON *stands behind her.*

SUTON *(tenderly)* Dearest Manohra, don't look so unhappy. I know you are looking forward to returning home to Krailas. But Pancala needs me now more than ever. My father's sickness and the bandit raids keep me here against my will.

MANOHRA Forgive me, my Prince. I understand your concern for Pancala, but I am thinking of the time when you will be away from me.

SUTON Aren't the servants treating you properly?

MANOHRA Oh, yes, my Prince. They're wonderfully kind. *(Through tears.)* Only, when you are with me . . .

SUTON *(sits on the bench beside her)* I know. It is not my wish to be away from you, but you know that I must. My thoughts are constantly with you wherever I am.

MANOHRA And my thoughts are always with you.

SUTON Except that sometimes they fly back to Mount Krailas? I promise we will be there together someday.

MANOHRA I promise I will never leave you, my Prince, unless . . . you wish me to go.

SUTON Manohra, how could you say such a thing! Nothing can ever keep us apart, not even death.

CHAIYUT *(out of breath, bursts into the room from down left and kneels)* I beg your pardon, my Prince, my Princess, but the

141

bandits and their allies have destroyed three of our border outposts and are marching rapidly on Pancala itself.

SUTON (*strides quickly to* CHAIYUT, *pulling him to his feet*) Can they be so bold? Are you certain?

CHAIYUT I rode out to see for myself. They have burned and sacked every small village in their path. Our border army has been completely routed.

SUTON What about the reinforcements I ordered you to send?

CHAIYUT We were too late, your Highness. The King authorized the army only three days ago.

SUTON What can we do?

CHAIYUT The King has called an emergency meeting of the councilors and has sent me to request your presence.

SUTON I shall go right away. (*Turns to* MANOHRA.) My dearest, I will return as soon as possible. I shall send in the dancers to entertain you. (SUTON *claps his hands twice*.) Come, Chaiyut, let us go to the King.

CHAIYUT *and* SUTON *exit down left as* MANOHRA *sinks to the bench with crying gestures. Ten female* DANCERS *enter, wearing gold satin dresses trimmed with silver, long gold fingernails, and black and gold headdresses. The ringing sound of the xylophone, small cymbals, and ankle bells of the* DANCERS *accompanies their movements. They form two lines of five* DANCERS *each and perform the* sat chatri, *similar to the Prologue dance. Sitting on their heels, they lift their hands to the heavens and then to the audience in a graceful salutation. The music starts slowly, with a distinct thumping beat from the drum. The* DANCERS *move their shoulders to the rhythm; then their bodies move from side to side. The* DANCERS *are now on their feet, legs deeply bent, arms extended to the side and alternately sweeping over the head and then down. The pattern is varied with the right hand to the forehead, forefinger and thumb extended together and the other fingers bent back; the left arm is extended to the side, the hand in the same articulation as the right. The left elbow bends and snaps into place; then right and left arms reverse positions. The two lines of* DANCERS *come together and part, echoing the courtship dance of* SUTON *and* MANOHRA. *The lines come together again, curved hands and bent arms moving in opposition. Then the lines form a circle,* DANCERS *facing in, arms to the center, with the same use of the elbows and hands. The circle moves first one way and then the other and breaks again into two lines. As the volume and the tempo of the music increase, the coming-together pattern is repeated. The dance ends abruptly. The* DANCERS *make the wai gesture to* MANOHRA *and exit up center. The brilliance of the* DANCERS' *smiles and the happy sounds of the music bring* MANOHRA *out of her doldrums. She bows graciously as the* DANCERS *exit.* SUTON *re-enters and crosses to* MANOHRA.

MANOHRA (*bravely*) What has the King decided?

SUTON My father cannot lead any force in his present condition. Chaiyut volunteered to lead the army, but I have decided to command it myself.

MANOHRA My Prince, I shall miss you so very much.

SUTON Chaiyut!

CHAIYUT *enters quickly, bowing.*

CHAIYUT Yes, sire?

SUTON Chaiyut, I want you to remain behind to guard Manohra. I fear that when I am gone, Purohit will make his move. On no condition are you to leave the Princess alone. I don't think he will try anything until he has done away with me. (*Confidently.*) Which he can never do!

CHAIYUT Can't I go with you?

MANOHRA (*urgently*) Please take him, my Prince. I shall feel so much safer if Chaiyut goes with you.

SUTON Don't worry, dearest. I can take care of myself. My only concern is for your safety. No, Chaiyut, you must stay here.

CHAIYUT Yes, my Prince. (CHAIYUT *bows deeply.*)

SUTON Manohra, my love, let us say our good-byes.

The two lovers walk off slowly, knees bending in time to the drumbeat. The light quickly fades. Stagehands changing scenery are silhouetted by the light of the forest backdrop.

Scene 2

The setting is Pancala Plaza. A throne, center, stands before a backdrop of red silk banners embroidered with Thai designs. The throne is represented by the red bench that has appeared throughout the play. The triangular pillow is placed in the middle of it, separating the KING *and the* QUEEN *when they sit cross-legged on the throne. A royal procession enters up left, led by* PUROHIT; *his son and henchmen follow. Next comes a black chariot, decorated with elaborate Thai designs in gold, carrying the* KING. *It is pulled by two* GUARDS *dressed in the standard soldier-costume of red panung and white vest.* SUTON *follows the chariot,* MANOHRA *at his side. They are on foot, as is the rest of the procession. The* QUEEN *comes next, followed by seven* MAIDS *in blue and eight more* SOLDIERS. PUROHIT *and his followers group themselves right of the throne.* SERVANTS *and* SOLDIERS *stand stage left. The chariot stops and the doddering* KING *dismounts in front of the throne.* SUTON *stands on his right,* MANOHRA *and the* QUEEN *on his left. The* KING *tries vainly to be heard over the noise of the crowd. Finally,* SUTON *signals and all is quiet.*

KING My people, citizens, loyal subjects: we are threatened by an enemy which is coming ever closer to Pancala. They have sent emissaries demanding our surrender; we have answered them, Never! (*The crowd cheers.*) My son, Prince Suton, will lead our army against this rabble; he will need many volunteers to defeat them. We plead with you to join him and defend the honor of Pancala.

General approval from the crowd.

PUROHIT *(enjoying the spotlight)* Heed our prayers and exhortations, mighty ones. Accept our humble sacrifice and grant us victory over our enemies.
SOLDIERS Grant us victory!

PUROHIT *steps forward to read the following passage from a scroll.* PUROHIT JUNIOR *tries to lead the people in "Grant us victory," but his cracking voice is always heard a beat too late.*

PUROHIT Vishnu, lend thy cunning to our Prince Suton so he may lead our enemies to their doom as thou once did to thine enemies.
SOLDIERS Grant us victory!
PUROHIT O Brahma, preserve him in thy all-knowing palm of righteousness and justice. Safeguard Pancala and all of its people. Bring our Prince safely home to us and grant us everlasting peace.
SOLDIERS Grant us victory!
PUROHIT Demonstrate your wills to us, O mighty ones.

PUROHIT *signals two* SOLDIERS *to bring on a free-standing tree trunk and place it center stage.* SUTON *draws his sword and dances around the tree, demonstrating his prowess to the approving crowd.* SUTON *finally strikes the trunk, as if to chop it in two, but the sword breaks instead.* PUROHIT *and his men are delighted. Momentarily* SUTON *is shaken, but he recovers quickly.*

SUTON *(reassuring the crowd)* We shall defeat them, my people. Sire, the omen is good. With our triumph over this bandit army, we shall have peace. *(The people shout their approval.)* Is that not so, Purohit?
PUROHIT *(outmaneuvered)* It is just so, my Prince.

SUTON   Thank you, wise Jurisconsult.

The KING *picks up a large sword and gives it to* SUTON.

KING   The gods have spoken! This magic sword belongs to
our ancestors. Ever since the great war in which much blood
was shed, this sword has never been unsheathed, for its power
is too terrible to imagine. Now is the time. Power is in your
hands—use it wisely, my son.

SUTON *(strongly)*   Your Majesty, I will.

The people cheer SUTON *with great fervor.*

MANOHRA *(calmly)*   Lord of my life, I am confident you will
defeat the enemies of our people. My thoughts and prayers
will be ever with you.

SUTON   I leave my beloved wife in your care. Let no harm
come to her.

KING *and* QUEEN   We promise, my son.

PUROHIT   May the gods smile upon you, my Prince. *(Aside.)*
May you never return alive.

Eight SOLDIERS *dance their skill in battle, to music that is
stronger and louder than any previously played. Drum and
rhythm sticks set a vigorous tempo.* SUTON *dances among the*
SOLDIERS, *demonstrating his prowess with the magic sword. A*
SERVANT *follows him, carrying an umbrella high overhead, twirling it whenever* SUTON *moves. A* FLAG-CARRIER *dances center
stage,* SUTON'S *second-in-command. Then* SUTON *inspects his
troops, dances back upstage to the throne area, and watches.
The* SOLDIERS *square off in two lines of four each. Each pair of
men wields a different weapon: bow, spear, sword, and knife.
They engage in mock combat: legs bent, they lift one foot and
then the other, bringing the foot flat to the ground with a
loud slapping sound. One line kneels as the other towers over
it; then the pattern reverses.* SOLDIERS *with the same weapons*

present themselves two by two to the audience and pantomime their skill in fighting. They form a marching column two abreast. At this point PUROHIT *sneers at the audience and exits.* SUTON *calls in the elephant that appeared in the first scene. With the beast leading the way,* SUTON *and his entourage march off to war, circling the stage in a broad figure-eight as the curtain falls.*

Act Three

Scene 1

A garden of the palace. Trees seen earlier and several large rocks set the scene. As the curtain rises, the stage is flooded in deep-red light. Two MAIDS, *wearing blue panungs and sleeveless blouses of blue and white check, come in up left.*

FIRST MAID (*awed*) Oh! Look at the beautiful sunset.

SECOND MAID (*worried*) I don't like it. The sky glows blood red, as if the entire heavens were on fire.

FIRST MAID Sssh! You'll upset the Princess. She is so worried about Prince Suton, and he's only been away three days.

SECOND MAID Did you notice her Highness has barely touched her food? No matter how much Chaiyut tries to console her, she still worries about Suton.

FIRST MAID Speaking of Chaiyut, have you seen him today?

SECOND MAID No, but I saw some of those handsome guards outside the palace.

FIRST MAID Be serious!

THIRD MAID (*dashes in from down left*) Oh, oh . . . let me catch my breath.

FIRST *and* SECOND MAIDS What happened? What is it?

THIRD MAID The streets are filled with fleeing villagers. They're saying our army has been defeated by rebels. Prince Suton——

FIRST MAID It can't be. Nothing has happened to him?

THIRD MAID Some say he has been captured. Others believe he's hiding with a small band of soldiers.

SECOND MAID Poor Manohra! What shall we tell her?

CHAIYUT *overhears the last lines from up left. He crosses to the* MAIDS, *stage center.*

CHAIYUT Nothing! No one is to whisper a word to the Princess. It is a meaningless rumor. Do you understand?

CHAIYUT *sees* MANOHRA *entering down left. He dismisses the* MAIDS *and they exit down right.* MANOHRA *crosses to him, walking aimlessly.*

MANOHRA (*with forlorn voice*) Rumor, what rumors, Chaiyut? Krailas, so far away—how I need my sisters today to while away the lonely hours. They could fly where my Prince is and tell him how much I long to be by his side. Chaiyut, when I was very young, I played games of hide-and-seek with my sisters, and I used to hide in a big cave. I used to feel very brave when I entered it, but one day as I sat there waiting for my sisters to give up their search, I felt as if I were alone in the world—funny, isn't it? The sky is blood red again tonight. Chaiyut, it was so yesterday, wasn't it?

CHAIYUT Red is the color of war, death, and destruction!

MANOHRA Chaiyut, it doesn't mean victory for anyone, only suffering and bloodshed. (*A* GUARD *enters quickly, whispers in* CHAIYUT'S *ear, then exits.*) What has happened?

CHAIYUT (*a bad liar*) Nothing of great importance, my Princess. We can only investigate the matter.

MANOHRA (*shocked at what she sees*) Chaiyut! A falling star! No, a comet! Chaiyut, has anything happened? What news have you been keeping from me? I command you to speak.

CHAIYUT I have kept nothing from you.

As CHAIYUT *attempts to evade* MANOHRA'*s urgent questions, he pulls away.* MANOHRA *follows.*

MANOHRA Old seers on Mount Krailas say whenever a comet appears, it is a sign from the gods, an omen of change. Sometimes it marks the death of a great man. (*Demanding.*) Chaiyut, tell me what is wrong.

CHAIYUT (*tentatively*) It is rumored the Pancala army has been defeated and the Prince has been captured.

MANOHRA There could be some truth in it. Three days now the sky has been painted with blood and villages have been destroyed. (*Exasperated.*) Suton may be in danger, and you stand there and say it's only a rumor.

CHAIYUT The Prince gave me explicit instructions to look after your safety. I am only trying to fulfill my duty. The dangers we face are internal. Purohit is the man to fear.

MANOHRA (*defiantly*) I'm not afraid of Purohit. Chaiyut, you must leave immediately for Suton's camp. You must protect him.

CHAIYUT Prince Suton has ordered me to stay with you. But if your Highness commands, I have no choice but to obey.

MANOHRA (*strongly*) I do command, Chaiyut; go now!

CHAIYUT My Princess.

CHAIYUT *bows and exits down left, happy to be joining* SUTON. MANOHRA *falls to her knees in prayer.*

MANOHRA (*pleading*) Dear gods, protect my Prince always from danger, let not his foe prevail, and bring him safely back to me. (*Sinks back on her heels.*) No moon tonight, eh! How many more such nights as these?

The lights slowly fade to black.

Scene 2

Blue silk banners upstage indicate an interior room in the palace. It is the bedchamber of the KING, *dimly lit in the middle of the night. The* KING *dreams fitfully on the red bench. During the scene the light gradually brightens. The* KING *groans and trembles. Suddenly, he springs out of bed.*

KING (*screaming*) Guards! Guards! (*Runs frantically around the stage.*) Where are they? Guards! (*A* GUARD *runs on from down left, the* QUEEN *from down right. She fusses over the* KING, *checking his forehead and pulse, and looking at his tongue. He speaks breathlessly.*) Sleeping on duty, eh? Next time you'll lose your head! Tell Purohit to come here at once. Hurry!

GUARD At once, your Majesty. (GUARD *exits down left.*)

KING (*almost hysterical*) What a nightmare! I can still see it!

QUEEN Are you all right, Adhitavongse? Did you take your medicine tonight? Oh! You must have a cold. Come lie down.

KING Chan-Devi, I cannot go back to bed until Purohit interprets my dream. (*Pacing.*) Oh, why doesn't he come?

QUEEN (*scolding*) You must have been drinking again. Every time you drink, you have bad dreams. And in your condition, too. Shame on you!

KING No, my dear, I did not touch a drop. I've never had such a dream before. It frightens me.

QUEEN Your Majesty had quite a dream when Suton was born. Maybe . . . (*Pats her stomach.*)

KING No, no! It was not that kind of dream. This one is quite different. It may signify something horrible is going to happen to me.

QUEEN There is no danger to Pancala; that I'm sure of.

PUROHIT *enters from down left in a mock-solemn manner. He bows deeply to the* KING *and* QUEEN. *The* QUEEN *ignores him.*

PUROHIT (*hiding his glee*)   May the gods smile with continued favor upon you. Your Majesty's humble servant is glad to see his Majesty is looking exceptionally healthy and well.

KING (*distraught*)   I am so glad that you are here, Purohit. I have had a terrible dream I want you to interpret for me.

PUROHIT   Your Majesty, I feel something evil in this room. A ghost, a demon—some foreboding presence is here. It treads like an enemy and not a friend. Spirit of the night, away with you! (PUROHIT *makes a show of conjuring away the evil spirit: he sweeps about the room, gesturing and rubbing his hands.*) It is gone, your Majesty.

QUEEN (*skeptical*)   I didn't see anything.

KING   My dear Chan-Devi, of course you cannot see it; you don't have Purohit's occult powers.

PUROHIT (*fawning*)   You flatter me, your Majesty. Shall I now interpret the dream?

KING   Of course, of course! I——

QUEEN   Is it a long dream? The last one took three days and three nights to interpret.

KING   Chan-Devi, please let me tell my dream. (*The* KING *and* PUROHIT *walk down left together. The* QUEEN *follows closely.*) Purohit, I dreamt I was standing out in space with the world before me, and as I stood there, my intestines began to encircle the globe; and when the globe was fully encircled, I was awakened.

QUEEN (*laughs skeptically*)   Anybody can make predictions. Why, Purohit will soon tell us that we might die tomorrow.

KING   Stop making fun of Purohit. I trust him completely.

PUROHIT (*aside*)   Damn! The dream portends victory for Suton. Yet, the stupid King will believe anything I tell him. (PUROHIT *turns to the* KING *with an elaborate flourish.*) The dream fills me with such fear, your Majesty, I do not have the courage to speak to you.

KING Not speak? Speak, man, speak! What is it? Tell me!

QUEEN Oh! Come now, my dear Jurisconsult; what unspeakable horrors have you concocted for your King this time?

PUROHIT Your Highness is pleased to jest! Such a dream occurs once in centuries. The last time, a great earthquake opened up to swallow the entire city.

KING (*completely given over to* PUROHIT's *mastery*) Purohit, tell me. I must know. What can it mean? That the gods are angry with me? Have I forgotten to worship one of them?

PUROHIT Your Majesty, I dare not even whisper it.

KING I command you! Tell me!

PUROHIT I dare not, your Royal Majesty.

KING Speak or die!

PUROHIT (*calmly*) My fear for your Majesty thus prompts me to speak. (*Dramatically*.) Sire, within the period of the crescent moon and the star of death, the two have never collided. Within seven days the crescent moon and the star of death will meet. Then, sire . . . (*Pause*.)

KING Tell me!

PUROHIT (*grandly*) Then, sire, you will die and the city of Pancala will be beset by great natural disasters. The city of Pancala will be no more.

KING (*hysterical*) I knew it! I knew it! Didn't I tell you, Chan-Devi? I could feel it in my bones, my very being. Purohit, what can you do to stop it? There must be something you can do!

QUEEN (*growing desperate with her obsessed husband*) My King, what disasters can be in store for Pancala, or for you? Don't be silly. Why should you trust in his opinion? Call in the other seers and ask their opinions, too.

KING Be quiet, Chan-Devi! I believe in this man. He has served me faithfully through the years. I will not let you or anyone else in my kingdom make such slurs on his capability.

PUROHIT Your Majesties! If the Queen has any doubts, bring in others to interpret your Majesty's dream.

KING There is no need! Tell me what you can do to stave off this disaster.

PUROHIT (*slyly*) Very well, your Majesty. I have several remedies, but what I am about to suggest is of such grave importance, it can be heard by your Majesty alone.

QUEEN (*outraged*) You mean you don't want me to hear. Oh! The nerve of you to even suggest such a thing. Whatever you have to say, say it! I want to hear what you say to my husband!

KING Chan-Devi, go!

QUEEN You order me to?

KING Yes! Go now!

QUEEN Well! (*She storms out down right.*)

PUROHIT From now on, your Majesty, no one should be allowed to disturb us. To begin the ceremony to purify the city and prevent disaster, the entire inner palace must be sealed off from all visitors. During these crucial days no one should talk to your Majesty except myself.

PUROHIT *begins pacing, gloating in his mastery over the* KING, *who follows him closely.*

KING It shall be done. (PUROHIT *stops and the* KING *stumbles into him.*) Will that be enough?

PUROHIT That is the first step, your Majesty. Moreover, a ceremonial altar will have to be established. The sacrifice must be purified in the ritual manner, making it of higher value to the gods. (PUROHIT *begins his pacing again. The* KING *follows.*) I shall need one hundred four-legged animals, equally divided according to sex; one hundred two-legged animals; and . . . (*Pause.*)

KING What else?

PUROHIT One hundred persons, fifty men and fifty women, will have to be sacrificed.

KING (*agrees quickly*) You have my permission.

PUROHIT (*stops abruptly and the* KING *almost falls to the floor, further making a fool of himself*) But we still lack one essential ingredient in this cure. In order to make it complete, we shall require the sacrifice of one of the celestial bird-maidens, a kinnaree.

KING (*blustering*) What is so difficult about that? Get one.

PUROHIT Your Majesty forgets that they live on the celestial mountain of Krailas, from whence no mortal has ever returned. They are extremely difficult to capture. We shall try, your Majesty, but I doubt we can find a kinnaree.

KING Can the city be saved if these sacrifices are undertaken?

PUROHIT Yes, your Majesty, but you will not live to see that day unless one of the bird-people is sacrificed.

KING (*pleading*) Is there no other way?

PUROHIT No, sire. The sacrifice of one of the bird-people would greatly please the gods. Your Majesty would be assured of a very long life if only there were some other way to get our hands on a kinnaree.

KING Well, there is no reason why we can't get one; that forester did. Go and instruct the men.

PUROHIT I obey, your Majesty. (*Aside, gleefully.*) Now, Suton, I have you. Stupid King! Ha! Suton, you won on the battle-field, but you shall lose at home. (*Laughs triumphantly and exits.*)

KING (*pacing*) Why should I die? I'm not ready to die yet. Suton is such a young boy; he is not yet ready to rule Pancala. (*The* QUEEN *enters, as if passing through.*) Chan-Devi, my dear, what should I do?

QUEEN I'm not supposed to speak to you!

KING (*hysterical again*) Oh! I'm sorry, but this is an emergency! I am going to die in seven days, and the only thing that will save me is the sacrifice of a kinnaree. What am I to do? I'm not ready to die; Suton is not ready to be king. Besides, he is married to——

QUEEN Manohra, the sweetest, most beautiful princess I've ever seen.

KING She is from Mount Krailas! She is a kinnaree! (*The* KING's *thundering inspiration carries him center.*)

QUEEN What are you thinking? Adhitavongse! Surely you can't mean . . . No, I won't allow it. Think of Suton. He did not leave Manohra here to be sacrificed to a crazy whim.

KING I am the King and I command!

QUEEN I will not allow it! Adhitavongse, you have gone too far.

KING Guards! (*Two* GUARDS *enter from down right.*) Escort the Queen to her chambers and confine her there.

QUEEN Adhitavongse. Don't!

KING Take her away! (*The* GUARDS *drag her out.*) Purohit, come here! Purohit! Where are you?

The KING *whirls around repeatedly until he gets dizzy and falls to the ground. The lights abruptly black out on the forestage area.* STAGEHANDS *begin the scene change.*

Scene 3

The setting is the ceremonial pavilion in the palace grounds. The pavilion is a platform covered with a burnt-orange canopy suspended by four poles. As the lights quickly come up, two WORKERS *in brown panungs and brown-and-white sleeveless tunics are seen sweeping at stage right.*

FIRST WORKER Psst! What's going to happen today?

SECOND WORKER (*leaning on his broom*) Something big, I'll betcha. Look at all the soldiers.

FIRST WORKER After yesterday, they'll need all the soldiers they can get!

SECOND WORKER The King must be out of his mind, killing all those children. I hope Prince Suton returns soon. He'll put a stop to this.

Manohra

The CHIEF WORKMAN, *a portly fellow dressed in the same costume as his co-workers, enters up right and surprises the lounging* WORKERS. *He brandishes his whip.*

CHIEF   All right, you two over there, cut out that noise and start work. Why couldn't I get some people who are good at sweeping? I lost my best sweeper when the army left. Now, get back to work or I'll use this whip on your lazy backs.

FIRST WORKER   Honorable sir, is it true our Princess——

CHIEF   Get to work!

FIRST WORKER   Rumor has it Princess Manohra will be sacrificed today.

SECOND WORKER   What for? The Princess has done nothing wrong!

FIRST WORKER   I knew he was crazy. What will the Prince think when he returns from the war?

SECOND WORKER   The people will never allow it.

The WORKERS *see the procession coming in down right and run off down left. The* CHIEF *chases after them.*

CHIEF   Stop! Where are you going? Wait till I get my hands on them.

The CHIEF *begins sweeping hurriedly with a broom left by the escaping workmen.* PUROHIT *and his group precede the* KING, *who is standing in his chariot pulled by* GUARDS. *The* QUEEN *and her* MAIDS *follow. As the chariot turns, the* KING *discovers that his back is to the audience, and he vainly changes position to face front.* PUROHIT JUNIOR *crosses down left to the* CHIEF WORKMAN.

PUROHIT JR.   You, workman, turn around and face me or I'll report you to the overseer.

CHIEF I am the overseer.

PUROHIT JR. Oh! I beg your pardon. Why are you doing the sweeping yourself? What has happened to all the servants?

Interrupting, PUROHIT *steps forward to center stage after all members of the procession are in position.*

PUROHIT The safety of the kingdom, your Majesty, has been preserved through the sacrifices. Pancala will not be destroyed. However, the dark cloud over your Majesty's own life has yet to be removed. The last step must be taken. Princess Manohra must be sacrificed before all will be well.

QUEEN (*protesting vehemently*) I will not allow it! Adhitavongse, because of your dream many are dead. Our city is no longer full of laughter. Don't take Manohra from us, too. Stop now, before it is too late, I beg of you.

Murmurs of support from GUARDS *and* MAIDS.

PUROHIT There is no other way.

QUEEN (*on her knees before the* KING) Adhitavongse, we have had a full and happy life. I have been satisfied. Let me now offer myself in Manohra's place.

KING That cannot be. You are my wife, and the Queen besides.

GUARD (*steps forward*) I offer my life in the Princess' place, your Majesty.

MAIDS (*all step forward*) And we, too, your Majesty.

KING I thank you for all your offers. But what can I say?

PUROHIT (*struggles for control*) To save the life of his Majesty, it is imperative a kinnaree be offered; else the gods would neglect the plea. Your Majesty, the time is getting short; Princess Manohra should be brought here immediately.

KING Guard, bring my daughter-in-law here.

The GUARD *exits.*

QUEEN I beg you, Adhitavongse, wait until Suton returns from the war. That isn't too much to ask, is it?

PUROHIT (*aside*) The old fool is weakening. I'd better do something fast. (*To the* KING.) The dream of your Majesty is powerful, and the results will be very sudden. Sire, I am afraid we tarry too long already. It is possible your Majesty will not be with us shortly.

KING How long do we have?

PUROHIT Until the sun reaches its zenith and coincides with the death cycle, your Majesty.

KING When will they meet?

PUROHIT At noon, your Majesty. (MANOHRA *is brought in. She kneels center, next to the sacrificial fire.*) Princess Manohra, the King will not live beyond the noonday sun unless you are sacrificed.

KING (*standing on the throne*) I ask you humbly, not as a king, but as a father. Not for me, but for Suton.

MANOHRA (*calmly*) Sire, Manohra calls Pancala her home, your Majesty her father, the Queen her mother. I had prayed that I could serve your Majesties until my death. I would gladly give all, even my life. But Suton is so far away. What will he say when he returns?

Loud crowd noises are heard offstage right and left.

KING What's all the commotion? Stop that noise!

GUARD (*enters from down left and crosses to the* KING) Your Majesty, the people want to come into the palace grounds. We cannot hold them off.

KING You must hold them back; they must not interfere.

The GUARD *exits down left.*

MANOHRA (*with all possible charm and sincerity*) Your Majesty, may I ask one last favor?

KING What is it, Manohra?

MANOHRA   I would like to fulfill a promise to dance as a kinnaree before I die. This dance will keep Manohra in your memories forever.

QUEEN (*sees* MANOHRA's *plan*)   Maid, bring Manohra's wings. Hurry!

A MAID *goes out up left.*

KING   Chan-Devi, it is not that I do not love our daughter. It is the will of the gods that she must die. Let it be remembered that by the grace of your actions, Manohra, Pancala was saved. We shall remember you always. You may begin, Manohra.

PUROHIT (*upset at* MANOHRA's *delaying tactics*)   Your Majesty, the sun is almost at its height.

The MAID *returns with* MANOHRA's *wings.*

QUEEN   Dance well, Manohra; they shall never forget it. (*Aside to* MANOHRA.) Fly away, my love.

The QUEEN *helps* MANOHRA *on with her wings, whispering advice to her.* MANOHRA *bows deeply to the* QUEEN *and begins her dance to the music of the piphat orchestra on the side stage. She expresses submission and sorrow at having to leave the world that* SUTON *inhabits. She circles the fire in ever wider arcs. Dancing gracefully, she pantomimes flying, hitting* PUROHIT *with her wings and causing him to turn a back somersault. Son and henchmen are bowled over into an amusing tangle of arms and legs.* MANOHRA *"flies off."* PUROHIT *and the* KING *are shouting at each other. All others wave good-bye to* MANOHRA, *cheering her journey back to Mount Krailas. Pandemonium as the stage fades to black.*

Act Four

Scene 1

The setting is near the lake in Himmaphan Forest where MANOHRA *was first captured. The old white-bearded seer,* KASSOP MUNI, *is seated on the porch of his hermitage, a small thatched hut, talking with the* ANIMALS *that appeared in the first scene of the play.* KASSOP *chants the following scripture in a ringing monotone.*

KASSOP *Musigo udsapo, payako saso nako ja spubbago auslego pijang wanaro kookukato sonasukkharo suppape sutata awera aneka apubpayapuchata sukee udtanung prihoranutu.*

BUN *and* SUTON *enter up right.* SUTON, *having conquered the enemies of Pancala, is now setting out to find* MANOHRA.

BUN Your Highness, there's Kassop Muni's hermitage.
SUTON Bun, I can never thank you enough.
BUN Never mind, Prince Suton. Bun glad he can help.
SUTON I shall ask the prophet whether he knows the way to Krailas Mountain, where my beloved Manohra is. Bun, this is as far as you have to come; you may return to your home now. I can find the way myself.
BUN (*upset*) Prince Suton, Bun not very brave, but he follow you anywhere.
SUTON You have said the way is rough and dangerous. There is no need for you to come with me. I must find Manohra

by myself to atone for my negligence. You have no need to
share my fate, worthy Forester. Return to your home.

BUN (*on his knees*) I beg to go with your Highness. No matter
what danger, Bun will follow Prince.

SUTON I command you to return home. I will go alone. I
must. Try to understand, my friend.

BUN (*almost in tears*) Yes, your Highness.

SUTON Return to Pancala and tell the King and Queen that
Suton will return when he finds Princess Manohra. Take
care of yourself, my Forester. May the gods always smile
upon you. Farewell!

BUN (*tearfully*) Farewell, my Prince. Bun always wait for your
return. (BUN *bows and exits slowly.*)

SUTON Farewell, good friend; I hope we shall meet again.

SUTON *crosses to* KASSOP's *hut, bows, and falls to his knees before the smiling old man. The* ANIMALS *gather around* SUTON.

KASSOP What man are you that braves the perils of Himmaphan Forest to come to me? Are you Suton, following the
kinnaree princess Manohra?

SUTON Yes, Holy One! Is it possible that your Worship can
point out the way to Krailas, so I may find the Princess?

KASSOP Does your Highness intend to follow the Princess
Manohra if there are no possibilities of success?

SUTON I am determined, Kassop Muni. I will follow my Princess no matter what the obstacles. I will not return to Pancala
until I have found her.

KASSOP (*warning*) Do not waste your life in such an impossible
task, Suton. The way to Krailas is too difficult, too dangerous, for mere mortals.

SUTON (*determined*) To live is but to die, Muni. No man can
escape this. But we may all choose the manner of dying.
Holy One, I cannot turn back on my quest.

KASSOP Since you are so determined, I have no choice but to

161

give you my aid. The paths are dangerous and the way rugged with obstacles almost impossible to overcome. But before I tell you the way, I have something for you. (KASSOP *pulls* MANOHRA'S *ring out of an old, shabby bag. It is tied with a red ribbon.*)

SUTON Did she leave it here? What did she say? How did——

KASSOP Slow down, young man. (*Speaks deliberately.*) After escaping from Pancala, Princess Manohra flew here, leaving these instructions for you: "I leave this ring so you may remember me always, my Prince. Do not try to follow me to Krailas. Our fate did not mean for us to be together. Suton, you were not to blame. Return to Pancala. Farewell, my beloved." With these words she flew on to Krailas.

SUTON I will never turn back, Manohra. Never! Tell me the way to Krailas. I shall start tonight.

KASSOP From here to Krailas the dangers are tenfold. No mortal has ever penetrated the forest and returned. (KASSOP *presents a small monkey to* SUTON.) Take him with you and eat only what he eats. With your prowess there is very little danger from wild beasts, but take all precautions. By the forest of vines is an ancient tree that reaches up to the heavens itself. On it, giant birds come to rest. Tie yourself to their backs and they will fly you to Krailas. Follow the monkey; he will show you the path to the tree. Wait! (KASSOP *drops to his knees. Going into a trance, he speaks in a high, moaning voice.*) The omens are favorable, but many obstacles must be overcome. It will be a long time, Prince Suton, before you reach the heavenly mountain. It will be seven years, seven months, and seven days.

SUTON Whether it is seven or seventy, Suton will never lose hope. I am indebted to you forever. (SUTON *bows deeply.*)

KASSOP Thanks are not necessary. To help others is enough thanks. My blessings go with thee, Prince Suton.

SUTON Come, my little friend, let us begin our journey. Farewell, Kassop Muni.

SUTON *takes the monkey's paw and circles the stage. Striding with great determination, he marches off down right.* KASSOP *and the remaining* ANIMALS *exit up right as* STAGEHANDS *remove the hut.*

Scene 2

SUTON *returns immediately, with the monkey leading him.* SUTON *circles the stage, pantomiming movement through a thick forest. Lighting changes from red to green to yellow to purple, to suggest* SUTON's *emotions. He walks in Thai dance movements as he wields a sword, fighting the clinging undergrowth.*

SUTON (*calling loudly*) Manohra! I am coming, Manohra! My darling, how you must have suffered. But such is our fate; our parting is but the penance for wrongs in our past existence. We can do no more than live with them. Manohra! (*Sees an imaginary* PUROHIT *and attacks with his sword.*) Purohit, your jealousy is the cause of this. You wanted to be king, but why did you try to kill my Manohra? For this your life is forfeit; I shall kill you, Purohit. (*Stops, speaks quietly.*) No, Suton, to kill once is to kill again and again. One answers for all one's deeds in the future life. Purohit, I shall let you live in bondage. Watch over him, Chaiyut. (*Hears* MANOHRA's *voice.*) Don't cry, my love. (*Searching.*) Where are you, Manohra? Don't hide from me. Manohra! Manohra! (*Thinks he sees a leopard.*) What's that? Don't come near me. (*Scares it away and laughs bitterly.*) I hope he's not as hungry as I am. Why must I go on? Only for a woman? How everyone in Pancala must be laughing at me. To be in this intolerable forest for seven years, seven months, and seven days is ridiculous. Come, let us go on. We are almost at the tree Kassop Muni mentioned!

SUTON *and the monkey march offstage as if pushing their way through tall grass.*

Act Five

Scene 1

The scene is the foot of Mount Krailas. As the lights come up, SUTON *is sleeping on a bench down right. The strips of cloth that earlier served as the lake now are lying diagonally across the stage, representing a stream to which the* MAIDS *come for water. Seven* MAIDS *enter in groups of two and three, speaking as they appear. They make sinuous circles about the stage, indicating a narrow footpath.*

FIRST MAID Today is the last day for the ceremonies, isn't it, girls?

SECOND MAID Yes, isn't it exciting?

THIRD MAID Oh, I'm so happy for her.

FIRST MAID It's been such a long time! Imagine living within eyesight of the royal palace for seven years, seven months, and seven days! I wouldn't be able to stand it for a week.

The first three MAIDS *are now kneeling by stream's edge.*

SECOND MAID That's because you have somebody waiting at home.

THIRD MAID But do you notice the Princess sometimes as she gets a faraway look in her eyes? Every time that happens, she cries.

FOURTH MAID (*kneeling by the stream*) Yes, one time I played some music of the earth people, and she cried and cried for a long time.

FIFTH MAID Ssssh! Don't you know the Princess married one of the mortals? A prince, or so I hear.

SEVENTH MAID (*kneeling*) This cleansing ceremony is to rid her of those mortals.

FIRST MAID We all know that's silly.

SIXTH MAID Come, girls, we're wasting time. The Princess'll be waiting. She has waited so long already. Let's hurry.

They begin filling their jars.

SEVENTH MAID You know, I think the Princess would like to return to the earth place. I think her Highness loved the Prince very much.

THIRD MAID Forbid the thought. Returning to that place again! You must be out of your mind.

SEVENTH MAID Well, it was just a thought. Her Highness would be very happy if he were here. Besides, seeing the King and Queen for the first time since that awful day should make her very happy.

FIRST MAID No mortal can ever come to Krailas. It's impossible.

SECOND MAID How can a mortal cross the impenetrable forest? They don't have wings.

THIRD MAID Why don't you go and help him?

ALL MAIDS We know, we wish the same thing, too.

FIRST MAID Let's go. We mustn't keep everybody waiting for us.

All but the last MAID *leave quickly. She falls and spills the contents of her jar.*

SEVENTH MAID Oh well, after drawing water for seven years, seven months, and seven days, I can do it once more. (*She goes back to the stream after looking to see if any of the other* MAIDS *are waiting for her.*) After today the Princess Manohra

165

will be finished with the purification ceremony. I hope her Highness finds happiness.

SUTON (*has heard the last speech and is overjoyed*)   The cleansing ceremony of Manohra. This must be Krailas! Thank the Gods! I must let Manohra know I am here. How can I do it? (*He stops the* MAID *center stage.*) Little girl, could you stop a minute?

SEVENTH MAID (*very much afraid*)   What do you want?

SUTON   Don't worry; I won't harm you. Why are you carrying that water?

SEVENTH MAID   Don't you know? It's for the purification of Princess Manohra, who has returned from the mortal world.

SUTON   Manohra! At last!

SEVENTH MAID   Today is the last day of her purification ceremony.

SUTON   May I help you carry this jug? It looks rather heavy.

SEVENTH MAID   Thank you very much, kind sir. Are you from some kingdom on Krailas?

SUTON   Not exactly!

SEVENTH MAID (*aside*)   He looks like one of the mortals. I wonder if . . . (*to* SUTON.) Do you know of a city called Pancala?

SUTON   Perhaps.

SEVENTH MAID (*testing him*)   I have heard Prince Suton of Pancala is a very handsome man, but that he is very cruel.

SUTON   Oh, why so?

SEVENTH MAID   He left Princess Manohra to die because he wanted to marry somebody else. I wouldn't want to be married to someone like that; would you?

SUTON   The Prince did not want to leave the Princess to die, my little friend. He went to war to save his people. Certainly, it was not his intention to kill the Princess and marry another, because he loves her very much.

SEVENTH MAID (*gently scolding*)   Well, if he really loved the Princess, he would have followed her Highness, because the Princess . . . loves him very much, too.

SUTON (*knowing look at her*) Maybe he has followed her.

SEVENTH MAID Oh, I must hurry; the Princess will be waiting anxiously for me so the ceremony can begin. Thank you for your help. (*She begins to exit.*)

SUTON If it is the gods' will that we are reunited, let this ring be the symbol of our everlasting love. May the gods have mercy on both of us. (*Ecstatic, he dances his way along the path to* MANOHRA.) Manohra, I'm here. Oh, Manohra, if I could only catch a glimpse of your face! It has been a long time. But not too long, for the end is almost in sight.

SUTON *exits up left.*

Scene 2

The setting is the throne room in the Palace of Suvannakorn on Mount Krailas. The throne is up center and is backed by silk banners of gold and silver. Six KINNAREE, *the sisters of* MANOHRA, *sit on a long bench up right. The* MAIDS *sit in a straight line on the floor up left.* KING TUMARAJA *rises from his throne to address his* QUEEN, *Chankinnaree. The expository beginning this scene is recited as if it were part of the purification ritual.*

KING My dear, a long time has passed since our daughter returned from the mortal world. Hasn't the purification ceremony been completed yet? I seem to recall it should be almost finished.

QUEEN I'm surprised, Tumaraja, that you can't remember the day that our daughter will finally return home to us.

SECOND PRINCESS I think it is today. Don't you think so?

FIRST PRINCESS None of you can remember, but I can.

SECOND PRINCESS Tell us!

THIRD PRINCESS Well, it was seven years, seven months, and

seven days ago today our sister returned. Today is the day when she can come into our city.

The following byplay among the PRINCESSES *goes quickly, accompanied by much giggling.*

SECOND PRINCESS   That's what I said, silly.
THIRD PRINCESS   You did not.
SECOND PRINCESS   I did too.
FOURTH PRINCESS   She did not.
QUEEN (*mock serious*)   No quarrels, girls, or I'll take away your wings again. (MANOHRA *comes in down left with a* MAID. *The* QUEEN *crosses to comfort her, and the* KING *follows.*) Oh, look, there's Manohra now. How beautiful she looks.
KING   Come here, my little kinnaree. There, there, don't cry. There, dry your eyes, my sweet. Father is here.
QUEEN   I am here, too, darling. Manohra, are you all right?
KING (*continuing formality of the ritual*)   Manohra, tell me where and what happened after that forester caught you with the naga.
QUEEN   Please tell us, Manohra.

The three of them return to the throne and sit.

MANOHRA (*shudders*)   When the naga caught me, I almost died of fright. Especially when I saw all my sisters flying away. I was so afraid.
KING   And then you married a mortal?
QUEEN   A prince, Tumaraja. Was he handsome?
SECOND PRINCESS   Tell us; we are dying to know!
FIRST PRINCESS   It sounds exciting. Maybe I'll be captured, too!
ALL   Ssssh!
MANOHRA (*harboring a delicious secret*)   Well, Prince Suton is his name.
QUEEN   Prince Suton! What a nice name.

KING (*angry*) What a wonderful husband this Suton made! If he loved you as you say, Manohra, why did you have to escape? He probably told you to do so!

QUEEN Manohra, dear, why did you have to fly away?

ALL Yes, tell us!

MANOHRA You see, it was really Purohit who wanted to kill me. He is a very evil person.

SECOND PRINCESS He sounds nasty. I wouldn't want to meet him.

QUEEN You poor thing. Tumaraja, can't we do something to that evil man?

KING (*playing the devil's advocate*) Oh! Blaming everything on this Purohit. Manohra, you are just as stupid as you always were. Don't you know it was you your Prince whatever-his-name plotted to get rid of? Ha! That Prince is like the rest of mankind, corrupt and insincere. Stop thinking so well of those . . . animals.

MANOHRA But, Father, Suton is not like the rest of them. No one says an unkind word about him, except Purohit. Everyone loves him.

KING (*testily*) Stop praising your husband's worth. I don't want to hear any more. If your Prince is as good as you have said, he should be on his way to Krailas.

QUEEN Tumaraja, can't you see she's crying? Please, dear, stop making her unhappy. This is a day for great joy. Her return should be a happy occasion.

KING Well, all right. But if this Prince is all you think him to be, he will come to Krailas to fetch you. Why, I would even perform another wedding ceremony for you.

MANOHRA (*bursting with joy*) Father, can you please repeat what you just said?

KING If he really loves you, if he is brave enough, he should be able to follow you to our city.

MANOHRA And what if he follows me, your Majesty?

ALL PRINCESSES We doubt it.

FIRST PRINCESS No man has ever come up to Krailas.

SECOND PRINCESS How could he get through all those obstacles? Isn't that right, Sisters?

They nod in unison.

KING (*tossing it off*) If he does come, then I shall give you the greatest wedding Krailas has ever witnessed.

MANOHRA (*exuberant*) On your word of honor, Father dear?

KING On my word!

QUEEN I'll see that he keeps his word, Manohra.

MANOHRA (*proudly*) Prince Suton has persevered and followed me to Suvannakorn. At this moment he is waiting outside the palace.

KING Is that so? I don't believe it.

MANOHRA If it is not true, Father, I will offer my life in atonement.

KING (*disbelieving*) Well, send for him.

MANOHRA Go out to the pavilion and ask the Prince to come here. And hurry!

MAID *runs out down left.*

KING This is tomfoolery. No man can come to Krailas! It is impossible. (SUTON *strides in down left, led by* MAID. *The* KING *is flabbergasted.*) Are you the prince called Suton?

SUTON Sire, I am. (SUTON *crosses to the throne, kneels, and bows deeply, his hands in the wai position.*) It is a great honor to be able to pay my humble respects to your Majesties.

QUEEN Isn't that sweet? He's so well-bred, and handsome, too.

MANOHRA'S *sisters giggle with approval and embarrassment.*

KING Dear! No such open approval yet! They might say you are overanxious to have a son-in-law! (*Testing him.*) Prince

Suton, for what purpose did you come to Krailas? It must be something very important for you to have traveled such a long way.

SUTON (*calmly*) Your Majesty must already know from Princess Manohra that after her capture she became my wife. When Manohra left Pancala, I could not endure the loss. Because of my love for her, I endured the hardships of Himmaphan Forest to find her.

KING If you really loved my daughter, Prince Suton, why did she have to flee for her life?

SUTON I was tricked into leaving the city to fight a war. When I returned, Manohra had already escaped the ceremonial fire. I set out immediately for Krailas, overcoming all obstacles for seven years, seven months, and seven days to arrive this very morning.

KING Here are my daughters. Find the Princess Manohra and I will give her hand willingly to you. Since you are her husband, you should be able to recognize her, though seven years have passed. To fully prove your claim, you must pass this last test.

SUTON I shall try, your Majesty.

KING Do you think you can identify your wife?

SUTON It will be difficult, your Majesty, but I shall try to the best of my memory and love. (SUTON *walks on his knees past the throne, in accordance with Thai custom.* SUTON *stands in front of the* KINNAREE.)

KING Daughters, stand up and let the Prince try to find Manohra. (*The seven* KINNAREE *form a circle around* SUTON. *He dances with each one briefly. Finally, he dances with* MANOHRA, *recognizing her easily. They dance perfectly together. The* KING *is delighted.*) Let there be joy unbounded! Kinnaree, let us celebrate the reunion of Princess Manohra and Prince Suton.

Gradually, others join the exuberant couple in their dance of

Manohra

exultation. Even PUROHIT *joins in, as the entire company is now on stage. The rippling music of the piphat guides them as they dance their homage to the joy of life. The women kneel and the men dance their happiness. All strike a pose as the curtain closes slowly.*

Japanese Noh

Between the tenth and the thirteenth centuries, performers of a number of Japanese theatre forms vied for audience attention and for the patronage of Buddhist temples and the court in and around the important cities of Nara and Kyoto. Jugglers and acrobats, singers of epic romances, and players of various kinds of short plays and dances—especially those known as *dengaku,* literally field music, and *sarugaku,* monkey music—were part of the theatre scene. Both *dengaku* and *sarugaku* troupes performed sketches, songs, and dances, but as independent pieces. Around the middle of the fourteenth century, the *sarugaku* troupe leader Kannami Kiyotsugu (1333–1384) introduced into his performances a sung dance section, the *kusemai* or *kuse,* thus for the first time giving the dance a genuine dramatic function. In the *kuse* section of a play, a crucial tale of the past is narrated as the protagonist dances out the story. Kannami's new way of performing was called *sarugaku-noh,* and in time this was shortened to Noh.

Kannami's son, the famous Zeami Motokiyo (1363–1444), was twelve years old when he was seen performing Noh by Yoshimitsu, the *shogun,* or military ruler of Japan. Yoshimitsu was captivated by the boy's beauty and grace, and he brought Zeami to the palace in Kyoto to be his catamite. Zeami spent most of his adult life at the court, even after his patron died. In the sophisticated atmosphere of the *shogun*'s court, he raised Noh from a plebeian, almost rustic, theatrical form to an exceptionally subtle art. Zeami was not only the chief performer of his troupe (inheriting this position from his father) but also the writer of more than one hundred plays. And in a series of treatises on the practice of his art, he established the aesthetic basis of Noh. For four hundred years following Zeami's death,

Noh troupes were supported by feudal lords in Kyoto and in the outlying provinces, thus preserving down to the present the texts of Noh and the style of performance as well.

About two hundred and forty plays make up the Noh repertory that is performed today.* Another two thousand or so plays have been written, but are not performed. Plays are divided into five groups according to subject matter and style: god (*kami*) plays, congratulatory pieces praising the gods; warrior (*shura*) plays, in which the protagonist is usually a slain warrior who appears as a ghost and relives his sufferings; woman (*katsura*) plays, in which the protagonist is a woman; miscellaneous plays—one type concerns a woman driven mad by grief for a lost child or lover, another a character who is obsessed, and a third, known as living person plays, an unmasked male protagonist; and demon (*kiri*) plays, in which the protagonist is a demon, devil, or supernatural figure.

A day's performance in Zeami's time was made up of one play from each group, staged in order, and interspersed with comedies called *kyogen*. A program of five plays was viewed as an artistic entity. Atmosphere, tempo, and tension changed perceptibly from one play to the next. The god play was quiet and dignified, the warrior play active and strong, and the woman play radiated elegant beauty. Increased tempo marked the fourth play, and in the demon play, a furious battle between demon and hero was resolved with the demon being killed or subdued—thus bringing the performance back to a congratulatory mood similar to that of the first play. Zeami wrote that the five-play series should be organized according to the principle of *jo*, or introduction (first play); *ha*, or development (second, third, and fourth plays); and *kyu*, or scattering (fifth play). According to Zeami, also, each play was to be organized into *jo, ha, kyu*—beginning, middle, end—with the same principle of artistic progression in mind. Significantly, the *jo-ha-kyu*

---

* There are five schools of Noh troupes—Kanze, Hosho, Kongo, Komparu, and Kita. Some plays are performed by all five schools, others are the property of one, or several, of the schools.

concept is derived from *gagaku* court music, and not from literature.

Noh plays are deeply impregnated with the doctrine of Amida Buddhism, according to which human salvation is achieved through prayer and penance. The profoundly pessimistic Buddhist theme of the impermanence of life is common to a number of plays (not, however, to *Ikkaku Sennin*). A noble warrior is slain before achieving his dream of conquest; a beautiful young woman eagerly sought after in her youth wanders alone in her withered old age. In Buddhist thought, the soul that clings to earthly attachments after death dwells in a purgatory of ceaseless torment. Plays of the second and third type concern these tortured souls.

Only a small number of characters appears in most Noh plays. In a text they are designated by their role-type and not by their character's name. The *shite,* or doer, is the central figure, and is usually an aristocrat, a court lady, or a powerful spirit. The *shite* completely dominates a performance; other actors are mere by-players. It is the *shite* who always performs the *kuse* dance and other important dances. Normally the *shite* is masked. The *shite* may have attendant courtiers, retainers, or maids (*tsure*). In the play there may be a noble child role (*kokata*) or roles for other minor characters (*tomo*), all of which are acted by lesser performers associated with the *shite* actor's school. The *waki,* or supporting role, is most often that of a priest who initiates the action or the play. Only rarely is the *waki* an antagonist to the *shite.* The *waki* may have attendants (*wakizure*), acted by performers associated with the *waki's* school. *Kyogen* actors play roles of villagers or other commoners (*kyogen* actors also perform the *kyogen* farces between two Noh plays).

Plays are presented on a raised stage, about eighteen feet square, with a highly polished cyprus floor. Scenery is not used, but constructed props and hand props commonly are. A bridgeway (*hashigakari*) about thirty feet long, leading from stage right to the dressing rooms, is used for exits and entrances.

Japanese Noh

The tempo of song and dance is regulated by accompanying music, played by musicians who sit in view of the audience at the rear of the stage. One flute, two hand drums (one large and one small), and in some plays a stick drum compose the small Noh ensemble. A chorus of six to ten actors from the *shite* group sits on the left side of the stage. Several other actors, disciples of the *shite* and sometimes of the *waki*, assist their teachers on the stage. They give and take away hand properties, adjust costumes, and move larger set properties. All performers in Noh are male.

The most important influence on the aesthetics of Noh theatrical art is Zen Buddhism. From austere Zen came the principle that suggestion is preferable to flat statement, that subtlety is preferable to clearness, that the small gesture is preferable to the large, that, in short, the secret of beauty lies in restraint. Beauty in Noh is refined and it is everywhere: in the chaste planes of the masks, in the simplicity of the stage, in the rigor of the line of musicians or chorus on the stage, in the quavering tone of the actor's chanting voice, in the elegant movements of the performers. Zeami described the unique beauty which Noh strives toward in two terms: mysterious and sublime. Mysterious beauty, or *yugen,* is the ephemeral beauty that lies in impermanence. The cherry blossom, delicate and fragile, is touched by the wind and in an instant is scattered and gone. Elegance is tinged with the sadness of passing. The sublime would appear to be Zeami's more mature view. In sections of Noh that suggest the sublime, melancholy over the impermanence of life gives way to serenity and acceptance. The beauty of the sublime is the beauty of old age, restful, at peace with the world. It is silent, austere. That such a theory of beauty was developed for a theatrical art must impress us deeply. Indeed, there is no other form of theatre in the world in which the externals have been more thoroughly abandoned in favor of elliptical, concentrated, austere expression.

Noh is not a storyteller's art; it does not (in most cases) present the unfolding of a human action. Rather, through recollections of the past, it evokes a mood, an emotion, a religious state. Human characters appear on the stage, but they are not three-dimensional figures living the usual round of daily routine. At the most extreme they are quite literally momentary manifestations of the spirit world; at the very least, they exhibit an unworldly degree of composure and restraint. Through the gradual increase in tension created by the steady musical accompaniment, the chanting of the chorus, and the formal movements of the characters, content is subsumed to form, until the knowledgeable spectator perceives the occurrences before him, not as emotionally bound human actions but as elegantly formed patterns of sound and color that impinge on his emotions peripherally if at all. Noh is the purest of the art forms of theatre and consequently makes the most demands on its audience.

Suggested Reading

The best general introduction to Noh, superbly illustrated with nearly four hundred photographs, is Donald Keene, *No: The Classical Theatre of Japan* (Palo Alto, Calif.: Kodansha International, 1966). P. G. O'Neill's *Early No Drama* (London: Lund Humphries, 1958) is a scholarly account of Noh's beginnings. Excellent translations of thirty Noh plays are in the three volumes of *Japanese Noh Drama* (Tokyo: Nippon Gakujutsu Shinkokai, 1955 and 1960); the first volume is available in reprint as *The Noh Drama* (Rutland, Vt.: Tuttle, 1967). Donald Keene has recently brought out *Twenty Plays of the No Theatre* (New York: Columbia University Press, 1970). Makoto Ueda's *The Old Pine Tree and Other Noh Plays* (Lincoln, Neb.: University of Nebraska Press, 1962) contains a bill of five Noh plays. Zeami's chief theoretical work, *Kadensho*, has been translated by Chuichi Sakurai, *et al.* (Kyoto: Sumiya Shinobe, 1968).

Ikkaku Sennin
A Japanese Noh Play
BY KOMPARU ZENPO MOTOYASU

English translation by Frank Hoff

English verse adaptation by William Packard

Performance script by Aida Alvarez. English verse adaptation by William Packard, commissioned by the Institute for Advanced Studies in the Theatre Arts (IASTA) for use in the production directed by Sadayo Kita, of the Kita Noh School.

The play *Ikkaku Sennin,* or *The Holy Hermit Unicorn,* was written by Komparu Zenpo Motoyasu in the last half of the fifteenth century, one generation after Zeami's time. It may be performed as a play of the fourth group (because the hero is a living person) or the fifth (because the hero is a wizard with supernatural powers). It is in the repertory of the Kanze, Komparu, and Kita schools.

The action in *Ikkaku Sennin* supposedly takes place in an Indian kingdom, though there is nothing specifically Indian in the play except the single line stating that India is the place of action. The play dramatizes an ancient legend from India and China. A hermit priest, through his powers of meditation, traps the dragon gods of rain in a mountain cave. Then after a time drought threatens the land. In order to free the gods so they can make rain, the emperor orders one of his most beautiful court ladies, the Lady Senda Bunin, to visit the hermit and seduce him. The play begins as she (the *shite tsure*) arrives at the hermit's mountain retreat with a court official (the *waki*). They enter to the usual opening music (*shidai*) and the *waki* stands at the conventional name-saying place, upstage right. He announces who he is and the purpose of their journey (*nanori*). This is followed by a travel song (*michiyuki*), which accompanies the crossing of the *waki*'s group onto the main stage, a movement conventionally indicating arrival at their destination. With the *waki*'s group now in position, the *shite*—the hermit—appears within a hut, already placed on stage, and chants his opening lines (*sashi*).

In this, and in the play's subsequent development, *Ikkaku Sennin* follows the usual Noh structure. The *waki* is a minor character who simply guides Lady Senda on her journey. The

overriding importance of the *shite* is clear: the hermit absolutely dominates the performance, though in plot terms, he is
acted upon and is not an initiator of action. The play's climax
typically occurs in a dance section, in this case not a *kuse*
(there is no event out of the past which requires explanation),
but a violent *hataraki* dance, when the hermit battles the
dragon gods and attempts to prevent their escape.

The play illustrates how conflicts are often attenuated in
Noh. There is a direct and strong opposition between the
hermit and the court lady when he is first disturbed. In the
following scene, she gets him drunk and seduces him. These
scenes could be dramatized very effectively, as they are in the
Kabuki version of this story, *Narukami*. However, in the Noh
the incipient conflict between the hermit and Lady Senda is
almost immediately resolved when he allows wine to be served.
His seduction is only suggested in graceful dance patterns by
Lady Senda, and the indirection of this scene is further em-
phasized by the lyric verse of the chorus, "dance to the music of
flutes." The words are not strong narrative, as they might be
if the conflict were of greater concern. Lady Senda's formal role
is minor; she is only a *tsure*, or secondary player, and is given
but one line to speak in the play. Yet she dances several important sequences and is, within the overall theatrical pattern,
of considerably greater importance than the *waki* figure.

Ikkaku Sennin balances several qualities of Noh in fairly
equal proportions. There is some conflict, but not much. There
is beautiful dancing, but it does not have the central importance
that dance would have in plays of the third group. The play
is rooted in religious concerns, yet there is nothing truly spiritual about its story. There is a touch of the erotic that is not
explicitly developed. It is perhaps in the especially active finale
that the play's individuality is best seen. The dragon gods and
the hermit energetically whirl the long manes that surround
their fearsome, glaring masks. Movements and music rise to a
furious climax, then dissolve into stillness.

A translation of *Ikkaku Sennin* by Frank Hoff was adapted

for production at the Institute for Advanced Studies in the Theatre Arts by William Packard. Like all Noh texts, about half of the Japanese script for *Ikkaku Sennin* was composed in verse of alternating phrases of seven and five syllables. Usually two phrases are sung or chanted within the strict eight-beat Noh musical measure. Several metric patterns are possible. In the *hira nori* pattern, for example, the seven-syllable phrase fits into the first four beats of a measure and the five-syllable phrase into the second four beats. These rhythms create a constantly flowing sound pattern that is almost hypnotic in its effect upon the audience. In order to recreate this vocal effect in English, Packard followed the Japanese syllable count exactly in his adaptation.

The performance traditions of Noh have been maintained— with some minor changes of course—from Kannami's time down to the present, so each detail of blocking, gesture, dance, music, vocal style, costuming, and emotional interpretation for *Ikkaku Sennin* is rigidly set. For this production at IASTA a replica of a Noh stage was built, somewhat larger in area than a stage would be in Japan, but incorporating a bridgeway, pillars, and a smooth dancing area. Authentic costumes, properties, and masks for Lady Senda, the hermit, and the rain gods were brought from Japan. Actors and actresses (a departure from Noh's all-male tradition) were trained daily in basic movement by the Noh actor Sadayo Kita. Vocal intonations were patterned after the original Japanese and timed to taped music. The most significant change made in the text was the elimination of the chorus lines at the end of the play. They describe the battle between the hermit and the rain gods. The danced action was felt to be sufficiently clear without the lyrics.

Characters

IKKAKU SENNIN, *a wizard*
SHINDA, *a court official*
LADY SENDA, *a beautiful young girl*
TWO DRAGON GODS
CHORUS
LADY SENDA'S ATTENDANTS
STAGE ASSISTANTS

Ikkaku Sennin

The play takes place in the Kingdom of Barana, India. The season is autumn. The auditorium and stage lights are up full before the audience enters and remain so during the perform-ance to enable actors wearing masks to note their positions on stage through the pin-point eyeholes of the masks. The stage is a raised platform about twenty feet square, with square pillars at the four corners. The wooden surface of the stage has been rubbed smooth and is completely empty of scenery. The rear of the stage consists of a large wooden panel on which a beautiful twisted pine tree is painted. A passageway leads from the up right corner of the stage to the "mirror room," or dressing room, fifteen feet away. There is a low railing along the passage-way, and three pine saplings are spaced along its length to mark the position of actors during their entrances or exits or during any action that may take them onto the passageway. A silk cur-tain of green, white, and red vertical stripes covers the door leading to the mirror room; it is raised and lowered by two bamboo poles attached to the bottom corners. Stage left there is a low door, the "hurry door," used for entrances and exits of the CHORUS *and* STAGE ASSISTANTS.

The play begins with two STAGE ASSISTANTS *bringing on the first of the set props. The passageway curtain is lifted and a plat-form is brought down the passageway and placed lengthwise on the main stage left of center. The* STAGE ASSISTANTS *exit and return carrying two set props symbolic of the rock cave within which the* DRAGON GODS *are trapped. They are basket-woven and shaped in semicircles, covered with blue silk, and tied together lightly with white tapes. The* ASSISTANTS *lift the rock pieces care-fully onto the platform as actors playing the* DRAGON GODS *step onto the platform from behind, unseen. The silk is adjusted to*

Ikkaku Sennin

fully cover the hidden characters. The STAGE ASSISTANTS, *dressed unobtrusively in their black divided trousers over black kimonos, exit silently through the small door left. The hermit's hut has been waiting backstage to be set with* IKKAKU SENNIN *already inside. A curtain has been hung on the hut and tied in back at the top and bottom. As the curtain is three inches longer than the hut,* IKKAKU SENNIN's *feet cannot be seen. The two* ASSISTANTS *lift the hut on either side and enter. The hut is placed upstage center, and the front is lifted slightly to tuck the front end of the curtain neatly under the hut.* ASSISTANTS *move upstage right, behind the hut, and kneel. The action of the play begins.*

After a moment the music of a flute can be heard. On the first note of the music the passageway curtain lifts slowly, LADY SENDA *enters on the passageway, followed by two* ATTENDANTS *holding a frame representing a canopy and by* SHINDA, *a court official. She wears a silk kimono of orange, green, and gold, tied with a sash of gold and orange, and over it a wide, split skirt of orange brocade. She wears a smooth black wig and the white mask of a beautiful, sweetly serene young woman. The mask is attached with a headband of gold and orange material decorated with an intricate bow at the back. She wears a delicate crown and carries a gold and orange folding dance-fan. Her* ATTENDANTS *wear wide, split trousers of white over green and brown kimonos. They do not carry fans nor do they wear masks.* SHINDA *is dressed similarly but with a green and gold outer jacket tied at the waist with a black and white sash. He wears no mask but carries a blue and white folding fan decorated with a fish design. All move slowly down the passageway, gliding their feet in the stylized walk of Noh. The procession lasts a full two minutes.* LADY SENDA *stops center stage,* SHINDA, *upstage right. The music ends. In a rich baritone voice* SHINDA *almost chants his speech, his face immobile, explaining to the audience who they are and what they hope to achieve.*

SHINDA

The prince I serve is a great prince,
he is the emperor of Barana,
with many lands along the Ganges.

Now in the country of this prince
there lives a hermit
and he is a wizard,
he was born from the womb of a deer
and he has one single long horn,
a horn that sprouts out of his forehead;
and therefore we have named this wizard
Ikkaku Sennin, holy hermit unicorn.
Once Ikkaku Sennin and the great dragon gods
had an affair of honor,
and the wizard won;
he used his magic
to undo the dragon gods,
he drove them into a cave
and made them stay inside.
Away in that cave,
for many years they could not cause rain to fall.
Since then, my prince has come to grieve,
he sees that his whole countryside is dry,
and so now he knows
he has to free those dragon gods.

(SHINDA *pivots left slightly to face* LADY SENDA.)

Listen, this is the prince's plan,
this is the beautiful young girl
who is going to go up into the mountains,
there where the wizard lives,
the holy hermit unicorn,
and he may make a mistake
and think she's lost her way.
Then he may fall in love,
he may say this young girl is so beautiful,

he may lose his heart and art
and all the magic that he used to use.
It may work out that way,
that's what the prince is hoping for,
and so we're going to carry her up
to the unicorn.

ATTENDANTS (*still standing and holding the canopy frame over*
LADY SENDA, *they sing the following travel song*)
Mountains and mountains and mountains,
mists that cover over all the weary travelers,
cold winds that blow through the open woods,
as we keep going,
no sleep on the mountainside,
no sweet dreams for us.

SHINDA (*pivots front and speaks*)
Day after day,
we've hurried on our way,
traveling on this old road
that no one knows about;
now we are lost, we are all worn out.

Look, there are many rocks,
all lying on the ground
and piled up in a mound,
I wonder why?
—how sweet the breezes
as they blow over the rock pile;
I can tell the smell of pine.
Perhaps this is where the wizard lives,
the holy hermit unicorn,
perhaps this is the place.
We could keep quiet
and get close to it,
slowly, slowly,
get close so we can see
if the wizard is hiding inside.

(During his speech the STAGE ASSISTANTS *cross to the back of the hut unobtrusively and untie the curtain. They hold the curtain and wait for the proper moment to lower it.* SHINDA *turns again to* LADY SENDA *and asks her permission to stay.)*
   Gracious lady,
   if your patience will permit it,
   we would like to stay right here.

LADY SENDA *shows no sign that she agrees. She moves slowly to the downstage corner of the dragon cave and sits.* SHINDA *moves to the upstage corner and sits. The* ATTENDANTS *lower the canopy frame, place it against the back wall of the stage, and kneel facing each other. The* STAGE ASSISTANTS *lower the hut's curtain slowly to reveal* IKKAKU SENNIN *sitting with right knee up and holding a fan in his right hand, which rests on his knee. He is an extraordinary sight as seen through the bamboo poles of the hut. His ornate brown-and-blue kimono is covered by a light overgarment of sheer black material. A leaf-shaped apron is tied at his waist. A huge black wig stands out around his face in great wisps. A single horn, fixed into the wig, protrudes from his forehead. He wears a mask with a face very old and gnarled but at the same time tender. His nonfolding Chinese fan is blue, gold, and orange. He is not frightening; rather, he gives the impression of wisdom. The* ASSISTANT *right passes the curtain of the hut to the* ASSISTANT *left, who exits with it through the small door left. The remaining* ASSISTANT *unobtrusively nudges* IKKAKU SENNIN *through the cagelike bars of the hut to cue him. In a deep, rumbling voice, which seems to come almost from the ground,* IKKAKU SENNIN *tells* SHINDA *they should leave him to his solitary life.*

IKKAKU SENNIN
   I scoop water from deep streams
   with my magic gourd,
   I call forth all my art,
   I lift up clouds that have folded over forests

and I make them boil swiftly,
then I play music.
But I play alone.
The mountains rise up high above river banks.
Green leaves suddenly become the color of blood.
I play music and I play alone in autumn.

On the last two lines of IKKAKU SENNIN's *speech* LADY SENDA *and*
SHINDA *rise from their position, kneeling on one knee, pivot
slowly toward the hut, and move forward one step.*

SHINDA
Listen to me, listen,
this is a traveler;
we have lost our way
and we want to speak to you.

IKKAKU SENNIN
Who's there?—
I thought I would be free in these mountains,
I thought I would be able to escape
from the human race,
and now someone comes—
O please leave, please leave
as fast as you can.

SHINDA (*pleads to be allowed to stay*)
No, listen to me, listen,
we are travelers
and we are lost,
and the sun is setting,
and the road is dark,
so won't you let us spend the night
right here?

IKKAKU SENNIN
No, no, I told you to go,
this is no place for you to stay,
so go;

I say you should go far from here.
SHINDA (*adamant*)
    You say this is no place for us to stay,
    and is that because
    the holy hermit unicorn lives here?
    Come out, I say, so we can see your face!
IKKAKU SENNIN (*as yet motionless*)
    I am getting up,
    I am coming out of here,
    I am going to show myself
    to all these travelers!

Slow music of flute and drums. As the CHORUS *begins to sing with an almost sinister feeling,* IKKAKU SENNIN *slowly rises and opens the bamboo gate to the hut. He steps out, and his robe is adjusted as he does so.*

CHORUS (*offstage*)
    He takes the great grass gate
    and swings it to one side,
(MUSICIANS *inject cries of "Iya," and we hear drums whack.*)
    he takes the great grass gate
    and swings it to one side,
    now he is aroused—
    look, look at his face!
    Black hair snarled on his proud brow,
    a single long horn
    sprouting out of his forehead.
    See how he stands here—
    if he disappeared
    we would still see him stand here,
    strange and wonderful!

IKKAKU SENNIN *has pivoted to face* LADY SENDA *and* SHINDA, *and on the last line of the* CHORUS *all three slowly sink to the floor. The music ends.*

Ikkaku Sennin

SHINDA
> Are you the hermit
> we have heard about,
> which they call
> the holy hermit unicorn?

IKKAKU SENNIN
> I am ashamed to say it
> but I am he,
> Ikkaku Sennin.

SHINDA
> Here is some sake which we brought along with us,
> to cheer us up on our long journey.
> My lady kindly offers it to you,
> so do take a cup of this fine wine!

IKKAKU SENNIN
> We hermits prefer
> to eat the needles of pine trees,
> the clothes we wear
> are made of moss,
> and we do not drink anything
> but dew.
> Year after year,
> we do not age,
> we do not change,
> we do not even die.
> And that is why I say
> I do not want your sake.

SHINDA (*appealing to the* HERMIT's *innate courtesy*)
> You say you do not want our sake,

(*He pivots on his knee to indicate* LADY SENDA.)
> but then would you take just a little
> if my lady asks it as a special favor?

LADY SENDA *opens her fan, holds it horizontally in front of her to represent the sake, rises, and takes a few steps toward* IKKAKU

192

SENNIN. *In a clear, light voice she speaks her only line in the play.*

LADY SENDA
 The young girl rises,
 rises to pour out some wine;
 she urges the hermit
 to try some sake.
IKKAKU SENNIN (*unable to resist her beauty and charm*)
 When travelers ask a favor,
 how can anyone refuse?
 —impossible,
 only the devil would say no.

Music begins. As the CHORUS *sings its song of wine to the haunting melody of the flute,* LADY SENDA *crosses to* IKKAKU SENNIN. *She kneels beside him, pantomimes—with her fan—pouring him some wine, then opens the fan and sweeps it up and out to the side in a wide, graceful arc.*

CHORUS
 A cup of wine is like the moon
 in the night sky,
 a cup of wine is like the moon
 in the night sky.
 The hermit reaches out
 and takes the cup of wine,
 just as a hermit once
 plucked a chrysanthemum,
 the dew dropped down to the ground.
 O that was so long ago,
 so long ago,
 but I will love you for that long.

As there are no realistic movements in Noh, only a slight nod of

Ikkaku Sennin

the HERMIT's *head indicates he has drunk the wine after raising his body from the low stool on which he has been resting and which the* STAGE ASSISTANT *now quickly removes. A moment later the* HERMIT *drops his left knee to the floor abruptly, and we realize he is now intoxicated.*

IKKAKU SENNIN *(singing)*
 O blessed ecstasy,
 the cup of wine!
CHORUS *(continues the song of praise)*
 O blessed ecstasy,
 the cup of wine!
 —it is like the moon
 that circles in the night sky.
 Red leaves on the autumn hills,
 see the silk sleeves.
 Two leaves move,
 like two sleeves
 that are dancing together,
 dancing in a great court dance,
 blessed ecstasy.
(Music begins and accompanies LADY SENDA's *danced seduction of the* HERMIT. LADY SENDA *slowly rises from her kneeling position and crosses down center. There she bows ceremoniously, bringing both arms overhead. The music of the flute begins as she slides her feet smoothly on the mirrorlike floor. Her arms flow in beautiful movements, manipulating her fan. She dances alone until the* CHORUS *again is heard, accompanied by the dynamic sounds of the big drum. The* HERMIT *watches her seductive dance, and when she begins a second variation of steps, he rises to join her, always slightly behind in tempo. They dance together, sometimes in unison, sometimes in opposition.)*
 Dance to the music of flutes,
 dance to the flute music.
 Dance to the music of flutes,
 dance to the flute music.

Pass the cup around, around,
pass the cup around, around.

(*At the critical encounter of the dance the* WIZARD *places his left
hand across the breast of* LADY SENDA; *she repulses him by stiffly
lifting her right arm. The* WIZARD *staggers backward, then forward again; then he goes into a spin, takes two turns, and sinks
to his knees. He raises his right arm so that the kimono sleeve
covers his face, symbolizing that overcome by love and sake, he
has fallen into a stupor.*)

The hermit has fallen in love,
he has fallen in love.
See, his feet have grown weak,
and see how the hermit
is beginning to falter and fall,
he keeps turning in circles,
now he wraps his sleeve around him
and he sleeps.
The beautiful young girl is pleased;
she tells everyone to come away
and they all go down the mountain,
they go down the rough mountain road
until they are already at the court
of the prince.

(*Quickly* LADY SENDA *closes her fan and turns upstage to* SHINDA.
The ATTENDANTS, *having risen when the* WIZARD *began to falter,
cross down to her and raise the canopy frame over her head.
They all turn and move onto the passageway. There they pause
momentarily, then cross swiftly off as the passageway curtain is
lifted for their exit. The music ends. Suddenly there is a loud
"thwack" of the drum, and the* WIZARD *awakens. The* STAGE
ASSISTANTS, *who moved behind the rock cave when the procession
went off, quickly untie the tapes that hold the two pieces of rock
together and stand ready to push them apart.*)

Rumble rumble rumble,
where is it coming from?
Rumbles thunder from deep

Ikkaku Sennin

inside the cave,
rumbles cause earthquakes
and make all creation shake.

IKKAKU SENNIN, *kneeling, turns toward the cave and reproaches
himself for his weakness.*

Why have I been sleeping,
sleeping all this while?
—it was the wine,
it was the beautiful young girl,
it was the need for some sleep.

Rumble rumble rumble,
something's wrong,
what is it?
DRAGON GODS *(unseen within the cave)*
Holy hermit unicorn Ikkaku Sennin,
you have let yourself get lost in lust,
and you confused your mind with wine.
No wonder now you do not know you are undone,
no wonder now you have no power.
Now the sky strikes you down,
Ikkaku Sen-ni-in-n-n!

They vigorously announce that the WIZARD, *having succumbed
to human temptation, has lost his power over them. Ending
their chant with his name, they almost sing in elongated syllables. Music for their dance begins.*

IKKAKU SENNIN *rises, advancing to the center of the stage, a
sight cue for the* STAGE ASSISTANTS *to push apart the two pieces
of the rock cave in what seems to be an explosion.* IKKAKU SEN-
NIN *retreats up right to the edge of the passageway as the rock
falls to the floor and is swept up and carried off through the
small door left by the two* STAGE ASSISTANTS. *Two* DRAGON GODS
jump off the platform and move upstage center. They are an

impressive sight with their flowing red wings topped with dragon headpieces. They wear dragon masks and carry wands. Jackets of blue and gold and wide, split trousers of orange and gold are worn over their kimonos—one of green, orange, and white and the other of orange, blue, and white. They begin an exciting and militant dance of strong, sweeping movements. Symbolizing heaven and earth, they raise their wands majestically, then turn, swoop down on one knee, and point their wands to the floor. They circle the stage in unison, always retaining three feet of space between them. In a final diagonal cross they move from up right to the platform and leap onto it, then turn to face the WIZARD. IKKAKU SENNIN *speaks the final words of the play, intoning his self-doubt, stamping once for emphasis.*

IKKAKU SENNIN
 Now, holy hermit unicorn,
 I do not know what to do.

The HERMIT *accepts the challenge of the* DRAGON GODS. *The music becomes faster.* IKKAKU SENNIN *pivots by the passageway, receives a short wooden sword from a* STAGE ASSISTANT *at the same time that he passes the* ASSISTANT *his fan, and without breaking the flow of his movement, moves toward center stage. The* DRAGON GODS *leap from the platform to the stage; they cross the* HERMIT's *sword with their wands.* IKKAKU SENNIN *fights courageously, but he cannot defeat them. To rapid beating of the drum, in a "big rhythm," he backs falteringly upstage. He drops to one knee and lets the sword fall from his hand. In an instant a* STAGE ASSISTANT *moves in to pick it up and carry it off left. The* WIZARD *crosses to the passageway, defeated. On the passageway, and considered to be invisible, he moves swiftly off as the curtain is lifted for his exit.*

Triumphant, the DRAGON GODS *dance to bring the rain that will end the drought. They swoop about the stage and finally cross to the passageway as if flying through the skies. They stop at the third small pine tree. They stamp, signifying the end of the*

197

Ikkaku Sennin

dance. *Then they jump, turning in the air, as if leaping into the sea and returning to their dragon home. They raise their left arm and flip the sleeve up and over to hide their face, in a movement which symbolizes their invisibility. The music ends with a flourish of the flute and the final cries of the* MUSICIANS, *"I-ya-o-o, i-ya-o-o!" The* DRAGON GODS *turn, and as the passageway curtain is raised for them, exit in silence.*

The props are now removed in view of the audience and with no music. The STAGE ASSISTANT *who had exited with the* HERMIT's *sword re-enters, and together the two* ASSISTANTS *lift the hut and carry it off down the passageway. They re-enter and remove the platform the same way. The play is finished. There are no curtain calls.*

Japanese Kabuki

Kabuki began in dance, and the elements of dance and its accompanying music are still important to Kabuki theatre art. The founder of Kabuki is reputed to have been the priestess-turned-prostitute Okuni, who, around 1600, danced for pay on an improvised stage set up in a dry river bed in the capital city of Kyoto. The dance she performed was called Kabuki, a word probably derived from the verb *kabuku*, meaning to be inclined, strange, or out of the ordinary. Like any dance at its first appearance, Okuni's new dance shocked many people because of its novelty and its erotic appeal. She scandalized the staid and delighted the pleasure-seekers by daring to wear baggy pantaloons and to hang a Christian cross around her neck—exotic fashions copied from the red-haired barbarians recently arrived on the islands from Holland. As the most up-to-date performance in town, Kabuki soon set trends for the wealthy merchants and the young people. Numerous anecdotes attest to Kabuki's dominant place in Japanese popular culture during the next three hundred years. If an important actor wore a new kimono of his own design on stage, it became instantly fashionable. When one idolized actor created a sensation by submerging himself in a vat of water in the play *Sukeroku,* maidens rushed to buy dippers of the water as precious souvenirs.

In one sense Kabuki developed as an eclectic borrower from other Japanese performing arts. Okuni's musicians played Noh instruments and she danced on a Noh-style stage, primarily, one supposes, because there was no other choice. Noh was the main Japanese theatrical form at the time. Many early plays were based on Noh and *kyogen* pieces. A century and a half later the puppet theatre (*joruri,* or *bunraku,* its popular but later name) achieved artistic distinction. Puppet plays were staged as Kabuki, and the puppet theatre's chanting and musical style, as well as some acting techniques, were assimilated by Kabuki. In Kabuki's mature period, in the latter part of the nineteenth century, a number of Noh plays (like *The Subscription List*) and *kyogen* farces (like *The Zen Substitute*) were adapted. But at the same time that it borrowed, new and original types of plays were created in Kabuki—the racy prostitute-buying play (*keiseikai*), a slow-motion pantomime in the dark (*danmari*), dramatizations of scandals and other events of the day (*sewamono*), and plays of bizarre horror (*kizewamono*).

Despite its many borrowings, Kabuki remains very different from its Noh sources. All of Noh drama and its performance techniques are of a piece; Noh developed rapidly (in about a hundred years), crystallized into a highly defined formal structure, and eventually was considered a perfected art form. It has been performed with only minor alterations during the course of its history. Whatever variety may be found in Noh is a variety of degree rather than kind, as is shown in the program of five Noh plays, all cast in the same basic artistic mold. Kabuki's growth, on the other hand, extended for three centuries (until the beginning of this century), and several quite disparate play forms and performance styles, borrowed and original, were incorporated into the performances of Kabuki troupes.

This eclecticism is often commented upon. But if Kabuki were only eclectic, we would be faced with a jumble of disconnected scenes and styles in the theatre, and this in fact is not the case. Several unifying principles of Kabuki art provide the cohesive force that has enabled Kabuki to assimilate and to grow over three hundred years without losing its original character.

A particular system of play construction evolved from the circumstances of Kabuki performance. During the major period of Kabuki growth, roughly from 1650 until 1850, audiences came to the theatre expecting a full day's entertainment; they arrived at dawn and left only at nightfall when the theatre closed. The programs of Okuni's time were a loose succession of short plays, group dances, dance plays, and songs. These miscellaneous programs ended when the government banned female prostitutes from Kabuki stages (in 1629) and attractive boy sodomites (in 1652). All performers henceforth were to be adult males and performances were to be "totally of plays imitating things."

The task of creating plays that would last for approximately twelve hours was formidable, and a solution was found in breaking down the day's play into four parts. The first, the historical part (*jidaimono*), was usually of three to five acts. A dance act (*naka naku*) followed or was included in the historical part. (It could be either a pure dance piece without dialogue or a dance-drama with dialogue.) The third, a longer part, usually in several acts, was based on contemporary events and set in a humble milieu (*sewamono*). The day's performance concluded with a sprightly, often humorous, dance in one act (*ogiri*). The four parts were thought of as a single play. One title applied to the whole, though the final dance piece was occasionally given a title of its own. The acts were numbered consecutively and were, as far as possible, related thematically.

Plays were produced five times a year in conjunction with the five seasonal festivals, and it became customary to stage events that were connected with the seasons. For example, the legendary Soga brothers were the chief figures in New Year's plays in Edo (Tokyo). In the history part of a New Year's play the brothers might appear as themselves. A retainer of theirs would be featured in the second or dance piece. In the third part the Sogas would appear disguised as commoners, and the finale would be a congratulatory dance piece. Acts were connected by plot or theme, often tenuously because the chief playwright of a troupe farmed out acts to several assistants to write. However, the majority of full-length plays composed for Kabuki, including those by Kabuki's two chief playwrights, Tsuruya Namboku (1755–1829) and Kawatake Mokuami (1815–1893), were written within this framework. In time, a day's program made up of several independent plays, or of revivals of popular acts from long plays, supplanted programs devoted to the single, long play. Even if one attends Kabuki regularly at present, there will be few opportunities to see a full-length, all-day play.

But regardless of whether a Kabuki program consisted of one long play or several unconnected short ones, it was organized into the same four-part sequence of strong history piece, emotional dance piece, lighter contemporary story, and brilliant dance finale. The audience would view it just as a Noh audience would view five plays in *jo-ha-kyu* sequence. Japanese observers do not suggest Kabuki's four-part pattern is part of the *jo-ha-kyu* aesthetic of court music and of Noh, but there seems little doubt that they are actually analogous aesthetic systems.

While some aspects of Kabuki performance derive from Noh (the sliding step used in some dance plays) or from the puppet theatre (the narration in strict time to *samisen* music), the fundamental techniques of Kabuki are unique. Kabuki style is tremendously energetic. Its leaping exits, or *tobi roppo* (such as Benkei's in *The Subscription List*), lengthy and athletic battle scenes (*tachimawari*), stylized scenes of torture or murder, and tense, dynamic poses of actors to express violent conflict (*mie*) characterize Kabuki stage art. Two sets of wooden clappers (*ki*) beat out rhythms to which an actor enters or exits and to which the conventional black, green, and rust front curtain is drawn aside. Black-hooded assistants crouch on stage ready to hand a property to an actor or to remove it; in dance plays they dress in formal *samurai* garb to add to the visual attractiveness of the scene. The heart of Kabuki music is the *nagauta* ensemble, which consists of Noh drums and flute, a number of three-stringed *samisen*, and singers. The ensemble was created for Kabuki, and its music is the most complex of the several kinds of Japanese theatre music. During dance plays the *nagauta* orchestra sits on a raised platform at the rear of the stage and in view of the audience; otherwise it plays from offstage right.

There is constant concern in Kabuki with form, both visual

and aural. A line of dialogue may be arbitrarily divided between several characters, with the final phrase spoken by all in unison. The technique is not psychologically motivated, but derives from the desire to create a rhythmic, antiphonal sound pattern. Normally dialogue is written in prose, but dialogue may be written in alternating lines of seven and five syllables for the beauty of the aural effect. Costumes and make-up are lavish and colorful. The actor's physical appeal is important in Kabuki, and the most is made of it through the staging device of the *hanamichi*, a ramp which runs through the audience to the rear of the auditorium. The actor invariably poses during his entrance or exit at a place seven-tenths of the way toward the stage to impress the audience with the beauty of his figure, and he mimes or speaks a few poetic phrases, The actor is in the midst of the audience and at this moment is seen more as an actor than as a character. A procession moving more than one hundred fifty feet along the ramp and stage creates a tremendous sense of space, an effect which is unknown and impossible on a Western peephole proscenium stage with its usual box set.

Scenery, often elaborate, contributes to the beauty of Kabuki. Brilliant cherry blossoms in spring, glowing red and yellow maple leaves in autumn, and the melancholy of a quiet landscape with snowflakes drifting down on trudging wayfarers are favorite Kabuki scenes. At its best, a Kabuki performance is an overpowering visual and aural experience. It challenges the senses to the utmost, not with suggestion as in Noh, but with a rich flood of color, sound, and movement.

Suggested Reading

Kabuki (Palo Alto: Kodansha International, 1969), by Gunji Masakatsu, is a beautifully illustrated volume and an excellent introduction. Earle Ernst's *The Kabuki Theatre* (New York: Grove Press, 1956) is the best full-scale discussion of the history and characteristics of Kabuki. A. C. Scott's *The Kabuki Theatre of Japan* (London: Allen and Unwin, 1955) and Faubion Bow-

Japanese Kabuki

ers' *Japanese Theatre* (New York: Hill & Wang, 1959) are standard works. About one hundred play synopses are in Aubrey Halford and Giovanna Halford, *The Kabuki Handbook* (Rutland, Vt.: Tuttle, 1966). Of the few play translations available, see especially *Benten the Thief*, in Earle Ernst, *Three Japanese Plays* (New York: Oxford University Press, 1959) and *The Love of Izayoi and Seishin*, trans. Frank T. Motofuji (Rutland, Vt.: Tuttle, 1966).

The Subscription List
A Japanese Kabuki Play
BY NAMIKI GOHEI III
English adaptation by James R. Brandon and Tamako Niwa

The Subscription List (*Kanjincho*) is one of the two or three most popular plays in the Kabuki repertory. It is an independent dance play in one act and normally would appear in the second position on a program of four plays. It was adapted by Namiki Gohei III in 1841 from the Noh play *Ataka* for the famous actor Ichikawa Danjuro VII. In Noh classification *Ataka* is a play of the fourth type—a living person play—and it is one in which, for Noh, the conflict between *shite* and *waki* is unusually strong and direct.

The play dramatizes an incident in the life of Minamoto Yoshitsune, a historical figure who lived in the twelfth century. Yoshitsune is refined, handsome, and a great lover; he is also a skillful warrior. It was largely through his valor that his brother Yoritomo secured the position of *shogun*, or supreme ruler. Yoshitsune's popularity is so great that Yoritomo begins to fear him and orders him captured. The play begins with Yoshitsune and his party, led by the priest Benkei, fleeing toward the Ataka barrier station. The barrier guard, Togashi Zaemon, challenges them, but eventually he allows them to pass because, although he recognizes Yoshitsune, he is deeply impressed by Benkei's resourceful defense of his lord. In many Kabuki plays, the hero is matched against a villain, but in *The Subscription List* both Benkei and Togashi are worthy men and both excite our admiration. The conflict between *giri* (obligation) and *ninjo* (human sympathy) is a major theme in Japanese drama. In *The Subscription List* Benkei's *giri-ninjo* conflict arises out of his need to strike his beloved master. The only way Benkei can save Yoshitsune is to strike him as if he were a mere porter, but this would be an inhuman act. As

206

resolute heroes often do, Benkei suppresses his human feelings and carries out his duty.

The play is composed of three major scenes (not distinguished by breaks or set changes, however) of contrasting moods: an intensely dramatic initial confrontation between Benkei and Togashi, a slow, plaintive scene in which Yoshitsune's fall from power is recounted (a very Buddhist, very Noh-like theme), and a lighthearted dance by Benkei celebrating their success. Using Noh terminology to identify the characters, Benkei is the *shite* upon whom the burden of the play rests; Togashi is the *waki* antagonist; Yoshitsune is the *kokata*, or child role (played by an adult, however, in Kabuki); the retainers and the soldiers are *tsure* to the *shite* and to the *waki*. The play's basic structure is taken from Noh: for example, the play opens with the *nanori bue* flute music. Then the *waki*, Togashi, enters and announces himself (*nanori*). The *shite*, Benkei, and his party enters then, as the journey song (*michiyuki*) is sung by the chorus. Because of its Noh origins the play has a sustained dignity not often found in Kabuki. In fact, when *The Subscription List* was first performed, audiences thought it highbrow. The play attained its current popularity through subsequent revivals.

Although *The Subscription List* is based on *Ataka*, the two plays appear as very different theatre pieces when they are staged. *The Subscription List* has a vitality and intensity which is foreign to the Noh play. The highly dramatic Buddhist debate (*mondo*), which occurs early in *The Subscription List*, is not in the Noh version at all; it was added by Danjuro VII after he witnessed an immensely successful recitation of the scene by a well-known professional storyteller. The danced confrontation between Benkei and Togashi, which is rudimentary in the Noh, is developed in Kabuki, including long movements down the *hanamichi* and back again. Benkei's high-spirited drinking scene is typical of Kabuki and is famous in itself. The *nagauta* music for *The Subscription List*, an extended composition lasting about forty minutes, was composed by Kineya Rokusaburo

IV for the first performance. It is pure Kabuki music, owing almost nothing to the Noh music for *Ataka*, and is ranked as a masterpiece of *nagauta* composition. *The Subscription List* is rare because of its excellence of script, dance, and music, and so rises to the level of a major classic, not only of Kabuki but of world theatre.

The version of *The Subscription List* given here describes the play's first English production at Michigan State University in 1963. The aim of the production was to recreate as fully as possible the theatrical experience of *The Subscription List* at a Kabuki theatre in Japan. The technical aspects of performance were almost literally recreated. The Kabuki version of the Noh stage was built (this was traditionally used for Noh-derived Kabuki plays), and included a fifty-foot *hanamichi* through the auditorium. Costumes for the three major characters—Benkei, Togashi, and Yoshitsune—were purchased in Japan; the rest were constructed from Japanese patterns. Properties and make-up were authentic. *Nagauta* music for the complete performance was recorded in Japan, minus the vocal line in order that the English verses could be added over it. The chorus was placed on a raised platform at the rear of the stage in the traditional manner. They chanted their verses in strictly regulated rhythms and inflections that were timed to the taped music. The usual wooden clappers (*ki*) accompanied the action. Blocking, gesture, and delivery were based on the Japanese original. Two months of intensive rehearsal were used to train the cast in basic Kabuki movements: how to rise and kneel, how to walk, how to gesture, how to perform the *mie* poses in the play. Since beauty of form is a major part of Kabuki art, great attention was paid to drilling the performers until they had acquired control and fluency of movement.

Some changes in both text and staging were made in order to give the English performance the same degree of stylistic unity and dramatic coherence that would be found in a Japanese production. Total copying of the original would not accomplish this, because a Japanese audience is extremely familiar with the

Yoshitsune story while an American audience is not. So chorus lines were added to describe in detail the conflict between Yoshitsune and Yoritomo and to make explicit the fact that Togashi will commit suicide. This is not mentioned in the script, but a Japanese audience knows it. Yoshitsune's importance is not clearly apparent in the script, so he was given more movement, especially in the plaintive middle section of the play, where he shares with Benkei the dance depicting his wanderings. (He would be motionless in Japan.) In the original text Benkei squares off against Togashi after he has struck Yoshitsune. This order was reversed so that the danced confrontation between Benkei and Togashi would culminate in Benkei's striking Yoshitsune, thus establishing the act of striking as the high point of the scene. Benkei's *ennen* dance at the end, a pure dance that does not move the action of the play forward (as do the earlier narrative dance and mime sections) was shortened. Stage assistants were dressed in black rather than in formal costumes in order to distinguish them from other cast members.

Characters

The Subscription List

The traditional Kabuki curtain of broad green, rust, and black stripes is closed; the houselights are partially dimmed. In a few moments two sharp claps are heard from backstage, wood against wood, as the STAGE MANAGER *signals the start of the performance. The opening music begins; first, the quavering, high-pitched notes of a flute, then the measured beating of drums.* MUSIC CUE NO. I.* *Then two more claps of the* STAGE MANAGER's *sticks signal that the cast is in place. The drumming rapidly increases in tempo and a* STAGE ASSISTANT, *kneeling beside the left proscenium arch, begins to beat out a furious tattoo with two wood clappers on a board in front of him. Just as the crescendo of sound reaches its peak, another* STAGE ASSISTANT, *robed and hooded in black, runs swiftly across the stage, pushing the curtain before him.* FADE MUSIC NO. 1.

We see a simple and stylized setting, representing a Noh stage. On a backpiece and two sidepieces is painted a background of light-tan wooden planking, with a single gnarled pine tree flanked by bamboos. Except for a small area upstage left, where a small group of hand properties is placed—partially covered by a purple silk cloth—the entire area of the stage is available for the action of the play. There are three entrances. A colorful striped curtain covers the large entrance at stage right. On the opposite side of the stage is a small door, used by the STAGE ASSISTANTS *who are stationed on the left of the stage and by actors for less important exits. The main entrance, however, is the "flower way," or* hanamichi, *a raised ramp which leads from the rear of the auditorium, through the audience, to the right side of the stage, and which serves as an extension of the stage*

---

* Music cues indicate the cue numbers of a long-playing record available from Samuel French, 25 West 45th Street, New York, N.Y. 10036.

The Subscription List

proper into the audience. A CHORUS *of six chanters is kneeling on a red platform upstage.*

There is a moment of silence. Flute and drums begin again. MUSIC CUE NO. 2. *The curtain stage right flies open, and* TOGASHI, *three* SOLDIERS, *and a* SWORD-BEARER *enter in stately procession, using the sliding step of Noh dance. The foot never leaves the floor. Each controlled movement blends into the next, so that the character appears to glide rather than walk. This style of movement is used by all characters in the play.*

When TOGASHI *reaches center stage, he stops, pivots slowly, and faces the audience. It is obvious that he is a samurai, for he wears the sumptuous ceremonial dress of nobility. His voluminous outer kimono is of pale-blue brocade figured with white and silver cranes. Its sleeves almost touch the floor. His legs are encased in the long trousers of court dress that trail away a full four feet behind him. He carries a fan in his right hand. His face and hands are pure white except for black lip and eye markings.* TOGASHI *speaks directly to the audience in a stately, half-chanting style of speech.* FADE MUSIC NO. 2.

TOGASHI It is I, Togashi Zaemon, who stand before you here at the Ataka barirer gate, at the command of our most august and sovereign ruler of the land, our Lord Yoritomo. I stand guard to apprehend our lord's younger brother Yoshitsune, once favored, now fallen from that favor and reported fleeing to the North disguised as a begging priest. We are strictly ordered by our Lord Yoritomo to stop and investigate every passing priest. In faithful duty I guard this barrier for our lord! I command you all to be of this same mind. (*No flicker of expression has crossed* TOGASHI's *face, composure being one of the highest virtues of the samurai code.*)

FIRST SOLDIER (*strongly, but also without facial expression*) Already the heads of three doubtful priests hang from the trees!

SECOND SOLDIER As you command, every priest shall be brought before you!

THIRD SOLDIER Captured! Bound on the spot!

FIRST SOLDIER   We are alert . . .
THE THREE SOLDIERS   . . . ever on guard!
TOGASHI   Well spoken! Seize each and every priest who attempts
to pass! We shall put at ease the mind of our Lord of Kama-
kura. Now, all of you to your posts!
THE THREE SOLDIERS   As you command, sir!

MUSIC CUE NO. 3. *There is a shrill cry from the flute, followed
by metallic beats on the drum.* TOGASHI *turns and slowly leads
his small procession across the stage, this movement symbolizing
their arriving at the barrier. The* SOLDIERS *kneel in a row upstage. The* SWORD-BEARER *kneels directly behind* TOGASHI, *holding the sword before him in readiness. From under the purple
property cloth* TOGASHI's *personal* STAGE ASSISTANT *brings out a
black lacquered cask ornamented with gold.* TOGASHI *seats himself on it. Another* STAGE ASSISTANT *arranges the folds of his
costume. To flute and drum accompaniment and the plangent
music of plucked samisen, the* CHORUS, *seated at the rear of the
stage, tells the tale of* YOSHITSUNE's *wanderings.*

FULL CHORUS
　　Their travel garments are those of a priest . . .
　　Their travel garments are those of a wandering priest,
　　　　With sleeves wet by dew and tears.
　　The time is the tenth night of the second moon.
　　　　The tenth night of the second moon.
　　And so having left the capital on a moonlit night . . .
CHORUS LEADER   (*the lead singer continues the story of the past*)
　　　　Yoshitsune, Yoshitsune!
　　　　　Defeated armies,
　　　　　. For his brother's rule.
　　　　But family ties are never proof to jealousy.
　　　　Soon it was known,
　　　　　"Yoritomo turns his face
　　　　From the one
　　　　Whom all have learned to love."

> Forced to flee
> Silently,
> Yoshitsune and his band of five
> For three long years have fled
> Through distant places
> And seasons . . .

The curtain at the rear of the ramp flies up, and YOSHITSUNE *enters. Using quick, sliding steps, he moves through the audience toward the stage, then sees* TOGASHI *and the* SOLDIERS *at the barrier. He stops and turns back toward the audience. For a moment he poses, a subdued tragic figure. He wears a dark-purple kimono and pale-green trousers. His long hair is gathered together and falls down his back. His face, hands, and dancing socks are white. As part of his disguise he carries a large coolie's hat and a pilgrim's staff. The blue box strapped to his back supposedly contains* BENKEI's *sutras and other religious objects; actually it contains* YOSHITSUNE's *armor. Next,* YOSHITSUNE's *four* RETAINERS *stride purposefully down the ramp one by one. They pass their master and form a line between him and the stage. They wear priests' vestments and carry Buddhist rosaries. Each has a short sword at his waist.*

FULL CHORUS (*continuing the story of their journey*)
> By furtive ship,
> Through distant paths of waves,
> Arriving, now at last,
> At Kaizu Bay.

BENKEI *moves quickly down the ramp. He wears a priest's pillbox hat and vestments. He is an imposing figure dressed in a robe of black brocade silk, figured with gold, and stiff white trousers. As* YOSHITSUNE *turns to him, the* RETAINERS *kneel.* FADE MUSIC NO. 3.

YOSHITSUNE So, Benkei. The roads ahead are blocked, as you say. And this was our last hope. I know now I shall never see the North. For myself I have decided: rather than suffer an ignoble death at the hand of some nameless soldier, I shall take my own life first. But I must consider your wishes, too, as I did in disguising myself as a common porter. At this crucial moment have you any suggestions?

FIRST RETAINER My lord, why do we carry these swords? When shall they be painted with blood? Now is the crucial moment of my lord's life.

SECOND RETAINER Let us resolve! Cut the soldiers down! We shall fight our way through this barrier!

THIRD RETAINER The years of obligation to our lord shall be repaid today! We must pass through, my lord!

FIRST, SECOND, and THIRD RETAINERS (*they rise, hands on the hilts of their swords*) We shall pass through!

They turn to go, but the FOURTH RETAINER, *an older man, blocks their path with an imperative gesture.* BENKEI *speaks.*

BENKEI Stop! Wait a moment!

Reluctantly the RETAINERS *resume kneeling positions.*

YOSHITSUNE Yes, Benkei?

BENKEI A crisis is no time for rash action. If we fight, we shall pass this barrier, I know.

THE FOUR RETAINERS We shall!

BENKEI But the news will travel ahead, alerting the next barrier and the next. Our success will become our failure. We cannot fight through them all. (*To* YOSHITSUNE, *with deep respect.*) Oh, my lord, it pains me to see you degraded and reviled. But your life itself is all-important. I urged we dress as priests; then later, when this ruse became known, asked your lordship to dress as a common porter. I beg again, my lord, that you pull low your coolie's hat, and making a pretense of exhaustion from the weight of your load, follow behind us, far in the rear; and I am certain no one will suspect who my lordship is.

YOSHITSUNE I leave everything in your care, Benkei.

BENKEI Trust me, my lord.

YOSHITSUNE (*to the chafing* RETAINERS) We shall do exactly as Benkei says.

THE FOUR RETAINERS (*bowing slightly*) As our lord commands.

BENKEI Then pass peacefully on.

THE FOUR RETAINERS We obey.

MUSIC CUE NO. 4. BENKEI *passes* YOSHITSUNE *and moves onto the stage to the accompaniment of samisen music. The* RETAINERS *follow closely behind.*

FULL CHORUS
> And so the travelers,
> Bent upon passing through,
> Drew near the barrier gate.

Irregular metallic taps from the large drum. YOSHITSUNE *ties his hat low over his eyes, then moves slowly onto the stage, taking a position between* BENKEI, *who is almost center stage, and the* RETAINERS, *who are kneeling in a row upstage right. His personal* STAGE ASSISTANT *places a small stool for him to sit on and arranges his costume.* YOSHITSUNE *poses with his head low, clasping the pilgrim's staff over his shoulder. Though he remains motionless in this position throughout most of the play, his noble bearing is such that we are always aware of his presence.* FADE MUSIC NO. 4.

BENKEI (*faces front and speaks in a powerful voice*) Ho there! We are priests who wish to pass!

TOGASHI What's that? Priests, you say? (*Rises, strides forward, and addresses* BENKEI *in measured tones.*) Now, my friends, know that this is a barrier!

BENKEI (*facing* TOGASHI *and feigning deference*) I know, sir. Throughout the country priests are now soliciting contributions to rebuild the Todai temple in the Southern capital. It is our honored mission to be dispatched to the Northern provinces.

TOGASHI A praiseworthy project, indeed. However, the very purpose of this barrier is to stop priests like yourselves. You will find it very difficult to pass.

BENKEI This is hard to understand. What can it mean?

TOGASHI Relations between our Lord Yoritomo and Yoshitsune having become strained, three years ago Yoshitsune left his brother's service. Now he flees to the North, disguised as a priest, to seek the aid of his friend Hidehira. Hearing this, our Lord Yoritomo has caused these barriers to be raised. (*He draws himself up and speaks deliberately.*) Know you that I am in command of this barrier!

FIRST SOLDIER We stand guard with orders to detain all priests!

SECOND SOLDIER And now before us, behold, many priests!

THIRD SOLDIER We shall not allow . . .

THE THREE SOLDIERS . . . even one to pass!

BENKEI Your orders are to stop all those disguised as priests, are they not? They surely say nothing of stopping real priests.

FIRST SOLDIER (*roughly but in strong rhythm*) Say what you will, . . .

SECOND SOLDIER . . . we killed . . .

THIRD SOLDIER . . . three priests . . .

THE THREE SOLDIERS (*in unison*) . . . yesterday!

FIRST SOLDIER So your saying you are real priests will not excuse you!

SECOND SOLDIER And if you try . . .

THIRD SOLDIER . . . to pass by force——

FIRST SOLDIER Beware!

THE THREE SOLDIERS (*drawing the words out*) You shall not survive!

BENKEI (*mock horror*) And these priests you beheaded . . . was one Yoshitsune?

TOGASHI Who can say? (*Commandingly.*) It is useless for you to argue! No priest . . .

THE THREE SOLDIERS (*with great force*) . . . shall pass this barrier!

TOGASHI *imperiously turns his back on* BENKEI, *kicking the long, trailing ends of his trousers as he does so. He strides back to his former position stage left and resumes his seat.*

BENKEI Monstrous horror! (*Turning to the* RETAINERS, *but speaking loudly for* TOGASHI's *benefit.*) Why should such misfortune be ours? Human strength is powerless against such unforeseen fate! But at least we shall be killed with honor. Come, draw near. Let us perform our last rites!

THE FOUR RETAINERS We shall, sir.

BENKEI (*gravely*) This is our final rite!

MUSIC CUE NO. 5. BENKEI *moves majestically up right, where two* STAGE ASSISTANTS *tie back the long sleeves of his kimono and hand him a scarlet Buddhist rosary. The* RETAINERS *form a square at center stage, kneeling, their hands folded in meditation. With a quick glance at* TOGASHI, BENKEI *moves swiftly into the square, and as the* CHORUS *chants, dances a prayer to the gods.*

FULL CHORUS (*to full orchestra accompaniment*)
To detain here Yamabushi priests,
  Who are versed in the austere teaching of En no Ubazoku,
  Whose bodies and spirit are one and the same with the
    Lord Buddha . . .
(BENKEI *raises his arms in supplication to the heavens.*)
Surely the gods will look with disfavor upon this impious
    act,
  The wrath of god Yuya Gongen
  Shall strike this spot!

(In simulated anger BENKEI *leaps high in the air and stamps loudly upon the floor.)*

"On a bi ra un ken" . . .

So chanting, they rubbed the beads of their rosaries in prayer.

BENKEI *rises to his full height and with a sweeping upward motion begins to rub the beads of his rosary. The others follow suit. The beads of the rosaries buzz and chatter. Then the* RE-TAINERS *turn their backs to* BENKEI, *clasp their hands as in prayer, and kneel. Their tableau is like Buddha protected on four sides by kneeling guardian angels, implying their closeness to Buddha.* FADE MUSIC NO. 5.

TOGASHI *(suspicious and determined to test* BENKEI'*s story)* A noble decision, to die. However, you mentioned a mission of soliciting for the Todai temple. If this is so, surely you cannot be without a list of contributors. *(An order.)* Bring out this list! I demand to hear it!

BENKEI What? *(Momentarily stunned.)* You . . . you say, read the list of contributors?

TOGASHI Read it, I say!

BENKEI *(his confident voice betrays nothing)* It shall be done.

He moves upstage right, where a STAGE ASSISTANT *hands him a scroll.*

CHORUS LEADER

Ah, ah! Were there but a list of contributors!
*(*MUSIC CUE NO. 6.*)*
Instead, from the box he draws a single unused letter-scroll,
And calling it the list,
He boldly improvises.

Moving back to center stage, BENKEI *unrolls the scroll, and holding it so* TOGASHI *cannot see it, pretends to read the dedicatory*

219

The Subscription List

passage. As BENKEI *is a priest, he has a considerable knowledge of Buddhist ritual and is able to make up a plausible passage.*

BENKEI Even Buddha, like the autumn moon, has taken refuge in the dark clouds of death. (TOGASHI *rises and stealthily begins edging toward* BENKEI.) Who then, in this world, should be surprised that life is but a long night's dream! (BENKEI *senses* TOGASHI's *presence and whirls to face him. The two pose for a moment, glaring angrily at each other. Then* TO-GASHI, *his suspicions confirmed, strides back and regally resumes his seat. Uncertain whether he has been found out or not,* BENKEI *determines to brazen it out. With a flourish he unrolls the scroll once more and in even louder tones than before continues to "read" from the list.*) In the Middle Ages there once lived an emperor whose name was Shomu! Having lost his beloved wife, his grief became too much for him to bear. The tears flowed from his eyes in a continuous chain; his cheeks were never dry. To aid her advance as a bodhisattva, he then built in her memory the great Rushana Buddha, the same that burned to the ground in the era of Juei. I, the priest Chogen, lamenting the loss of this place of worship, have received the Imperial Order to solicit throughout the provinces to rebuild this holy temple. I appeal to priests, high and low, and to laymen alike. He who contributes even a trifling amount shall live in ease in this world and shall sit among thousands of lotuses in the next. I address you most reverently!

FADE MUSIC NO. 6.

CHORUS LEADER (MUSIC CUE NO. 7.) He reads as if challenging the heavens to reverberate!

BENKEI *rolls up the scroll with utter composure and is about to turn away.* FADE MUSIC NO 7. *There is little doubt in* TOGASHI's *mind that this is* YOSHITSUNE's *party, yet he is impressed by*

BENKEI's *bold improvisation. Rising, he decides to test* BENKEI *further.*

TOGASHI I see. I have heard you read from the list now, and should have no further doubts. Still, the rough warrior seldom has the honor to be instructed in the Way of our Lord Buddha. I shall avail myself of this unexpected opportunity to learn of our religion's subtleties.

FULL CHORUS
Subtle are the ways of religion,
Subtler still the ways of the samurai.

BENKEI With pleasure, sir.

TOGASHI The followers of Buddha are sworn to peace. And yet there are some whose warlike appearance casts doubt on their calling. (*He looks significantly at* BENKEI's *sword.*) Is there an explanation for this?

BENKEI (*fabricating a plausible answer without hesitation*) It is the stern prescript of our Holy Order, in which the principles of Buddha and Shinto combine, that its followers should nurture the twin virtues of stoicism and benevolence while outwardly they conquer evil and subdue heretical doctrines in a warlike manner. All is Shinto and Buddha . . . the one hundred eight beads of the rosary representing the multitudinous blessings of the gods!

TOGASHI (*pressing another question without pause*) You wear a priest's vestment. Why then do you wear a pilgrim's hat at the same time?

BENKEI The hat and vestments are like the warrior's helmet and armor. With the sharp sword of Amida Buddha at his side, and breaking a path with a staff, the pilgrim crosses the highest mountains and the most dangerous places.

TOGASHI But how does carrying a staff protect a pilgrim's body and limbs?

BENKEI A foolish question! The spirit of Buddha dwells within the staff! As a child grows in his mother's womb, so the spirit of Buddha grows within us all!

TOGASHI   How has this tradition been handed down?

BENKEI   Our predecessors carried it as the holy staff of our Lord Buddha when traveling in the mountains and valleys, and this has become the practice down through the ages!

TOGASHI   Though a priest, you wear a sword.

BENKEI   Like the bow of the scarecrow, it serves to frighten our enemies. At the same time we do not hesitate to strike down those evil beasts and poisonous snakes, and human beings as well, that violate Buddha's law, or the Princely Way. For with one death many lives may be saved!

TOGASHI   One can, of course, cut down a solid object that obstructs the eye, but what of those formless evils that may obstruct Buddha's law, or the Princely Way? With what would you cut them down?

BENKEI   What difficulty is there in destroying formless evils? One would dispel them with the nine-word Shingon prayer!

TOGASHI   Shingon prayer?

BENKEI   Shingon prayer!

TOGASHI   (*moving in, pressing another series of questions without pause*)   Now tell me, what is the significance of your dress?

BENKEI   It is patterned in the likeness of the ferocious deity Fudo!

TOGASHI   The meaning of your hat?

BENKEI   The headdress of the five wisdoms, its twelve folds symbolizing the affinity of cause and retribution!

TOGASHI   (*moves in another step*)   The vestment about your neck?

BENKEI   (*moves in toward* TOGASHI)   Signifying the nine stages of Buddha's paradise!

TOGASHI   Why the bindings about your legs?

BENKEI   The black leggings of the Shingon sect!

TOGASHI   The white of your sandals?

BENKEI   In the spirit of treading on the eight-petaled lotus!

TOGASHI   (*spitting it out*)   And the air you breathe?

BENKEI   (*face to face, he controls himself, trembling with anger*)

In the holy sutras the beginning and the end, the two reverend sounds—*A* and *UN!*

TOGASHI (*still pressing*) You mentioned, before, the nine-word Shingon prayer. My final question is, Explain to me its meaning—if you can!

FULL CHORUS

> A paradox, a riddle,
> Deepest of the deep.
> Not Buddha himself
> Knows the meaning of this prayer.

The question is beyond BENKEI's *knowledge of Buddhism; nevertheless, he launches into a brilliant improvisation of Buddhist jargon.*

BENKEI This nine-word prayer is a precious secret of the Shingon faith, and its meaning is most difficult to explain. But to still your doubt, I shall undertake to do so. The nine words are *Rin byoh toh sha kai chin retsu zai zen!* Before you draw your sword, first, you must strike your teeth thirty-six times with hands folded in supplication. Then, with the thumb of your right hand, you draw four lines from earth to sky and five lines from horizon to horizon. Simultaneously, you rapidly incant the blessing *Kyuu kyuu nyo ritsu ryoo.* So doing, all evil—the evil of worldly passions and the devil of heresy—will disappear like frost before the vapors of steam. Sharp and shining, the prayer cuts through to the very heart of the world's darkness. Now . . . have you any further questions regarding our religious practices? I shall reply to them all in full, that you may share in the power of their virtue, which is all-embracing and infinite! Engrave these words on your heart, but reveal their secrets to no one! O gods and bodhisattvas of Japan, I call upon you to witness the words I most reverently speak! I bow before you! (*He does, then turns to* TOGASHI.) I speak to you with utmost respect.

223

FULL CHORUS (**MUSIC CUE NO. 8**) The barrier guard seems impressed.

BENKEI *dances a few steps expressive of his success; then he and* **TOGASHI** *pose in tableau:* **BENKEI** *with scroll held high in triumph and* **TOGASHI** *with fan overhead.* **FADE MUSIC NO. 8.** **TOGASHI** *is certain they are* **BENKEI** *and* **YOSHITSUNE,** *yet* **BENKEI** *has not faltered in his defense of his master. Impressed,* **TOGASHI** *decides to let them pass.*

TOGASHI That I should have doubted such honorable priests even for a moment! I should like to be added to your list of contributors. Guards, bring gifts for the priests!
THE THREE SOLDIERS Yes, sir.

The mood relaxes. **MUSIC CUE NO. 9.** **TOGASHI** *returns to his seat stage left.* **BENKEI** *gives the scroll to his* **STAGE ASSISTANT** *and receives a rosary. The three* **SOLDIERS** *pick up gift trays just brought in through the small door stage left by* **TOGASHI's STAGE ASSISTANT.** *The* **SOLDIERS** *place the trays center stage and return to their kneeling positions upstage of* **TOGASHI.**

FULL CHORUS
On wide stands, brought forth by the guards,
A ceremonial skirt of pure white silk,
Many rolls of Kaga silk,
A mirror, and golden coins.

FADE MUSIC NO. 9.

TOGASHI Though the gifts are small, it would be accredited as a meritorious deed for me should you accept them on behalf of the priests of Todai temple. Respectfully, I beg you to accept them.
BENKEI (*before the gifts, speaks impressively*) You are indeed a

benevolent lord. There can be no doubt of your peaceful, happy existence in this world and the next. (*He rubs his rosary over the gifts in blessing.*) One thing more. We will be traveling through the neighboring provinces, not returning to the capital until the middle of the fourth moon. I beg you to keep the larger articles for us until then. (*He kneels before the gifts. When he rises, he takes only the two bags of money from the center tray. These he gives to two of the* RETAINERS.) Now, pass through!

THE FOUR RETAINERS Yes, sir!

BENKEI (*takes out his fan, flips it open, and holds it in front of him*) Go! Go now! Hurry!

THE FOUR RETAINERS We go, sir!

CHORUS LEADER (MUSIC CUE NO. 10)
>   Rejoicing within,
>   The warrior-priests
>   Quietly rise and move away.

BENKEI *moves swiftly down the ramp, followed by the four* RETAINERS. YOSHITSUNE *rises, and with head bent low, slowly begins to leave the stage. One of the* SOLDIERS *crosses to* TOGASHI's *side and whispers in his ear.*

TOGASHI (*rises abruptly*) What? That porter? (*With the help of his* STAGE ASSISTANT, TOGASHI *slips the kimono from his right shoulder, freeing his arm for action. Receiving his sword from the* BEARER, *he takes two deliberate paces forward and stops, hand poised on the hilt of his sword.*) Stop! Stop, I say!

The action now is very rapid. YOSHITSUNE *stops. As if pulled by invisible strings, he backs toward* TOGASHI. *He kneels, head low and staff held against one shoulder. At the same time* BENKEI *turns and rushes past the* RETAINERS, *toward the stage; but before he can reach* YOSHITSUNE, *the* RETAINERS *also turn and start toward the stage. They have their hands on their swords, ready to draw. With twirling rosary and outstretched arms,* BENKEI *blocks their headlong rush.*

BENKEI   No! Rashness will lose it all!

FULL CHORUS
> "Our lord is suspected!
>   Now is the moment
>   Between sinking and floating!"
> These are their thoughts as they turn.

Feigning rage, BENKEI *stamps on the floor. He twirls the rosary about his head and crosses in swiftly to* YOSHITSUNE. FADE MUSIC NO. 10.

BENKEI   You! Strong One! Why haven't you passed through?

TOGASHI   (*in a fearsome voice*)   Because I have detained him!

BENKEI   Detained him? What for?

TOGASHI   There are those who say he resembles . . . a certain person. That is why I have detained him.

BENKEI   One person often resembles another! (*Brazening it out.*) Who do you think he resembles?

TOGASHI   My soldiers say General Yoshitsune. He is to be held for questioning.

BENKEI   The General? The Strong One resembles General Yoshitsune, you say? (*Turning on* YOSHITSUNE *in feigned fury.*) This is something to remember a lifetime! Ohhhh! It's unendurable! We'd planned to reach Noto by sundown, and now, just because of a lagging porter . . . this has happened! If people begin suspecting you of being the General on the slightest provocation, you'll be the cause of the failure of our mission! (*Grinds his teeth.*) The more I think of it, the more despicable you become! (*He growls through clenched teeth; he leaps in the air and stamps on the floor.*) You are hateful, I say! Hateful! Hateful!! Now move on, I tell you!

CHORUS LEADER
> He berates him soundly,
>   Ordering him to pass through!

Shielding his face, YOSHITSUNE *rises and quickly crosses upstage right, where he kneels with his back to the audience; in effect, removing himself from the scene which follows.*

TOGASHI No matter how you plead his case, he shall not . . .
THE THREE SOLDIERS . . . pass through!

The SOLDIERS *stand in a resolute row with their hands on their sword hilts. The* RETAINERS *reach for their swords and are about to attack. Still trying to avert a conflict,* BENKEI *makes an excuse for the* RETAINERS' *actions.*

BENKEI For you to eye the porter's box as you do, you're not
    guards at all. You must be thieves! (*He strikes the staff on
    the floor and poses with it threateningly. The* RETAINERS *surge
    forward.* BENKEI *uses the staff to block their path.*) Here! Here!

MUSIC CUE NO 11. BENKEI *forces the* RETAINERS *back, but they
press forward again. He pushes them back a second time, holding them until they are calmed.* BENKEI *now turns to face* TO-
GASHI, *holding the staff before him in both hands.*

FULL CHORUS (*accompanied by full orchestra*)
        "How cowardly it is!
        To draw swords
        Against a lowly porter!"
    With such seeming thoughts,
    And god-frightening looks,
    The priests prepared for battle

*The two opposing groups surge forward and meet center stage.
On each side the men press against their leader. Then* TOGASHI
and the SOLDIERS *begin to advance, one, two, three slow-motion
strides forward. In unison* BENKEI *and the* RETAINERS *take one,
two, three strides backward. The two groups of men move as*

227

one, bound together by their fierce antagonism. Now BENKEI *summons his last resources, and as the* SOLDIERS *and the* RE-TAINERS *stand aside, he forces* TOGASHI *back step by step to his original position.* FADE MUSIC NO. 11.

BENKEI   If you still think this miserable creature is Yoshitsune, then hold him along with the gifts until our return; investigate him any way you wish! (*Raises his staff, face contorted in feigned fury.*) Or would you rather I beat him with this now?

FULL CHORUS
> Right, left!
> Right!
> The servant strikes his master!
> Unimaginable act!

BENKEI *strikes* YOSHITSUNE *three times, only the last blow, however, actually touching the hat enough to set it gently rocking.* BENKEI'*s lips quiver and he suppresses his tears.*

TOGASHI (*aghast, for he is certain it is* YOSHITSUNE)   Stop! Stop!

BENKEI   Then why do you doubt us?

TOGASHI   There is the complaint of my soldiers.

BENKEI (*raising the staff again*)   Then I shall kill him before your own eyes! Will that convince you?

TOGASHI (*visibly recoiling*)   Kill him?

BENKEI (*roaring*)   Yes!!

TOGASHI   Stop! Do not be hasty! Because of the baseless suspicions of my soldiers you have already severely beaten this person, who . . . is not the General. My doubts are now dispelled. (*Speaking brusquely to cover his emotion.*) Quickly now, pass through the barrier!

BENKEI (*continuing the pretense*)   You laggard, you've been lucky this time! Don't tempt the gods again!

TOGASHI   From now on, it is my duty to maintain even stricter

guard! (*His* STAGE ASSISTANT *fixes the sleeve of his kimono.*)
Come with me, men!

THE THREE SOLDIERS Yes, my lord.

BENKEI *and* TOGASHI *face each other in tableau. The air crackles
with emotion.* BENKEI *has succeeded; he knows this, yet cannot
show it. For* TOGASHI's *part, he knows who* BENKEI *and* YOSHI-
TSUNE *are, yet he cannot show this. Further, there is the im-
plication that having failed his own master,* TOGASHI *will take
his own life in the future. He averts his face. Just as he is about
to give way to tears, he shakes his head, dismissing the thought
of death from his mind. He draws himself up, pivots regally
about, kicking out the long, trailing ends of his trousers, and
strides off the stage.*

FULL CHORUS (MUSIC CUE NO. 12)
    Taking his soldiers with him,
    The barrier guard enters within the gate.

TOGASHI *and the* SOLDIERS *exit through the small door stage left.*
BENKEI *looks after them. The music becomes plaintive and
halting in tempo.* YOSHITSUNE's *hat and box have been taken
by his* STAGE ASSISTANT, *and he moves to left center stage, where
he kneels.* BENKEI *slowly moves to center stage right. He kneels
facing* YOSHITSUNE, *his head bent in grief. The* RETAINERS *kneel
in a line upstage between the two. They have symbolically
passed through the barrier and are now stopping some distance beyond it.*

YOSHITSUNE (*in spite of their success he seems subdued and
    melancholy*) Benkei, you acted with great presence of mind.
    Indeed, no one but you could have succeeded with such a
    daring plan. Without hesitation you struck me as recklessly
    as though I were a lowly servant and so saved me. I stand
    in awe for having received the divine protection of our
    patron, the god of war.

FIRST RETAINER   The barrier guard stopped us and we all felt, "Now is the moment to fight for our lord's safety!"

SECOND RETAINER   It is a sign the gods are protecting our lord. Our trip from here on to the North should be swift.

THIRD RETAINER   Yet without the quick thinking of Benkei here, it would have been hard to escape.

FIRST RETAINER   We were . . .

THE FOUR RETAINERS   . . . truly amazed!

BENKEI (*head bent to the floor*)   The seers have preached that the end of the world is soon at hand. Yet the sun and the moon have not yet fallen from their places in the heavens. Fate has been kind to Yoshitsune also. How grateful we all are. You speak of strategy, but the fact is, I have struck my own dear lord. The heavenly reprisals are frightening to contemplate. How wrong I have been! How wrong!

FADE MUSIC NO. 12.

CHORUS LEADER (MUSIC CUE NO. 13)
How noble, now,
Even Benkei,
Who has never given way before,
Finally shed the tears of a lifetime.

His body shaking with grief, BENKEI *bows his head and holds his hand before his eyes, weeping.*

FULL CHORUS
The General then took his hand.

Rising to one knee, YOSHITSUNE *extends his right hand to* BENKEI *in token of forgiveness.* BENKEI *starts forward to accept his master's gesture, then is overcome with the enormity of his crime. He pulls back sharply, flings down his fan, and bows his head to the floor. Seeing the rocklike* BENKEI *reduced to tears on his behalf brings home to* YOSHITSUNE *the hopelessness of their position. He, too, raises his hand to his eyes to cover his tears.*

YOSHITSUNE Why should it be? Why should Yoshitsune, nobly born, his whole life spent in devoted service to his brother, end his life as a corpse sinking unheralded beneath the waves of the Western Sea?

BENKEI (*picking up his fan and holding it before him formally*)
> Midst mountain places,
> And rock-bound coasts,
> Awake and asleep,
> The warrior spends his lonely existence.

FADE MUSIC NO. 13. MUSIC CUE NO. 14. *As the* CHORUS *tells the story of* YOSHITSUNE's *flight,* BENKEI *dances its meaning to the accompaniment of a plaintive melody played by the full orchestra. The pace is slow, the mood softly melancholy.*

FULL CHORUS
> The warrior,
> With armor and sleeve-pillow
> As sole companions . . .

(BENKEI *mimes sleeping, his head cradled on his kimono sleeve. He turns upstage.* YOSHITSUNE *rises and continues the dance.*)
> Sometimes,
> Adrift at sea,
> At the mercy of wind and tide . . .

(*He sculls a boat; his open fan flutters overhead as in the wind.*)
> Sometimes,
> In mountain fastnesses,
> Where no hoofprint breaks the white snow . . .

(*The upside-down fan becomes a mountain.*)
> While he endures it all,
> From small evening waves of the sea,
> Come whispers of disgrace and banishment.

(*To emphasize the strength of the thought,* YOSHITSUNE *draws the string of an imaginary bow. He gestures throwing a stone, indicating that his fortunes are being dashed to earth in the same way. For a moment he poses, left hand extended, right*

hand over his head. Two sharp claps of the STAGE MANAGER's
sticks.)
>　For three long years past,
>　　Like the roadside thistle,
>　　Which has begun to wither and die,
>　　Covered only by the frost and dew.
>　How pitiful it is!

BENKEI *indicates* YOSHITSUNE *with his closed fan. Then he and
the four* RETAINERS *bow low. Straightening up, they cover their
eyes to hide their tears.*

THE FOUR RETAINERS　Quickly now, my lord, let us withdraw!
FULL CHORUS
>　Pulling on each other's sleeves,
>　They seem anxious to be on their way.

But BENKEI *does not move. The fan falls from his nerveless
fingers; his head sinks to his chest.* FADE MUSIC NO. 14.

TOGASHI (*offstage*)　Wait! Wait a moment! (*As* BENKEI *rises instantly,* YOSHITSUNE *retires upstage right, where he is covered
from view by the four* RETAINERS. TOGASHI *and the* SOLDIERS
*enter through the main entrance stage right and cross to
their original positions stage left.*) Forgive my abruptness,
but I have brought some sake, and though it is nothing much,
I hope you will drink with me.

A small cup is placed on a tray before TOGASHI *by one of the*
SOLDIERS, *and filled.* TOGASHI, *the host, drinks. Then the cup on
the tray is ceremoniously placed before* BENKEI. *He accepts it
center stage, kneeling facing the audience. The cup is filled.*
BENKEI *looks at it with undisguised pleasure.*

BENKEI　My kind lord, I shall drink with you with pleasure!
CHORUS LEADER (*accompanied by a single samisen;* MUSIC CUE
　NO. 15)

Truly, truly, Benkei understands this gesture.
How can he ever forget
Having received this cup of human sympathy?

BENKEI *tosses off the drink in one swallow. In an expansive mood now that the crisis is past, he laughingly gestures for the lid of the big lacquered cask stage left to be brought to him and filled with wine. Two* SOLDIERS *do so, then watch in open-mouthed amazement as* BENKEI *buries his face in the lid and downs an enormous draught.* BENKEI *comes up for air, smacks his lips, and with a sly chuckle points out at the audience. The* SOLDIERS *lean forward, straining to see what is there; and as they do,* BENKEI *pushes them off balance and they tumble to the floor.* BENKEI *roars with laughter. Then he empties the lid and gestures for it to be filled once more. The* SOLDIERS *hesitate, but a menacing glare and a roar of mock anger quickly convince them to fill the lid at once. His eyes gleaming with delight,* BENKEI *raises the lid to his lips and drains it in a single breath-taking swallow. The* SOLDIERS *stand amazed. Now slightly tipsy,* BENKEI *puts the lid on his head like a hat; and as a* STAGE ASSISTANT *removes the lid, he rises unsteadily to his feet to dance, beating time with the closed fan. The fan is flicked open and it becomes a sake cup; it sails in a graceful arc across the stage and it is a sake cup floating down a mountain stream.*

FULL CHORUS

Floating the wine cup
Down the mountain stream.
The swirling water,
In eddies and currents,
Splashes the sleeves
Covering the reaching hand.

BENKEI *dances his unsteady way along the "river bank" after his "sake cup." He stumbles, almost falls, recovers his balance. Then, the dance over and his tipsiness gone, he retrieves the fan, folds it, and formally faces* TOGASHI. FADE MUSIC NO. 15.

BENKEI In gratitude, I come to offer you wine!

He holds out the open fan to TOGASHI, *symbolically offering a drink.* MUSIC CUE NO. 16. *The implied meaning is that* BENKEI *recognizes what* TOGASHI *has done for them and that he wishes to express his gratitude. At the same time, it is implied that* TOGASHI *recognizes the true meaning of* BENKEI's *words.*

TOGASHI *(facing front, speaking in a constrained voice)* Life is short, but when pure, it is glorious. Dishonored, life's briefness is the more to be desired. Dishonored . . .
FULL CHORUS . . . as Togashi is in Yoritomo's eyes.
TOGASHI Life's briefness, . . .
FULL CHORUS . . . self-inflicted, with cold steel . . .
TOGASHI . . . the more to be desired!
FULL CHORUS
    He knows! (BENKEI *faces* TOGASHI.)
    He knows! (TOGASHI *faces* BENKEI.)
    Between the two,
      Samurai to samurai,
    A fleeting moment, never to return,
    Of total understanding.
BENKEI *(kneels and faces* TOGASHI)
    Live myriad long years
    As the turtle dwells
    On the rocks!
    Aryu dondo!
TOGASHI Go now!
BENKEI *(rises and faces front)*
    The sound of the falling mountain-stream
    Reverberates on the rocks below.
    That which roars is the waterfall!
    That which roars is the waterfall!

BENKEI *strikes his staff resoundingly on the stage to signal* YOSHITSUNE *and the others to leave. They rise and their line parts.* BENKEI *swiftly moves between them and kneels upstage right, where* STAGE ASSISTANTS *help tie up his sleeves.*

FULL CHORUS
> The waterfall will roar,
> The sun will shine.
> But this shall be endless. . . .

(YOSHITSUNE *and the* RETAINERS *move rapidly down the ramp, through the curtain, and out of sight.*)
> So saying, Benkei shouldered the porter's box.

(*Two* STAGE ASSISTANTS *help* BENKEI *into the box harness. He moves quickly onto the ramp.* TOGASHI *rises, following his progress with an intent gaze. On the ramp* BENKEI *pauses, with legs spread wide apart, the staff held over his head in both hands.* TOGASHI *steps forward a pace, twirls the long sleeve of his kimono over his left arm, and raises his closed fan high in the air. They pose.*)
> Feeling as though
> They had trod on the tail of a tiger,
> And slipped through the jaws of a dragon,
> They departed for the province of Michinoku.

FADE MUSIC NO. 16. *The curtain is run closed behind* BENKEL BENKEI *pauses; all is silence. He cannot but think of the great sacrifice* TOGASHI *has made on their behalf. His eyes are drawn back toward the place where* TOGASHI *was a moment ago. Then his thoughts abruptly return to the many difficulties still lying ahead.* MUSIC CUE NO. 17. *He resolutely faces front. He twirls the staff round his head, and poses. He remains poised for a long instant on one leg, bending and flexing it. Then he makes a powerful leap forward to the other leg. Bending and flexing again, he prepares for the next leap. With a twirl of the staff he makes another bound. Again the bending and flexing, then another leap, and another, and another. Faster and faster he goes, arms and legs flashing in all directions. By the time he reaches the end of the ramp, he is moving at full speed in pro-*

digious leaps and bounds, a brilliant and theatrical projection of masculine strength. As BENKEI *disappears from sight through the ramp curtain, the music and clapping of the sticks reach a crescendo, then taper off.* FADE MUSIC NO. 17. *The play ends as it began, with a few minutes of quiet drum-and-flute music.* MUSIC CUE NO. 1 *can be repeated here.*

The Zen Substitute

A Japanese Kabuki Farce

BY OKAMURA SHIKO

English adaptation by James R. Brandon and Tamako Niwa

The Zen Substitute (Migawarizazen) is one of the most recent plays to enter the standard Kabuki repertory. It was adapted from the *kyogen* comedy *Hanako* (or *Zazen*) in 1910 and quickly became the most popular of all one-act Kabuki dance comedies. Because *The Zen Substitute* is a comic piece, it would normally be placed as the fourth or concluding play on a program.

The plot of *The Zen Substitute* concerns a love triangle. In the first half of the play Lord Ukyo hopes to get permission from his wife to go out, to visit temples he says, but actually he wants to visit his mistress. She allows him to sit in the garden and do Zen meditation instead, whereupon he changes places with his servant Tarokaja. His wife comes to the garden, discovers her husband's deception, and takes Taro's place. The rest of the play concerns Lord Ukyo's return from his night of bliss, merrily tipsy, to tell "Taro" about the joys of being with his young mistress. Eventually his wife can stand no more and chases him off the stage, a traditional ending to many *kyogen* plays. The strong plot focuses on direct conflicts of husband and wife, husband and servant, wife and servant, and again husband and wife. The comedy is derived in part from character, in part from incident, and is never artificial or forced. The three main characters—Lord Ukyo, Lady Tamanoi, and Tarokaja—have strong individuality.

A few commentators have suggested that in spite of the excellence of *The Subscription List,* it is not truly Kabuki, for its spirit is closer to the gravity of Noh than to the erotic sensuousness of Kabuki. *The Zen Substitute,* however, falls naturally into the Kabuki orbit because it is pleasantly hedonistic and comic.

A more emotional style of Kabuki music than *nagauta,* the

238

tokiwazu style, is introduced during the second half of the play —when Lord Ukyo returns from his tryst with Hanako—to enhance the sensual quality of the performance.

When a *kyogen* is adapted to Kabuki, some small changes, such as cutting unneeded lines, are inevitable. The most prominent change is usually the addition of songs and dance sections, which radically alter the dialogue of the original. In *The Zen Substitute* two maids—who do not appear in *Hanako*—are added, and it would seem that the reason is largely to allow the two dances they perform to be inserted. Taro, too, is given several short dance sections. The second half of the play is almost entirely dance and mime to song accompaniment. It is interesting to note that though *Hanako* contains thirteen short songs (*kouta*)— extremely unusual for *kyogen*—only three are retained in *The Zen Substitute*. The reason the songs from *Hanako* were not used is because an original score is composed for a new Kabuki dance play, regardless of the source of the script.

The Zen Substitute was first performed in 1963 at Michigan State University, where it was played after *The Subscription List*. The same set was used for both plays, as would be the case in Japan. The same chorus and stage assistants were used, and some cast members appeared in both plays. Although women do not appear on the Kabuki stage, actresses were cast in the women's roles. The approach to this play was the same as that described for *The Subscription List*. The actor playing Lord Ukyo proved to be gifted in learning Kabuki movement, and consequently the lengthy dance and pantomime sections were retained almost in their entirety. A few short sections of verse that seemed repetitive during rehearsal were deleted.

Characters

LORD UKYO
LADY TAMANOI, *his wife*
TAROKAJA, *his servant*
HANAKO *(mimed by actor playing Lord Ukyo), his mistress*
CHIEDA ⎤
SAEDA ⎦ *Lady Tamanoi's maids*
CHORUS LEADER
CHORUS
STAGE MANAGER
STAGE ASSISTANT

The Zen Substitute

The houselights are up full. MUSIC CUE NO. 1.* *Leisurely drum-beats and the clear sound of a flute. The drumbeats quicken, the flute grows louder. The curtain rises. The scenery is the standard Kabuki representation of the Noh stage: a buff-colored backpiece and two sidepieces painted to represent a single spreading pine tree flanked by groves of straight green bamboos set against plain wooden planking. There are two entrances to the stage. One is stage right, hung with a brightly striped silk curtain. The other is a raised ramp that runs straight through the audience to the rear of the auditorium. The stage proper is free of any props or set pieces.* FADE MUSIC NO. 1. *Six* CHORUS *members in black formal kimonos and brown winglike outer garments are seated on a red platform upstage.*

From offstage right a sharp, resonant clap of the STAGE MANA-GER's *sticks signals that the performance is to begin. There is a moment's silence. Nothing moves. Then the* CHORUS LEADER *reaches down, picks up the closed fan in front of him, and places it across his right knee. Half chanting, half singing, he gravely declaims his lines, his face an unmoving mask.*

CHORUS LEADER
> Public tranquillity!
> Domestic concordity!
> Our land lives in peace!

* Music cues indicate the cue numbers of a long-playing record available from Samuel French, 25 West 45th Street, New York, N. Y. 10036.

The Zen Substitute

The other CHORUS *members pick up their fans and join the* CHORUS LEADER, *singing in high, sweet tones. No hint of the irony of their words can be seen in their impassive faces.*

FULL CHORUS

> Peace without!
> Peace within!
> No outside gale ruffles
> > The harmony of the home.
> The spread of green matting
> > Lies quiet as the sea.

As they finish, they place their fans again before them on the platform. MUSIC CUE NO. 2. *To booming drumbeats the striped curtain stage right flies up and* LORD UKYO *enters. He cuts a magnificent figure in his voluminous court robe of pale-blue silk brocade patterned with silver and gold. The enormous sleeves almost sweep the floor; the long trousers, which fold under his feet and trail behind him, swish back and forth as he struts across the stage. In samurai style his head is shaven bare, except for a long, lacquered topknot. He carries a closed fan in his right hand. His face and hands are a delicate white. It is an imposing façade until we notice the hint of a pixilated smile on his red lips and a touch of the comic in his upturned jet-black eyebrows. Center stage he faces front and speaks rapidly, buoyantly.*

LORD UKYO I live in the outskirts of Kyoto. But, ohhh, I had a fine time out East a while ago. Stayed at a place near Lake Biwa called the Bide-a-while. A girl named Hanako served me. Poured my wine, took care of me . . . you know! Ho ho— you can say a country girl if you like, but what a face! What a figure! Tender words. Warm heart. Why, when she heard I was back the other day, straightway she came to Kyoto to live, right nearby in Kitashirakawa. (*A broad smile.*) She writes me all the time, "I miss you. I want to meet you so."

But how? That's the problem. My wife, dear old thing, won't bear an instant's separation. Ahh, it's hard! (FADE MUSIC NO. 2. *He sighs.*) But I've just got to meet her, somehow. Hmmm-mmm. (*He closes his eyes in concentration.*) Ah! I have it! (*Slaps thigh with fan. A smile spreads over his face.*) Where is the old shrew? (*He sharply pivots right, twirls the kimono sleeve over his right arm, points offstage with the fan, and speaks out eloquently.*) Are you there, my love? Are you there, my sweet? (*Kicks out the trailing ends of his trousers and crosses swiftly to left of center, where he faces front, waiting for his wife to enter.*)

FULL CHORUS

His words allure.
His tones drip sweet.
She comes in
Joyfully.
They look so like two cooing doves!
But underneath it
Lies, such lies!
Fickle man!
Amorous!
There are two sides
Two sides
Two sides to the human heart!

On the last lines the curtain at stage right flies up and LADY TAMANOI *enters, followed by two maids,* CHIEDA *and* SAEDA. *She wears a kimono of cream and white, embroidered with gold. Her long hair, tied with a simple colored ribbon at the back of the neck, falls down to her waist. Except for her red daubed cheeks, her face is pure white, as are her hands and dancing socks. Her left arm is extended in front of her in the standard Noh stance, and as she enters, she moves with the rhythmic gliding steps of Noh dance, in which the foot is never raised from the surface of the floor. It is immediately apparent that this lovely exterior belies a veritable monster of a woman. Phys-*

243

ically she is huge, as solid as granite. And behind the façade of Japanese feminine submissiveness lies a will of granite to match. Yet for all that, she is a woman, a woman in whom feminine instincts and an iron will are constantly in conflict.

LADY TAMANOI (*nods ever so slightly in the direction of her husband*) You called, my dearest? What can I do for you?

LORD UKYO First, come over here beside me a moment.

He moves center. She crosses past him to his left, and the MAIDS *move to his right. They all kneel. The women drape the long left sleeve of their kimonos over their lap.*

LADY TAMANOI (*so polite*) What is it, my dear?

LORD UKYO Oh, it's nothing, really. I, ah . . . well, I didn't want to worry you, but I've been having nightmares, terrible nightmares, the past few nights. I, ah . . . I've been thinking a good pilgrimage might be just the thing to purify my soul. Ha ha! Yes, that's it, yes. That's what I wanted to say.

LADY TAMANOI What do you mean by a pilgrimage? (*Suspicious.*) How long would it take?

LORD UKYO Yes, well. I've been thinking of visiting different temples . . . all around the country, you see; so, ah, oh, I don't know, it might take a year . . . ha ha ha. . . . (*Sees her shocked look. He puts on a forlorn air.*) It might even take two years.

LADY TAMANOI (*half rising*) Two years? Oh, you can't mean it. It'll break my heart! Chieda! Saeda! Stop him! I won't let him go! (*She beckons them to come.*)

CHIEDA *and* SAEDA Yes, my lady.

CHIEDA *and* SAEDA *bow with elaborate politeness, rise, and approach* LORD UKYO. *They pantomime holding his sleeves, but he brusquely shakes them off. They subside to respectful kneeling positions behind him.* LADY TAMANOI *sinks back to the floor, on the verge of tears.*

LORD UKYO Ha ha, I'm really glad you object; my dear, it shows how much you care for me. You know, my love, it's not that I want to go. It's just these hideous nightmares. I don't see any other way out.

SAEDA Then at least, to make her happy . . .

CHIEDA . . . can you not perform austerities here at home?

SAEDA *and* CHIEDA Yes, my lord, please do. (*Placing their palms on the floor before them, they bow low.*)

LADY TAMANOI Is that possible? Can that be done?

SAEDA Why, yes, my lady.

SAEDA *and* CHIEDA Of course, my lady.

MUSIC CUE NO. 3. *The* MAIDS *bow, then rise and come down center stage, where they dance the words of the* CHORUS. *At the same time* LORD UKYO *moves left. He sits on a black lacquered cask brought out for him by a* STAGE ASSISTANT. *The* ASSISTANT *adjusts the folds of* LORD UKYO's *costume and retires unobtrusively upstage.* LADY TAMANOI *remains where she is to watch the dance.*

FULL CHORUS (*metallic drumbeats punctuate a rhythmic melody played on several samisen*)
> From the beginning,
>> Twelve roads of escape
> Have been known
>> To break the wheel of Karma.
> And one of these
>> Is to submit the flesh
>> To austerities.
> A million prayers honor the Lord Buddha.
> Voices chant the Lotus Sutra.
> The beads of the rosary flash and whirl
>> Round and round and round.

(*The girls weave patterns of graceful, supple movement. Their*

245

*arms swing in wide arcs. They kneel and rise. In unison they
circle the stage. The sounds of a bass drum and tinkling bells
mingle with the music of the samisen.*)

> The deep-booming drum.
> The tinkling bell.
> The beat of the hollow gourd.
> Echo, *Namu Amida Butsu!*
> "All praise the Lord Buddha!"

FADE MUSIC NO. 3. *Dance finished, the* MAIDS *tuck their fans in
their sashes and retire upstage right, where they kneel respectfully.*

CHIEDA (*like the* CHORUS, *the sweetness of her voice belies the
meaning of her words*)   And there are other marvelous austerities as well, my lord. There is exposure to the wintry gale,
bathing in ice water, living in total silence . . .

SAEDA   . . . moxa-burning of the arms, my lord . . .

CHIEDA   . . . or of the face if you prefer.

SAEDA   So please, my lord . . .

SAEDA *and* CHIEDA (*bowing low with utmost humility*)   . . .
consent to perform some simple austerity here at home.

LORD UKYO   Ice water? A man of my position? (*Appalled.*)
Never.

LADY TAMANOI   As you like, but you're not going to leave this
house! (*She fixes him with a determined glare.*)

LORD UKYO (*holds his own for a few moments, then turns away*)
Damn! (*His head falls to his chest. Then he gradually
straightens up. Raptly thinking of* HANAKO, *he rises and unconsciously drifts right until he is standing directly in front
of his wife.*)

FULL CHORUS

> Wandering heart,
> Amorous heart,
> Hunting Hanako.

(LORD UKYO *raises his arm, pointing off into the distance. His long sleeve blocks* LADY TAMANOI's *view.*)

> But all our dreams
> Are empty dreams,
> Caught by thorns at home.

(*In one motion* LADY TAMANOI *rises to her knees, sweeps the offending sleeve aside, and pops her malevolent face into his. His idyllic dream is shattered. He backs off distastefully, then sinks to a heap on the floor.*)

> Spirits crushed,
> Head bent low,
> He thinks dejectedly:
> "What shall I do?"
> "What can I do?"

LORD UKYO (*slaps his thigh with his closed fan and looks up suddenly*) Ah ha! I have it! (*Turns to his wife.*) My dearest, my sweet, if you really don't want me to go out, all right, I won't. What I'll do is perform a seven-day-and-seven-night Zen meditation right here.

LADY TAMANOI In the family temple?

LORD UKYO The temple in the garden.

LADY TAMANOI Ah, that's a good idea. Then I can stay by your side through it all. I'll bring you tea, and I'll bring you hot water. And I'll——

LORD UKYO (*waving fan at her*) No, no, no! Woman is evil. In religion, I mean. A mere glance from you and my mind would utterly desert Buddha. You must not be there!

LADY TAMANOI Well, if I'm not going to be there, you aren't either. (*In a sulk, she turns her back on him.*)

LORD UKYO How can you say that? How can you refuse this single small request of mine? Please, my dear. Please, my love. (*He presses his palms together in supplication. He bows meekly to the floor.*)

CHORUS LEADER

> The code of the ancients remains:
> A woman's life is to obey

> .Three men,
> Her father
> Her husband
> Her son.

FULL CHORUS

> We must advise you not . . .

CHORUS LEADER

> . . . to tamper with the wisdom of the ages!

CHIEDA Ohh! See how he implores you, my lady. He is even bowing before you.

SAEDA Should you really keep saying, "You can't do this," "You can't do that"?

CHIEDA It's only a little Zen.

SAEDA Won't you say yes?

SAEDA *and* CHIEDA Please. Say yes, my lady. Please. (*They bow to the floor.*)

LADY TAMANOI Hmph! (*She turns to him.*) Well, if you insist, you have my permission. Tonight you may immerse yourself in the spirit of Zen. (*Coldly, she rises and turns to go.*)

LORD UKYO Tonight? Only one night?

LADY TAMANOI Did I say two nights?

LORD UKYO I see. Well, then if that's the way it must be, it's *zazen* tonight, all night.

LADY TAMANOI Until tomorrow morning, my dear. Early. (*She turns away.*)

LORD UKYO (*rising on his knees and gesturing firmly with his fan*) Remember! You are not to come to see me, you hear? You are not to disturb me when I'm seeking Nirvana.

LADY TAMANOI I promise. But remember, your meditation is just for one night.

LORD UKYO Absolutely—no visits, my dear! (*He shakes his fan at her, then holds that pose.*)

LADY TAMANOI Positively—one night, my sweet!

She faces front and strikes a commanding pose. For a moment they both freeze.

FULL CHORUS
> She bestows her
> Gracious consent!

LADY TAMANOI *breaks the tableau and starts to go off right. Suddenly she remembers something and stops. She throws him a haughty look over her shoulder. Instantly he executes an elaborate bow, touching his head to the floor. He holds this humiliating position as a flicker of satisfaction crosses her usually stern face. She turns toward the* MAIDS, *and they too bow obediently to the floor. Mollified, she sweeps grandly off.* CHIEDA *and* SAEDA *rise and follow. The instant they are through the doorway,* LORD UKYO *leaps to his feet.*

LORD UKYO *(alone, his personality changes)* Ho-ho! I fooled her! I fooled her, didn't I! She's clever, that one, but after all only a woman! Ha ha! Now, where's that Taro? *(With a flourish of trouser ends he turns and calls off right.)* Heh, Taro! Tarooooooooooo! *(Without waiting for any response, and bubbling with good spirits, he swiftly strides stage left.)*

TAROKAJA *(skittering on)* Yes, my lord.

LORD UKYO *(in mid-stride)* It's you, Taro?

TAROKAJA Yes, my lord.

LORD UKYO You're here?

TAROKAJA Yes, sir.

LORD UKYO You're really here.

TAROKAJA *(with a little bow)* Before you, sir.

LORD UKYO Well, what do you know! *(Turns to him, face beaming.)* You're fast today, Taro.

TAROKAJA And you, my lord, seem happy today.

LORD UKYO With good reason, Taro. With good reason. Ho ho! What do you think? *(Moves in close to* TAROKAJA. *Confidentially.)* I got the night off! The whole night, and I'm going to see Hanako!

TAROKAJA Oh, that's wonderful, sir! *(He begins to laugh, then quickly catches himself.)* How did you manage that, sir?

The Zen Substitute

LORD UKYO Well, you know the dear shrew. (TAROKAJA *nods.*)
She'd never just give me the night off. So I gave her this cock-
and-bull story about nightmares and how I had to do *zazen*
all night to cleanse my soul.

TAROKAJA Ohh, that was clever, sir!

LORD UKYO Yes, wasn't it! I thought so, too. Now, Taro, there's
just one thing I want you to do for me.

TAROKAJA (*bows respectfully*) Yes, my lord.

LORD UKYO I forbade her, absolutely, to come meddling
around while I'm in Nirvana. But you know the old busy-
body she is. (*One conspirator to another.*) Sure enough, in the
middle of the night she'll come sneaking through the bushes
to spy on me. And if she doesn't see someone in meditation,
she'll be fit to be tied. Now I know it may be a bit uncom-
fortable, Taro, but it's only till morning. How about you taking my place and being religious tonight?

TAROKAJA (*swallows hard and bows respectfully*) Of course,
anything for my lord. But please, sir, not this.

LORD UKYO Ehhh? (*Commandingly.*) What's this?

TAROKAJA Sir! it's your wife's . . . terrible temper.

MUSIC CUE NO. 4. TAROKAJA *bows low to* LORD UKYO, *then moves
downstage and faces the audience. As the* CHORUS *sings, he mim-
ics* LADY TAMANOI *in dance-pantomime. His movements are half
feminine, half loutish.*

FULL CHORUS (*drums punctuate the samisen melody*)
    The dear thing loves you so.
    When you're at home,
    Her face is wreathed in smiles.
(*Kneeling before an imaginary mirror,* TAROKAJA *coyly adjusts
the hang of his kimono. He pats powder on his beaming face.*)
    Her chubby cheeks glow
    And burst with joy
    Like eternally smiling Otafuku.
(*Rising,* TAROKAJA *puffs out his cheeks, mocking the looks of*

Otafuku, the overweight goddess of happiness. Angry and amused at the same time, LORD UKYO *reprimands* TAROKAJA *by tapping him smartly on the forehead with his fan.* TAROKAJA *is undaunted, but he makes an attempt to hide his mirth as he turns away and continues his dance.*)

But when she's angry,
She's a raving demon.
And when she hates,
She's a witch!
A fiend!
A devil!
Like a gargoyle perched on a rainspout!
If she ever finds out
About a trick like this!
This Taro's as good as dead!

(TAROKAJA *cowers, then beats himself wildly on the head with both hands. Finally he sinks in a heap to the floor, as if dead. His act finished, he bows.*)

"So excuse me just this once," he said.
He begged.
He bowed.
He implored.

FADE MUSIC NO. 4.

LORD UKYO (*tucks the fan under the collar of his kimono and steps forward threateningly*) So! You're afraid of her but not of me! Eh, Taro? That mistake will cost you your head! (*He rears back, stamps, and grasps the hilt of his sword. Legs wide apart, he poses.*)

TAROKAJA (*throws up his hands to ward off the blow*) No, no, no, my lord! Wait! I was wrong. My lordship is the frightening one. I shall do whatever you say. (*He bows low but almost immediately pops up again, as he realizes he is presenting an inviting target for his master's sword.*)

LORD UKYO (*without moving*) You're sure of that, Taro?

TAROKAJA   Yes, my lord!

LORD UKYO   Truthfully?

TAROKAJA   Yes, yes, my lord.

LORD UKYO   Positively?

TAROKAJA (*frantic, he bows again and again*)   Yes, sir! Yes, sir!

LORD UKYO (*with a hearty laugh, drops his pose and crosses center*)   Then I won't kill you today. It was only a joke, Taro.

TAROKAJA   It was a bad joke, sir.

LORD UKYO   Sometimes you need a good frightening. Now here. Sit. (LORD UKYO *motions for* TAROKAJA *to sit on a black lacquered cask a* STAGE ASSISTANT *has placed left of center stage.* TAROKAJA *does so.*)   On with the robe.

LORD UKYO *and the* STAGE ASSISTANT *drape a robe of golden silk over* TAROKAJA'S *head.*

CHORUS LEADER
> A brilliant colored robe
> Hides the seated form.

LORD UKYO *circles* TAROKAJA. *He examines the robe from all angles, adjusting a fold here, a drape there. He returns to center stage and stands back a few paces, the better to survey his handiwork. The* STAGE ASSISTANT *kneels behind the cask, where he remains unobtrusively throughout the remainder of the play.*

LORD UKYO   Perfect. From the front, the side, the back, you'd never know it wasn't me.

TAROKAJA (*pops his head out*)   I think "Zen meditation" is just a fancy way of saying "torture," my lord. I can tell it already.

LORD UKYO   Be brave! It's only one night. (*Glances fearfully off in the direction of his wife, then tiptoes up to* TAROKAJA. *Confidentially.*)   Remember. If she shows up, keep the robe on and you'll be all right.

TAROKAJA Yes, sir.

LORD UKYO And whatever you do, God help you, don't open your mouth.

TAROKAJA Yes, sir.

LORD UKYO (*glowing with anticipation*) Well, then! I'm off!

TAROKAJA Hurry back, sir. Please, sir!

LORD UKYO Good-bye! (*He turns and starts to go off.*)

TAROKAJA Good-bye!

LORD UKYO Good-bye!

TAROKAJA Good-bye!

BOTH (*their alternate "good-byes" increasing in speed until they are speaking as rapidly as possible and finally in unison*) Good-bye, good-bye, good-bye, good-bye, good-bye, good-bye, good-bye!

TAROKAJA Just a moment, sir! (LORD UKYO *stops downstage right.* TAROKAJA *crosses to his master. The robe falls to his shoulders.*) Excuse me, sir. I know it's a bother, but . . . when you get to Lady Hanako's, would you please say hello to her for me? To Kobai, her maid?

LORD UKYO Hehhh? You mean, you and Kobai . . . ? While I was . . . (TAROKAJA *nods happily.* LORD UKYO *bursts out in delighted laughter.*) Ha ha ha!

TAROKAJA (*rhythmically repeating the laughter*) Ha ha ha!

LORD UKYO (*pokes* TAROKAJA *playfully in the chest with his closed fan*) Ho ho ho!

TAROKAJA Then you will say hello for me, sir?

LORD UKYO Of course, I—(*Suddenly catches himself.*)—Here now, what kind of Zen meditation is this? Are you trying to walk to Nirvana? (*He stamps his foot in mock anger and shoos* TAROKAJA *back to the cask.*) Sit, sit, sit, sit! And meditate! (*He carefully scrutinizes the covered form as the* STAGE ASSISTANT *adjusts the folds of the robe on all sides.*) Now, not a word. I'm off.

TAROKAJA (*peeping out sadly*) I'll be waiting, sir. Hurry back, please.

The Zen Substitute

LORD UKYO (*happy as a lark, moves right, toward the ramp*)
Good-bye.

TAROKAJA   Good-bye.

LORD UKYO   Good-bye.

BOTH (*same rhythmic speaking as before*)   Good-bye, good-bye,
good-bye, good-bye, good-bye, good-bye!

As he is about to step onto the ramp, LORD UKYO *stops and casts
one last glance at the huddled figure center stage. Free at last,
he sighs; a fatuous grin covers his round face. As the* CHORUS
sings, he moves with simpering dance steps onto the ramp.

FULL CHORUS
>   Away, away!
>   Wet by dew,
>   And the warmth of love,
>   He dreams, he dreams.

LORD UKYO *pauses for a moment on the ramp. He smiles a love-
sick smile and bashfully lowers his eyes. Then he charges into
action: he straightens up, stamps loudly on the floor, whirls the
long kimono sleeve around his right arm with a great flourish,
and points off down the ramp with trembling fan.*

LORD UKYO   Whee! I'm off at last! Going, going, going, going,
gone! (*He races out of sight, and the ramp curtain flies closed
after him.*)

TAROKAJA (*watching his master disappear into the distance, he
rises and drifts unconsciously toward the ramp*)   Come back
soon, sir. While she doesn't know. Please, sir! And give my
love . . . Kobai . . . won't you . . . sir . . . (*He gazes off
forlornly, in silence.*) What am I doing! Talking during
zazen! (*He crosses hurriedly back and sits on the cask. The*
STAGE ASSISTANT *drapes the robe over his head.* TAROKAJA *holds
the collar of the robe straight out in front of him, with both*

*arms extended. As long as he doesn't drop his arms, the audi-
ence can see every expression on his face.*) How uncomfort-
able! What a bore! (*He groans, then lapses into silence.*)

FULL CHORUS
>An empty robe,
>A husk remains.

(*The curtain stage right flies open and* LADY TAMANOI *enters.*)
>Her heart goes out to him—
>Poor lonely soul,
>Performing his act of piety.

LADY TAMANOI (*comes downstage, right of center, and faces the
audience*) Imagine, the poor dear, sitting out in the cold all
night long, thinking about Buddha. Alone. What an ordeal.
How can I keep away? I must see his sweet, suffering form.
(*She takes a halting step toward him, symbolic of crossing
through the garden. She cocks her head in his direction. Her
hand flutters to her massive breast. She staggers back a pace
and looks beseechingly at the audience.*) Oh, he looks so miserable! It's worse than I thought. I can't stand it. I've got to
help him. Chieda! Saeda! Bring the food at once, as I told
you. (*She lumbers right, frantically gesturing to the* MAIDS
offstage.) Hurry! Hurry! Hurry! (TAROKAJA *peeks out and
sees the dread form of* LADY TAMANOI. *He begins to shake
with fright, then ducks quickly back under the robe as the*
MAIDS *enter,* CHIEDA *carrying a small black lacquered tray
piled with cakes, and* SAEDA *carrying one with a cup of ceremonial tea.* LADY TAMANOI *kneels respectfully, to* TAROKAJA's
right; the MAIDS *kneel behind her.*) I know I promised not to
come, but you looked so pathetic. Let me serve you a cup of
wine. It will strengthen your religious resolve. (*The robe
nods vigorously a few times, then suddenly reverses itself and
shakes "no."* TAROKAJA *pulls the robe tightly around him.*)
No? Then at least have some tea.

The robe shakes "no" again. LADY TAMANOI *beckons to* CHIEDA
and SAEDA *to bring the cakes and tea. They approach* TAROKAJA,

kneel, bow, and place the two trays at his feet. They bow again, rise, and glide back to their positions upstage right.

CHORUS LEADER
>   Surely Buddha can't begrudge
>   Such selfless
>   Generosity!

FULL CHORUS
>   Imploring him, urging him!

LADY TAMANOI   Just a cup of tea, my lord, only a cup of tea.

TAROKAJA *shakes his head vigorously, but silently.* MUSIC CUE NO. 5. *To the singing of the* CHORUS LEADER *and slow samisen music,* LADY TAMANOI *rises and dances.*

CHORUS LEADER
>   "You tread the path,
>   You seek the light
>   Of eternal Buddhahood.
>   Ignoring me, your dear sweet wife,
>   Who serves you here
>   And now. . . .
>   Are you really more the man, more pure this way?"

(LADY TAMANOI *determines to take matters into her own hands and put an end to her husband's misery. She beckons* CHIEDA *to come over and take the robe off the seated figure.* CHIEDA *does not move. Even after* LADY TAMANOI *pulls her to her feet and pushes her center stage, she politely refuses. She is not getting mixed up in anything as unpleasant as a scrap between her lord and her lady. When* LADY TAMANOI *tries to take the robe off, herself,* CHIEDA *first blocks her path and then holds her back by force, grasping the broad sash of her lady's kimono. Actions that might be violent are muted; the performers move slowly, with graceful, stylized motions. At the end of the dance* CHIEDA

moves stage right. LADY TAMANOI *stands for a moment, irresolute.*)
>Sightless eyes,
>>Wordless lips;
>>He holds to Buddha's way.
>Tear-soaked eyes,
>>Blubbering lips;
>>Yes, this is woman's way!

(Feminine tenderness asserts itself. LADY TAMANOI *falls clumsily to her knees. Her huge bulk heaves up and down in passionate sobs. Her right hand covers her eyes in the symbolic gesture of weeping that is almost touching in its attempt at daintiness.)*
>And in the end,
>>Happily,
>She nuzzles up to him.

She minces over to his side, kneels, and rests her head coquettishly on his thigh. When he doesn't respond, except for shudders, she grasps his knee and violently shakes him, rather like a playful Saint Bernard with a rag doll. TAROKAJA's *response is to shudder all the more.*

LADY TAMANOI   At least, then, a glimpse of your precious face, my love.

The samisen music increases in tempo. The MAIDS *approach. The* STAGE ASSISTANT *whisks away the two trays and places them safely upstage. The terror-stricken* TAROKAJA *takes one quick look at the three of them descending on him and ducks back under the robe. Scrunching down as far as he can, he pulls the robe tightly around his frail, quaking body.* LADY TAMANOI, *on his right, and the* MAIDS, *on his left, pull the robe first one way, then the other. Desperately he holds it fast. His feet beat out a nervous tatoo on the floor. Pulling harder and harder, the women lift him to his feet. The* STAGE ASSISTANT *snatches the*

257

cask out of their way. The women whirl TAROKAJA *in a circle —once, twice.*

FULL CHORUS

> They pull, he tugs,
> They jostle, he struggles!
> Round and round they go!
> In a flash it's off!
> A thunderbolt!
> It's Tarokaja!

As the robe flies off, CHIEDA *and* SAEDA *flee upstage right.* TARO-KAJA *gasps and falls prostrate on the floor.*

LADY TAMANOI (*stamps thunderously; the words pour out in a torrent*) It's you? You? You? You wretch! Where did he go? Where did he go? Where did you let him go?
TAROKAJA   I . . . I . . . I . . .
LADY TAMANOI   Answer me! Answer meeeee!
TAROKAJA (*trying to stem the tide*) He went to Lady Hanako's. He went to Lady——
LADY TAMANOI   Lady? You dare say "Lady"? Say hussy! Say hussyyyyy! (*She stamps viciously for emphasis.*)
TAROKAJA   Yes, hussy. Hussy, hussy, hussy, hussy, hussy, hussy! He made me wear the robe so he could slip away. (*He bobs up and down in pathetic little bows.* LADY TAMANOI *wrings the robe as if it were* TAROKAJA's *neck, and fixing him with a murderous gaze, step by step she begins to advance on him. Half kneeling, half duck-walking, he edges away. Moving in unison, she advancing, he retreating, they make a half circle of the stage until they have exactly changed positions.* FADE MUSIC NO. 5. TAROKAJA *bows low.*) I couldn't help it. It wasn't my fault. He drew his sword, my lady. Don't kill me, madam. Please. (*He bows again, then sensing he is getting no response from* LADY TAMANOI, *he scrambles to his feet and*

dashes over to the MAIDS.) Saeda, Chieda. Help get me off.
Apologize for me. You know how.

He takes SAEDA *by the arm and tries to drag her center. In dance
motions they struggle back and forth; then she escapes.* TAROKAJA
pulls CHIEDA *to her feet and tries to lead her center. She pushes
him into* SAEDA, *who in turn gives him another push. He stumbles across the stage, off balance. Just as he is about to crash into*
LADY TAMANOI, *he regains his balance. Immediately he prostrates
himself before her.*

LADY TAMANOI He actually said he'd kill you if you didn't
obey?
TAROKAJA (*bowing low*) Oh, yes, my lady, he did.
LADY TAMANOI (*wavering between hurt and anger*) Humph!
Why didn't he tell me the truth straight out, that he wanted
to see this Hanako creature? For one night I'd have let him
go. Maybe. But no, he tried to make a fool of me. (*She shakes
the robe in a fury, then throws it to the floor and stamps violently. The* STAGE ASSISTANT *scurries forward to retrieve the
robe, folds it, and retires upstage.*) A fool of me! A fool of
meeeeeeeee . . . (*Her cry of rage dissolves into sobs. She
sinks to her knees, blubbering.*) . . . eehee . . . eehee . . .
eehee. . . .
CHIEDA Such an evil master.
SAEDA So very evil lately.

They bow to the floor.

LADY TAMANOI Taro, you've honestly confessed, and so I've decided to forgive you . . . on one condition.
TAROKAJA Oh, thank you, my lady! Anything.
LADY TAMANOI I'm going to take your place. I want you to
cover me with the robe, just the way he covered you.
TAROKAJA But . . . but . . . my lady, he'll kill me when he
finds out!

The Zen Substitute

LADY TAMANOI You said "anything."

TAROKAJA (*swallowing hard*) Anything but this. Oh, please!

LADY TAMANOI You're afraid of him, then, but not of me? (*She rises abruptly, stamps twice on the floor, and poses. Face twisted in anger, arms cocked threateningly, fingers stretched like claws, hair falling across her shoulders, she looks like some kind of witch.*) You will do as I say if you value your life! Or shall I kill you?

She makes a sudden move, and TAROKAJA *throws his hands up to ward off the blow.*

TAROKAJA Oh, no, no, no! Whatever you say. Anything for my life.

LADY TAMANOI Then do it now! Quickly! Quickly, I say!

TAROKAJA Yes, madam. Yes, madam.

He bows repeatedly. He and the MAIDS *rise and quickly cross center stage to carry out her orders.*

LADY TAMANOI (*fluttering with excitement*) Faster, faster, faster!

The STAGE ASSISTANT *places the lacquered cask where it was before.* LADY TAMANOI *plumps herself down on it, stamping and fuming all the while.* TAROKAJA, *to her left, and the* MAIDS, *to her right, take the robe from the* STAGE ASSISTANT, *unfold it, and drop it over her head. The* MAIDS *retire upstage right. Just as his master did,* TAROKAJA *inspects the robe first on the left side, then on the right. He kneels and bows respectfully.*

TAROKAJA My lady, you look his exact image, believe me. Like two peas in a pod.

SAEDA The very image.

CHIEDA Indistinguishable.

The two MAIDS *bow.*

LADY TAMANOI (*lifts the robe a bit, beaming*) I do look like him, then? Oh, splendid, splendid! Now, as long as he doesn't see you, he'll never suspect. Hmph, I suppose you're tired, Taro?
TAROKAJA Thank you, my lady, thank you.
LADY TAMANOI All right. You can all go now.
ALL (*bowing respectfully*) Yes, my lady.

TAROKAJA *is the first to rise. He tiptoes cautiously right, half expecting to be called back. When he reaches the exit and realizes he is safe, he lets out a sigh of relief. He turns for one last look at* LADY TAMANOI *huddled under the robe. The irony of the scene to come flashes through his mind. Smothering his laughter as best he can, he dashes off right.* CHIEDA *and* SAEDA *demurely rise and follow.*

FULL CHORUS
                The three of them bow . . .
CHORUS LEADER
                . . . quietly rise . . .
FULL CHORUS
                . . . and leave the room.

There is silence for a moment. Then the second half of the play begins. MUSIC CUE NO. 6.

FULL CHORUS (*flute and drum accompaniment*)
                How wonderful!
                    To loosen her silken gown!
                How glorious!
                    Down to the inner sash!
CHORUS LEADER (*slow, plaintive melody*)
                He ambles home tipsily, hair

> Awry
> Mussed
> And tumbled.
> Hanging disheveled
> Like weeping
> Willow strands.

(LORD UKYO *appears at the end of the ramp in a knee-length, black silk outer garment tied at the waist with a pink sash. He is in a happy fog of dreams and alcohol, a self-satisfied smile spread across his moon-face. He staggers down the ramp toward the stage, humming to himself. His comic actions are in marked contrast to the sentimentality of the accompanying song.*)

> Her fragrance clings
> Still to his sleeve.
> Her image yet
> To his heart.

FADE MUSIC NO. 6. *On the ramp, near the stage, he shuffles to a stop, suddenly overcome by melancholy. He looks back and points longingly into the distance with his closed fan. His eyes mist over; when he speaks, his tongue is thick and slow.*

LORD UKYO She came with me a long, long way. But when I looked back, where her visage once stood, there lingered only a sliver of a moon.

The fan drops from his fingers; he lurches forward a step. MUSIC CUE NO. 7. *Abruptly the orchestra switches to a lively tune.* LORD UKYO's *cheerful mood returns. Flipping open his red and gold fan, he begins to dance. He twirls around on one leg; trouser ends and dangling hair fly through the air. Tipsy and gay, he prances about. Again the music becomes plaintive, lingering.* LORD UKYO's *tousled head sinks to his chest; his arms hang loose.*

FULL CHORUS
    We see in the scattered remnants of a cloud,
    A reminder of this morning's parting.
CHORUS LEADER
            Splayfooted and staggering . . .
LORD UKYO Ah, at last. (*He lurches to a sudden stop and
    belches decorously.*)
CHORUS LEADER
                    . . . he weaves his way
                    Virtuously home.

Regally LORD UKYO *draws himself up and slaps his thigh with the
closed fan in a gesture of lofty resolution. He stamps once and
whirls to face the stage. Then, as if it is just too difficult to maintain, he drops the high-and-mighty pose, and with mincing gait,
toddles onto the stage proper.* FADE MUSIC NO. 7. *Seeing the
robed figure of* "TAROKAJA," *he stops, turns, and speaks directly
to the audience.*

LORD UKYO Isn't it good to be master of someone else! There
    he sits. Just as I ordered. Absolutely miserable! (*He laughs
    delightedly. On tiptoe he gingerly approaches* "TAROKAJA"
    and pokes him with his fan.) Psst. Heh, Taro. I'm back. Psst!
    Did the old biddy come? (*As* LADY TAMANOI *flashes bolt-up-
    right, we see her shocked and outraged face. Then she whips
    the robe down over her face once more and shakes it "no."*)
    She didn't? (*The robe shakes "no" again.*) What luck. Ah!
    It was wonderful tonight, Taro. Wonderful. How about you?
    Was it a bad night? (*The robe shakes "no."*) It wasn't too
    uncomfortable? Good fellow! Good fellow! You know, I
    think it's true what they say about love: what's inside shows
    on the outside. And that's just what I'm afraid of. When I
    think of tonight . . . why, if she were even to catch a
    glimpse of my face . . . (*He giggles.*) But you're the only

The Zen Substitute

one around here, aren't you, Taro? So you be a good fellow
and listen to my story, eh? (*The robe nods.*) You will listen?
(*Again the robe nods.*) But first, let's get rid of that ridiculous robe. (*He puts his hand on her head and is about to
take off the robe. She jerks away so violently, he is knocked
off balance.*) Oh, I see. You'd be embarassed, wouldn't you
. . . Taro? (*He hides his face behind his open fan, and
simpering, moves a few steps to the right.*) And I'd be embarrassed, too! (*She glares at him from the robe and shakes
it in anger. Just as he turns back, she pulls the robe closed.*)
Then I'll tell you just as you are. Right? Right! (*The robe
nods.* LORD UKYO *steps forward formally, if tipsily, and speaks
directly to the audience, slowly and deliberately.*) First, I
approached her domicile. Second, I drew near and went
knock, knock at her door.

*He strikes the back of his outstretched left hand with the closed
fan. Then, placing the fan on the floor before him, he kneels.
A* STAGE ASSISTANT *approaches him from behind and helps him
slip his right shoulder out of the black outer robe, freeing his
arm for the dance movements to come.* MUSIC CUE NO. 8.

CHORUS LEADER (*one samisen plays a bittersweet melody*)
    The nightingale's call
    Echoes from the valley.
    Sighing her welcome,
    Hanako opens the door.
(LORD UKYO *now dance-mimes the story of their meeting as
sung by the* CHORUS, *acting out both his own role and* HANAKO's.
He begins by pantomiming HANAKO's *actions in graceful, linked
movements as "she" bows in welcome, covers her face demurely
with her open fan, and takes his hand to lead him into the
room. Samisen, drums, and flute play a delicate melody.*)
    Scent-laden breezes
    Drift through the blinds.

Awakened affection wells
From her heart.
Spontaneous love is a gift freely given!

*Arching her back, her fan sweeping in an arc overhead, "*HAN-AKO*" swings back the blinds. She kneels and coyly bows. He returns the bow gallantly, but the blood rushes to his head, and he topples over on his face giddily, trouser ends flying through the air. Next,* HANAKO *lights a pipe for him, a traditional gesture of welcome by geisha and others, and passes it to him. He accepts the pipe in a lordly manner. For the actor it is a genuine tour de force to alternate dancing these two totally different characters.* LORD UKYO *puffs contentedly on the pipe a few times before* LADY TAMANOI *explodes in a tantrum of stamping and robe-shaking.*

LORD UKYO You be quiet! Now listen *(With a fatuous grin.)*
Then the sweet creature looked into my eyes and said reproachfully . . .
CHORUS LEADER *(to samisen accompaniment)*

"My pleading letter
Brings no reply,
My tearful entreaties
No visit.
Is my letter discarded?
Am I forgotten?"

HANAKO *kneels, opens her fan, and writes on it with an imaginary brush. She rolls the fan closed, as if it were a letter scroll. Hand pressed to her breast, her heart is breaking; hand to her eyes, she is weeping. The music increases in tempo. Rising, she mimes ripping the fan to shreds, then throws it indignantly to the ground.*

265

FULL CHORUS *(with drums and flute only)*
>>> Yet see how far
>>> He comes to see you,
>>> Soaked in the evening's rain.

>>> Can you be bitter?
>>> Can you threaten him
>>> With womanly tears?

(The open fan flutters to the floor, symbolizing the falling rain. Haughtily, she shakes off his advances; she brushes the raindrops from her sleeves. CHORUS *continues to samisen and drums.)*

>>> Her pouting face mirrors
>>> A heart
>>> Unwarmed by love.

(She turns a cold shoulder.)
>>> But soon he melts
>>> Her shield of anger
>>> With tender smiles and laughter.

FADE MUSIC NO. 8.

LORD UKYO   After that, we went inside and we . . . *(He chuckles tipsily at the happy memory of what happened next.)* She slipped off her robe and presented it to me. *(He begins to loosen the pink sash. A* STAGE ASSISTANT *comes forward and helps him take off the black robe.* LORD UKYO *gathers it up and hugs it fondly, thinking of* HANAKO. LADY TAMANOI *stamps wildly on the floor.)* I said, be quiet and listen! *(Beaming in recollection.)* Then we drank a bit and we ate a bit. And we talked. And we talked, and we talked. And we sang, oh, yes, we sang, and we danced.

The STAGE ASSISTANT *disappears into the wings with the black robe. As the music begins,* LORD UKYO *sinks to his knees and mimes playing the samisen, happily bouncing up and down.* MUSIC CUE NO. 9.

FULL CHORUS (*rhythmic melody played by samisen and drums*)
>Through the night we shared
>>Untold joys
>>And pleasures.
>The dawn came all too soon.

(LORD UKYO *dances over playfully and lets his hand drop on the robed figure. His hand is rudely shaken off.*)
>In the grove the early-morning birds
>>Warned us
>>Of the time.

(LORD UKYO *returns to stage right, grotesquely flapping his arms. Because of his long sleeves and trailing trousers, he does present a certain resemblance to a bird, a mad bird, in flight.*)
>We rose. I made
>>An early farewell.

(LORD UKYO *mimes a grandiloquent farewell.*)
>She tugged at my sleeve,
>>"You cannot go!"

(HANAKO *puts her kimono sleeves to her eyes to stem the flow of tears, then tugs his sleeve imploringly.*)
>>"I must! I must!
>>A fiendish monster
>>Waits at home!"

LORD UKYO (*he sinks to the floor in a dejected heap*) How annoying! Damn, damn, damn! (*He kicks his heels against the floor.*)

CHORUS LEADER
>>In fact,
>>He loves his wife.
>>He longs to see
>>Her dear face so!

FADE MUSIC NO. 9. LORD UKYO *sits up with a start and looks out at the audience incredulously.*

LORD UKYO What's that? Want to see the face of that old hag? Yaips, what a thought! (*The thought is too much for him;*

The Zen Substitute

> *he rocks back and forth, holding his head in both hands.*
> *Then he looks up and points to the audience with his closed*
> *fan.*) I will tell you what I think of her to the tune of an old
> folksong!

MUSIC CUE NO. 10. *A resounding arpeggio.*

CHORUS LEADER
> Such a very
> Strange face!

Samisen, flute, drums, bass drum, and bells strike up a rollick-
ing country melody. The bouncy rhythm soon has LORD UKYO
on his feet, miming the words of the CHORUS.

FULL CHORUS
> A bashed-in nose!
> And banjo eyes!
> A black-as-pitch
> Complexion!
(LORD UKYO *makes circles with thumb and forefinger, and looks*
through them.)
> Why, she looks for all the world like
> A broken-down
> Mangy
> Old monkey!
(LORD UKYO *scuttles over beside the robed figure and poses: his*
face purposely hideous, his fingers extended like claws over
LADY TAMANOI's *head. She stamps her feet repeatedly and*
bounces about on the cask.)
> Yes! Yes!
> A decrepit old monkey who scratches around
> In the forest all day,
> All drenched by the drizzling rain!

FADE MUSIC NO. 10. LADY TAMANOI *knocks him far over to stage
right. But he is so caught up in his act that he scarcely notices,
and after circling the stage once in a loping monkeylike gait,
he collapses to the floor, exhausted. Bit by bit her rage subsides.
Finally he speaks—the picture of jovial intoxication.*

LORD UKYO I think that's enough for a first installment, don't
you, Taro? Remember, not one word of this to the old lady,
or you don't hear the rest of the story. Right? (*The robe
trembles, then nods.*) Right! You can take off the robe now,
Taro. (*He crosses to her and is about to snatch the robe, but
she pulls away.*) You don't want to? You can't go on wearing
it forever, you know, just because you feel like it. (*Her response is to pull it tightly around her.*) What a fellow you
are. Come on! Let's see your face! (*No response.*) Off with
it! (*No response.*) No? Then I'll do it for you!

He grabs the robe from the right side. They struggle briefly.

FULL CHORUS
　　　　My God! Not Taro!
　　　　Out pops the devil herself!

Two STAGE ASSISTANTS *whisk off the robe. One of them moves
the cask out of the way as* LADY TAMANOI *leaps to her feet. There
is dead silence.* LORD UKYO *freezes in fear. Then he turns and
tries to steal away. One, two, three, four steps. The dam bursts
and* LADY TAMANOI *lets loose a flood of abuse.* LORD UKYO *drops
to his knees as if shot.*

LADY TAMANOI You villain! You villain! Try to fool me and
run off, will you! Where did you go?
LORD UKYO I . . . I . . . I . . . I . . . (*He bounces up and
down on his knees like a puppet on a string, his hands waving helplessly in the air.*)
LADY TAMANOI Where did you go? Where did you go?

The Zen Substitute

LORD UKYO To . . . to . . . to . . . to . . . the . . . the . . . temple of the Five Hundred Buddhas!

LADY TAMANOI In one night, three hundred miles to Kyushu? (*She actually growls.*) Liar, liar, liar! If you don't tell the truth, I'll tear you to pieces! (*She crosses to him and stamps savagely.*) Tell me!

LORD UKYO Yes, yes, yes! (*On the verge of tears.*) I went to the . . . the . . . the . . . Z . . . Z . . . Zen . . . Zenko temple in——

LADY TAMANOI It's all lies! Lies! Ohh! Catch him, somebody! Somebody catch him! (*She beats her breast and stamps the floor. He feels his end is near. He tries to rise and flee, but his legs are paralyzed. Frantically he clasps his hands before him and prays for all he is worth.*)

LORD UKYO Lord Buddha, save me, save me, save me! Save me, Lord Buddha, save me!

MUSIC CUE NO. 11. *In a flash* LADY TAMANOI *is on him. She seizes his ear, throws him to the ground, and beats him soundly. The sound of blows mingles with his prayers and her continued torrent of abuse. The action is stylized and performed in strict time to the singing and music of the orchestra.*

FULL CHORUS (*to samisen music*)
> "Forgive me,
>   Forgive me,
>   Forgive me!"
> Wild excuses
>   Pour from
>   His lips!
> A cascade
>   Of rambling
>   Gibberish!

(LORD UKYO *makes no attempt to resist, and at length she falls back out of sheer exhaustion.* LORD UKYO *sees this as his oppor-*

tunity to escape, and seizing the robe for protection, he stum-
bles to his feet. But he isn't fast enough. She grabs the trailing
end of the robe and stops him short. First he pulls, then she
pulls, in rhythmic movement, as they struggle for possession of
the robe. They both jerk hard at the same time, and the robe
flies from their hands. They fall to the floor, momentarily
stunned, he stage left and she stage right. A STAGE ASSISTANT
scurries forward and spreads the robe out full next to where
LORD UKYO *lies sprawled on his back.*)

> "Lying
> Deceitful
> Philanderer!
> I won't forgive!
> I won't!
> I won't!"
> She thunders furiously!
> Hard on his heels
> She chases!
> In panic
> He flees!
> He flees!

The remainder of the play is a pure dance-pantomime per-
formed to a rhythmic folk melody, its metronomic quality ac-
cented by booming offstage drums. They lie sprawled on the
floor. When his head pops up, hers bobs down; when his bobs
down, hers pops up. One, two, three times. Jerking on every
fourth strong beat, they seem like marionettes with all the
strings cut but one. Now they begin to move their arms and
legs as well, in angular, jerky movements. The effect is that of
a series of stopped motion-pictures. He tries to escape her by
burrowing under the spread-out robe and worming his way
across the stage. Simultaneously, she heaves and drags herself
along the floor, supported on one arm, the other wildly groping
the air for him. As he inches right, she flounders left, until they
cross paths and stop center stage. They are inches apart, back

271

to back, unaware of each other's presence. *She pauses to catch her breath; she looks frantically about—has he escaped? He gingerly pokes his head out from under the robe—has she gone? The robe slips to his shoulders, and with a smile of relief, he sits up. The music tapers off. Silence. In unison they look back over their shoulders. They see each other at the same time and fall back in surprise. The music begins again with a crash of drums and takes up the same melody as before. Once more* LORD UKYO *staggers to his feet and tries to move away. The robe starts to fall off; his hair is in wild disarray; his face is quivering in terror.* LADY TAMANOI *rises to her knees, then to her feet, violently shaking with rage. Her arms are outstretched, her fingers curled into claws that grasp for his tender flesh. By degrees he begins to inch his way stage right, and step by step she follows. In rhythm to the music, they move in unison: she chases; he flees. They are still working their way across the stage as the light Kabuki curtain of traditional rust, green, and black stripes is run swiftly before them by a black-hooded* STAGE ASSISTANT. *For a moment the music continues, then stops.* FADE MUSIC NO. 11. *The play is over.*

Copies of the original text of this play, in individual paper-covered acting editions, are available from Samuel French, Inc., 25 W. 45th St., New York, N. Y. 10036, or 7623 Sunset Blvd., Hollywood Calif. 90046, or in Canada, Samuel French (Canada) Ltd., 27 Grenville St., Toronto, Ont.

Chinese Opera

Traditional theatre in China is usually called opera in the West. While this has caused some discomfort to specialists— who rightly insist that traditional theatre blends singing with acrobatics, stylized movements, and chanted dialogue—still singing is so much the central artistic feature of Chinese theatre that it seems a good idea for the English title to indicate this. It is notable that in Asia sung drama is an important art form. This is especially true in China and in adjoining areas like Vietnam. Songs are part of Sanskrit drama. In Indonesian shadow plays they introduce important scenes or describe emotional states. Throughout Noh and in some Kabuki plays (dance plays in particular) song is important. However, song in these instances is either incidental or supports the dance. It is not the chief medium of expression as in Chinese opera.

The first mention of an actor is found in Chinese records of the seventh century B.C. Theatre is thus very ancient in China, as old as, and possibly even older than, theatre in Greece or in India. But theatre did not flourish in ancient China as it did in the other two countries. It developed slowly and without much official recognition for many centuries. We first hear of troupes being given royal patronage under the famous emperor Ming Huang (A.D. 712–755). He established a theatre-training school in the royal palace, apparently in the palace pear garden if we are to take literally the name of the school. During the Yuan dynasty (1280–1368), the new Mongol rulers of China proved to have an insatiable appetite for dramatic performances. Scholars, who formerly had disdained writing for the theatre because they thought it vulgar, composed hundreds of highly literate dramas. Performances in a lyric musical style and based on melodies played on the lute and the flute came to be very much appreciated in southern China during the Ming dynasty (1368–1644). These softly romantic, poetic operas called *k'un ch'u,* set the standard of excellence until the appearance of the most recent form of Chinese theatre, *ching hsi,* or Peking opera. During the reign of the emperor Ch'ien Lung (1736–1795), several types of local opera in northern China contributed to the formation of a new opera style in the capital city of Peking. Peking opera is simple in its literary style; its music is strongly rhythmic and often of ear-splitting intensity. Its popular appeal was very great and it quickly became the leading form of opera both in and out of court. For the past two hundred years it has been the national opera style in China, as distinct from the many local or provincial opera styles.

The Peking opera repertory is divided into two groups of plays, which are distinguished by subject matter and style of performance. Military plays *(wu)* are based on old stories and legends, and are akin to history plays. They emphasize heroic action and intrigue; their battle scenes are particularly spectacular. Some military plays concern gangsters and thieves. Civil plays *(wen)* are love stories, or concern daily social problems. The two styles are often combined in a play.

As a rule a performer specializes in a single role-type: male *(sheng)*, female *(tan)*, painted-face *(ching)*, or clown *(ch'ou)*. He devotes his entire life to perfecting the technique of performance for that particular role. This, and the fact that opera texts are not considered literature, places heavy emphasis upon the actor and his art. Josephine Huang Hung, translator of *The Price of Wine,* writes, "texts of Chinese opera were written in an unadorned style. Colloquial expressions that appeal to all classes of people are commonly used. Since the Chinese audience is usually familiar with the plots that are mostly taken from novels, history, the dramas of earlier Yuan and Ming dynasties, or from folklore . . . it chiefly finds enjoyment in the interpretation of the individual actor."

Different roles require different talents. The young male

role (*hsiao sheng*) requires a handsome figure and elegant movements. It is the most difficult role to sing, for the voice must rise, then break and fall several octaves to indicate adolescence. The warrior (*wu sheng*) must be an acrobat in order to perform the soaring dives, leaps, and somersaults that enliven battle scenes. Among the female roles, two are most important. The flirt (*hua tan*) dresses in red or other brilliant colors. Her silken jacket and trousers allow vivacious movements. Her opposite is the virtuous woman (*ch'ing yi*), who dresses in subdued colors, looks demurely at the floor, and whose tender songs require the finest voice among performers of female roles (usually actresses nowadays). The painted-face roles, so called because of their bold, vivid make-up—have more individuality than the others; each major character has a unique pattern of make-up that represents his personality and moral character symbolically through color: for example, red means bravery, black honesty, white treachery, and blue cruelty. A resonant voice and a manly bearing are essential. Actors of these roles need not sing especially well, nor are they called upon to execute acrobatics, but they must look, move, and speak impressively.

The dramatic structure of Chinese opera has not yet been fully described, but we can say that song, recitative, and dialogue alternate with entrances, exits, pantomime scenes, and, in military plays, battles performed to instrumental music. Songs are usually solos, but alternate verses may be taken by two or more characters. Group singing does not have a place in Chinese opera as it does in Noh and Kabuki.

The traditional method of staging Chinese opera is on a platform stage backed by a stylized silk backdrop. The stage is bare of scenery and properties, except for a table in the center, which has an embroidered cloth over it. Two or more chairs, similarly covered, are placed on or near the table to symbolize a throne, wall, well, or mountain, or some locale. Conventional costumes indicate types of roles rather than particular characters. Symbolism is a notable device in Chinese opera staging. A black flag symbolizes strong winds, a light-colored one snow. To symbolize a person riding in a chariot, the actor walks between two flags on which wheels have been painted. Mime is used extensively to suggest a physical world beyond the person of the actor: a young girl will thread a needle and sew (pricking her thumb, of course); a door is opened carefully and the high threshold crossed; a man circles the stage and arrives in a new place; a blind will be rolled up to let the sun stream in; two people, swaying, cross a river in a ferryboat. The actor's movements are so realistic that they easily suggest the physical environment. The high level of technical and artistic proficiency required of the Chinese opera performer never fails to delight the opera connoisseur.

Suggested Reading

Elizabeth Halson's *Peking Opera: A Short Guide* (London: Oxford University Press, 1966) is brief and clear. A more impressionistic introduction, illustrated with forty-four color photographs, is Kalvodova-Sis-Vanis, *Chinese Theatre* (London: Spring Books, n.d.). The best full-length study is A. C. Scott, *The Classical Theatre of China* (London: Allen and Unwin, 1957). Scott's two volumes of *Traditional Chinese Plays* (Madison, Wisc.: University of Wisconsin Press, 1967 and 1969) contain annotated translations of four operas. Five plays are translated in Josephine Huang Hung, *Children of the Pear Garden* (Taipei: Heritage Press, 1961).

The Price of Wine

A Peking Opera Comedy

AUTHOR ANONYMOUS

Adapted and translated by Josephine Huang Hung

The Price of Wine (Mei Lung Chen) is a comedy by an anonymous playwright and is believed to have been written in the sixteenth century. Scripts were not necessarily written out in full, and in any case, because opera was not recognized as literature, it was customary for playwrights' names to go unrecorded. Several centuries after it was originally composed, *The Price of Wine* was adapted to the style of Peking opera. It is one of the very popular *wen*, or civil, plays in the repertory. Like most plays which are performed today, it is short. Its two roles are for the young man (*hsiao sheng*) and the flirt (*hua tan*).

The plot of the opera is simple. The Emperor, disguised as a soldier, meets a beautiful and vivacious wine girl in a garrison town. He flirts with her and, though she enjoys it, she cleverly fends off his advances. In the end he reveals himself as the Emperor; she begs to be taken into the court as one of his mistresses and he consents. In reading the text, the plot and dialogue do not seem out of the ordinary. The pace seems swift, for no incident is developed extensively, each resolving quickly into the next. In production, however, the play will come across much more deliberately paced. The regular, punctuating sounds of drum and gong provide a strong aural framework for this light comedy. And the conventionalized patterns of movement that intersperse sections of dialogue provide the play with a variety not immediately apparent in the words of the text. Josephine Huang Hung suggests how important these movements are. "The two actors move according to their character types. Emperor Cheng Teh, being a gentle and noble character, makes slow and dignified movements with the help of the long, white undersleeves attached to his robe; while Li Feng, the wine girl, being vivacious and flirtatious, makes short, lively and graceful ones with the help of a big filmy handkerchief. When Emperor Cheng Teh enters the stage for the first time, he tidies his headdress, strokes his black beard and sways his long sleeves to make himself presentable according to the tradition of performing before the Emperor in the T'ang and Sung dynasties. Then he takes slow 'square steps,' with the toes pointing sideways and the feet at right angles with each other . . . and explains the situation of the play before he sits down to introduce himself in the 'poem of sitting.' When the girl enters the stage for the first time, she also tries to make herself presentable by touching her hair and glancing at her heels in a dance pattern accompanied by the little drum and the small gong. She takes short, mincing steps, with the toe of one foot following the heel of the other."

The version of *The Price of Wine* in this collection is by Josephine Huang Hung, who has incorporated into her original text the stage directions used in the production of the play at Grinnell College in 1963. Most songs are not differentiated from dialogue in translation. "The reason for this," the translator writes, "is that Chinese songs usually rhyme, or at least have a rhythm which is almost impossible to duplicate in English." The songs that are indicated were taken from tapes and recordings. Student musicians played the percussion accompaniment on the large and small drum, gong, wooden clappers, and cymbals.

For the Grinnell production authentic *sheng* and *tan* costumes were available. The play was produced using the traditional bare stage, table, and two chairs. Actors were trained in Chinese gesture and pantomime. Musicians sat in the wings, as in China, visible to the audience at times and in a position to watch the performers. A property man, dressed in black, moved the table and chairs as needed during the play. By convention he is assumed to be invisible. The only prac-

The Price of Wine

tical hand properties were a wine cup and pot, empty and symbolizing the Emperor's full meal, and an unlit candle on the table indicating night. Otherwise properties were pantomimed by the actors.

Characters

CHENG TEH, *an emperor of the Ming dynasty*
LI FENG, *a wine girl*
PROPERTY MAN
MUSICIANS

The Price of Wine

Scene 1

The anteroom of a small inn in the town of the Plum Dragon,
with back and side curtains for background. The stage is al-
most bare, except for a table center stage, on which are placed
an unlit red candle to indicate it is night, a small wine cup,
and a wooden block; a chair behind it; and another one up-
stage left. The table and chairs have red coverings with painted
yellow floral designs. Downstage left sit three MUSICIANS. *They*
face stage right. One plays the small drum, one the small gong
and wooden clapper, and one the big gong and cymbals. Their
music regulates the timing of almost every movement of the
actors throughout the performance. Overture music Ta Kuo
Men *is played.*
    CHENG TEH, *famous emperor of the Ming dynasty, enters from*
downstage right. Tall and handsome, he is disguised as a sol-
dier in the military uniform of the Ming dynasty: a long blue
robe, fastened under the right arm, with a white collar and
long white undersleeves. He wears a long black beard and a
black soft hat with yellow painted designs, a yellow tassel on
either side, and a big red flower in front. He has a red hood
with yellow lining over the back of the headdress. This shows
he is traveling. He wears a pair of black boots with thick white
soles. He carries a folded fan, which he uses often to fan him-
self in meditation or in satisfaction. Before he starts to walk,
he makes the stylized cough of a scholarly-male role, to show
his dignity. He takes square steps; that is, with his toes turned
outward, the right foot is lifted forward and the left foot is
brought up to the right heel and at right angles to it. After

The Price of Wine

a short pause the movement is repeated with the left foot lifted forward first. The steps are from side to side and in measured pace with two light, quick taps on the drum; four beats together on the drum and the small gong; one light, quick tap on the drum; one beat together on the drum and the small gong; ending with one beat on the wooden clapper. When he reaches right center stage, on the same plane as the drummer sitting stage left, he makes himself presentable by lightly touching his temples with both of his hands as though straightening his headdress. He strokes the right side of his beard from top to bottom between index and middle finger, ending with an upward sweep as he looks to the right. He waves his long white sleeves outward with a twist of the wrists. This movement is accompanied by the drum and small gong, one beat; clapper, one beat, repeated three times; drum, two beats; and small gong, one beat. This practice of Cheng-chuan, or tidying-up before the Mouth of Nine Dragons, the position of the drummer, is carried over from the T'ang dynasty: when Emperor Ming (712–755) beat the drum to train his performers, they had to tidy themselves in front of his Majesty. CHENG TEH continues to walk slowly downstage center, with the drum and small gong beating each step. He stops with one beat on the drum as he waves his right sleeve. He then speaks the four opening lines of the play. This is the formal entry of a leading-male role.

CHENG TEH (half sung, half recited)
 I have left my palace to seek wise men among the commoners
 And to find out the actual conditions of my state.
(Drum and small gong, two beats.)
 Also, it will give me a chance to see for myself
 The famous beauty spots in my kingdom.
(Drum and big gong, one beat; drum and small gong, one beat. Takes a step forward, turns clockwise, goes to the chair behind the table, and sits to drum and small gong, one beat; clapper, two beats; alternate beating of the drum and small gong and the clapper.) I (small gong), Emperor Cheng Teh

of the Ming dynasty (*small gong, one beat; clapper, two beats; small gong, one beat*), am alone here in this little Li Lung Inn, in the town of the Plum Dragon. Whenever I knock on the table with this wooden horse, I will be served tea or wine. (*Drum, four beats.*) Since I have entrusted the nobles of my court with state affairs, I have some time to enjoy myself. But (*drum, three beats*) I'm lonesome (*drum, two beats*), very lonesome! (*Shaking his head in frustration. Drum, four beats. He knocks on the table with the wooden horse. Drum and two wooden clapper beats.*) Hey, Innkeeper!

LI FENG (*off*) Coming! (*Carrying a tray on her left hand and a big pink handkerchief in the other,* LI FENG *enters from upstage right. She is a pretty, young girl, charming and lively. She wears an apple-green jacket and trousers, a pink apron, and a long sash on her left shoulder. There are flowers and brilliants in her hair. She walks with graceful, mincing steps to the accompaniment of the drum and small gong. Halfway on the stage, to make herself presentable, she touches her hair and alternately glances at her heels and waves her big silk handkerchief from one side to another. She sings a leisurely aria in* Erh-huang-ping-pan, *one of the two main musical modes of Peking opera. She dances around the right side of the front stage, which is imagined to be the back yard, and then to center stage.*) I was born and brought up in Plum Dragon town. My brother told me there's a soldier in the anteroom. Now, I'll serve him some tea. (*She turns and mimes raising the imaginary door-blind. Then she lifts her right foot to cross the imaginary threshold and lowers the blind, accompanied by the drum and small gong. She moves to his right and puts the tray down on the table. Bashfully she raises the handkerchief in her left hand to hide her face.*)

CHENG TEH (*seeing her, puts the fan on her hand in order to see her face, but she mimes spitting in his face, and he gets up laughing*) Ha, ha! Ha, ha! (*Drum, one beat; two pauses; drum and small gong, one beat.*)

The Price of Wine

LI FENG (*with mixed feelings of fear and bashfulness, walks quickly away to the front stage*) Ai-ya-ya! I'd better hurry back to my room and finish my sewing. (CHENG TEH *walks up and deliberately steps on* LI FENG'S *long sash. He holds it firmly while she struggles to free herself. She tries to pull away three times. Three drumbeats.* LI FENG *cries out.*) Look!

Small gong, one beat. She points behind CHENG TEH. *Thinking someone is coming, he lets loose of the sash.* LI FENG *slips away. She mimes raising the blind, lifts her right foot to cross the threshold, lowers the blind, and runs offstage left to beats of the drum.*

CHENG TEH (*laughing*) Ha, ha! Ha, ha! Ha, ha, ha, ha! What a pity such a beautiful, dainty flower should be allowed to grow up in a remote, unsophisticated market town. Amazing that my good nobles haven't discovered her for me! (*Sings an aria in moderate tempo in Erh-huang-ping-pan. He goes back to his chair.*) Let me sound the wooden horse for the second time.

Wooden clapper beats as he knocks. LI FENG *enters from upstage left and walks downstage center, stepping over the threshold to enter the room.*

LI FENG Here comes the innkeeper! (*She walks toward* CHENG TEH'S *left.*)
CHENG TEH (*showing respect by saying "Big Brother" and "Big Sister"*) Big Brother Innkeeper! Big Brother Innkeeper! (*Drum, three beats; drum and small gong, one beat.*)
LI FENG (*moving away to the front stage*) There is no Big Brother Innkeeper—only a Big Sister Innkeeper.
CHENG TEH (*aside*) Ah, ai-ya! This little lass calls herself Big Sister Innkeeper. I'll call her that and see how she reacts! (*He nods and fans himself.*) Big Sister! Big Sister!
LI FENG (*businesslike, comes back to him and stands on the left

side of table, with her left hand on her hip) Yes, Mister Soldier, what can I do for you?

CHENG TEH *(thoughtfully, stroking his beard with his left hand)* I want to know, Who is that tall, slim young man who was here just now?

LI FENG *(proudly)* He's my brother.

CHENG TEH What's his name?

LI FENG *(matter-of-factly)* Li Lung.

CHENG TEH Big Sister, what's your name?

LI FENG I? *(Takes a few steps forward and shyly lowers her head.)* I don't have a name.

CHENG TEH *(strokes his beard and fans himself)* Why, everyone has a name. How is it possible you don't have one?

LI FENG Well, I have one, but I don't want to tell you. *(Points coquettishly at him.)* If I do, you will call me by name, and I don't like it. *(Waves her big handkerchief and puts both her hands on her hips.)*

CHENG TEH I promise you I will not call you by your name.

LI FENG *(walks up to him)* You know my surname is Li, don't you?

CHENG TEH I know that, but what is your given name?

LI FENG *(stands with her left hand on her hip)* Feng, which means "phoenix."

CHENG TEH What an exquisite name! *(Shakes beard and closes his eyes. Dreamily.)* Oh, Li Feng! *(Three soft beats of the drum.)* Li Feng! *(Three more beats.)*

LI FENG *(stamps angrily)* Now give it back to me! *(Walks around to his left.)*

CHENG TEH Give back? What is it you want me to return?

LI FENG My name! *(Small gong.)* Give me back my name! *(Stamps her foot.)*

CHENG TEH The name is still yours, but once a word is uttered, it blows away like the wind. *(Extends both of his hands and arms to the sides in a circular movement.)* How can I return it to you?

The Price of Wine

LI FENG (*excited and angry*) But just now you promised me you wouldn't call me by name. (*Small gong.*) Why did you do it? (*Drum and small gong.*)

CHENG TEH Oh, I see. All right, I won't call you by your name any more, Big Sister.

LI FENG (*walks to his right*) You mustn't do it again. (*Businesslike.*) Now what can I do for you?

CHENG TEH Ah, Big Sister, what kind of wine and food do you serve here?

LI FENG (*in a businesslike manner, holds up three fingers of her left hand*) We serve three classes of wine and food here.

CHENG TEH What are they?

LI FENG (*in the same tone*) High-class (*puts up her right thumb; big gong, one beat*), middle-class (*puts up the third finger of the left hand; small gong, one beat*), and low-class (*puts up her right little finger; two beats of the drum and one faint beat of the small gong*).

CHENG TEH Serve me first-class food and wine.

LI FENG First-class food and wine are for officials.

CHENG TEH Then what about middle-class?

LI FENG That's for merchants.

CHENG TEH Who is the low-class for?

LI FENG Low-class? (*Walks away and coyly holds up her handkerchief with her left hand.*) I don't want to tell you. (*Drum, pause; drum, pause; drum, pause; drum and small gong.*)

CHENG TEH Why don't you want to tell me?

LI FENG Because (*three beats on the drum*), because I'm afraid you'll be offended. (*Big gong, one beat.*)

CHENG TEH I promise I won't be offended.

LI FENG (*going to his left side*) Are you sure you won't be angry with me?

CHENG TEH (*firmly*) I won't.

LI FENG (*taking a few steps away from him*) All right, I'll tell you. The low-class is for people like you (*points to him*), soldiers who live on our taxes! (*She puts her hands on her hips.*)

CHENG TEH (*aside, as he rises, surprised, and holds up his left sleeve*) Ah, ai-ya! (*Light taps on the drum; drum and small gong, one beat; drum, one beat.*) So soldiers are to be ill-treated. All right, when I return to the court, I'll give a million pieces of gold to the armed forces as a special bonus. (*Goes to* LI FENG.) Big Sister, please serve me high-class wine and food.

LI FENG (*looks him up and down with suspicious scorn, to drumbeats*) So you want high-class food and wine, eh? (*Big gong, one beat.*)

CHENG TEH Exactly.

LI FENG (*following ancient custom of teasing through a riddle*) Let me ask you a riddle and see if you can figure it out.

CHENG TEH (*confidently*) Go ahead! (*He goes back to his seat.*)

LI FENG (*comes and stands on his right*) Before you go on board the ship (*small gong, one beat*) . . .

CHENG TEH You must pay the passage. (*Big gong, one beat.*)

LI FENG When you spend a night at an inn (*small gong, one beat*) . . .

CHENG TEH You must pay for the lodging. (*Big gong, one beat.*)

LI FENG Now, if you want to have a drink (*small gong, one beat*) . . .

CHENG TEH You just drink your fill. (*Big gong, two beats.*)

LI FENG Pshaw! You can't even say, "You must pay for the wine." "Drink your fill." Ha! (*She waves her big handkerchief at him and puts her hands on hips. Big gong, two beats.*)

CHENG TEH (*standing up*) Are you insinuating you want me to pay you for the wine?

LI FENG It's not I who wants you to pay.

CHENG TEH Then who wants me to pay?

LI FENG When my brother comes back, he will ask me for the money.

CHENG TEH If you want money, it's easy. (*Sits down.*) Roll up the bamboo blinds and let the moonlight shine into the room.

LI FENG Yes, Mister Soldier. (*She goes downstage center and mimes rolling up the imaginary bamboo blinds, ties off the*

*cords, then comes back to the table. Her movements are
accompanied by the drum and the small gong.)*

CHENG TEH *(with ease and satisfaction)*

> I take out a piece of silver
> To pay Big Sister for the wine.
> Now take it.

Small gong and cymbals. He stretches his hand to her.

LI FENG *(sensing he wants to touch her hand, angrily)* Put it
on the table.

CHENG TEH

> The table is slippery
> And the piece of silver is smooth.
> If it falls on the floor,
> It will be lost.

LI FENG

> If it falls on the floor,
> I can easily pick it up.

CHENG TEH I'm afraid. *(Small drum, three beats.)*

LI FENG What are you afraid of?

CHENG TEH I'm afraid you'll hurt your willowy waist.

LI FENG What is it to you if I should hurt my waist?

CHENG TEH I won't be able to bear it. It'll break my heart to
see you harm yourself.

LI FENG If I can bear it, why can't you?

CHENG TEH *(piqued)* Huh! You don't deserve my sympathy!
Here, take it. *(Small gong and cymbals. Again he stretches out
his hand and tries to cover her hand with his fan.)*

LI FENG I know! You don't want to part with the piece of silver!

CHENG TEH I certainly am willing to part with it, but I'm
afraid you don't want to take it from my hand.

LI FENG *goes downstage right to drum, three beats, and small
gong, one beat. Lifts the handkerchief in her left hand to the*

level of her face. Clapper, one beat; small gong, one beat; drum, one beat; clapper, one beat.

LI FENG (*aside*) Ai-ya! Let me see. (*Circling her index finger in front of her right temple, accompanied by three beats on drum and small gong.*) It is obvious this soldier is not a gentleman. Let me play a trick on him. (*Points to the audience and nods with delight. Goes back to* CHENG TEH.) Have you seen the ancient paintings in our hotel?

CHENG TEH Ah, I love ancient paintings. Where are they? (*Stands up.*)

LI FENG (*pointing to the back of the stage; three beats on the drum and one on the small gong*) There!

CHENG TEH Where?

Three beats on the drum and one on the small gong. The instant CHENG TEH *turns his head, she snatches the piece of silver from his hand.*

LI FENG (*triumphant and laughing*) Here! (*Small gong, two beats. Showing the piece of silver on her palm.*)

CHENG TEH (*turning around*) This little lass tricked me, after all! (*He sits down again.*)

LI FENG Now that I have this piece of silver, may I ask how many plates I should serve?

CHENG TEH (*waving his long sleeves*) One for me and one for my horse.

LI FENG This is too much silver to serve one person. It is too much, sir, too much.

CHENG TEH Meat and rice for me and hay for my horse. (*Waving his left sleeve.*)

LI FENG It is still too much.

CHENG TEH Then go and buy some flowers for your hair with the rest.

LI FENG Thank you, sir. This way, please. (*Picks up the candle and points to the left at back of stage.*)

The Price of Wine

CHENG TEH (*stands up and follows her*) Where to?

LI FENG (*lifts foot, indicating crossing the threshold; three beats on the drum and one on the small gong*) This way to the dining room. (*Pointing left.*)

CHENG TEH (*crossing threshold in the same way*) Let's go to your bedroom. (*Pointing right.*)

LI FENG (*pointing left; seriously, firmly, slowly*) To the dining room! (*Three beats on the drum and two on the big gong.*)

CHENG TEH Ay? Dining room? (*He points right.*) Big Sister, whose bedroom is that? (*One small beat; two beats on the drum and one on the small gong.*)

LI FENG It's mine.

CHENG TEH That's exactly where I want to go. Come on. (*He starts to walk right.*)

LI FENG (*very seriously, excitedly*) Mister Soldier, you know that men and women, in giving and taking things, should not touch even hands! (*She hands the candle to him, indicating she does not want to go with him.*)

CHENG TEH (*aside, lifting his left sleeve*) Hm! This country lass even knows the rudiments of etiquette. She knows men and women should not touch hands when giving and taking things. (*Laughing.*) All right, I'll go to the dining room. The doors in this town of the Plum Dragon are stuck very tightly.

LI FENG Ay. (*Pushes him toward the left; mimes crossing the threshold as she goes back to the anteroom and closes the door.*)

CHENG TEH (*disappointed*) Big Sister, you are very tight, too! (*Laughing, CHENG TEH exits to the left. The small gong marks his steps.*)

LI FENG (*sighs with relief*) Ah-h-h! I have closed the doors. (*She sets the table with imaginary dishes and plates, wine pot and cup. A PROPERTY MAN in a long dark-blue gown puts another unlit candle on the table and disappears immediately, accompanied by soft beating of the cymbals.*) I'd better set the table here. Now I'll call the soldier to dinner. (*She mimes opening the door, goes out of the room by crossing over the threshold, moves left, and calls off, to drumbeats.*) Mister Soldier, dinner is served! Sir, please come out! (*Amazed but helpless.*) Ai-ya-ya! What a funny fellow! When I asked him to that room just now, he didn't want to go. When I call him to come out, he is reluctant to leave it! (*She re-enters the room, stepping over the threshold, and turns to the right side of stage.*) In preparing his dinner, I have dirtied my hands. Let me go and wash them!

As she mimes washing her hands, accompanied by the small gong, she faces right and does not see CHENG TEH *come out from the left, cross the threshold, and tiptoe toward her, accompanied by the clapper played alternately with the small gong and drum in beats of five and ending with two clapper beats. As she mimes pouring a basin of water out of the window, he embraces her. Big gong and cymbals. She pushes him away.*

CHENG TEH (*walking away left*) The people in this Plum Dragon town are so proper!

LI FENG (*approaching him*) Proper! (*Clapper, one beat.*) Proper! (*Clapper, one beat.*) I'll hit you a plateful! (*Big gong, one beat.*)

CHENG TEH Why this abuse?

LI FENG Ever since you entered our inn, you've stared at me from head to toe. What is there about us women that you think is so good-looking?

CHENG TEH You are very good-looking, Big Sister, and I love to look at you.

LI FENG If you love to look, then look a few times. (*With her right hand on her hip she stands sedately and serenely before him.*)

CHENG TEH Big Sister is loosening up! That being the case, I'll look as closely and thoroughly as I can. (*With his hands behind his back he walks clockwise around* LI FENG *and feasts his eyes on her. Drumbeats, ending with one beat of the small gong.*)

The Price of Wine

LI FENG Look at me again! (*She puts both her hands on her hips.*)

CHENG TEH All right, I'll look again! (*Walks counterclockwise around her.*) Hmm, good (*small gong and drum*), splendid (*drum, two beats; drum and small gong, one beat; small gong, one beat*), magnificent (*drum, two beats; drum and small gong, one beat; small gong, one beat; big gong, one beat*), incomparable model of excellence! (*Big gong, two beats.*)

LI FENG (*left hand on her hip*) Look again!

CHENG TEH Enough, enough!

LI FENG If you weren't a customer in our inn, I'd curse you! (*Angrily, both hands on her hips.*)

CHENG TEH Oh? You want to curse me?

LI FENG Not only curse you, but hit you! (*Cymbals, one beat; drum and small gong, one beat.*)

CHENG TEH I have never been hit by anyone since I was born. But if you, Big Sister, want to, hit me a few times.

LI FENG (*raising her hand to a crescendo of four drumbeats*) Is that so? Then I want to hit you. (*He turns his face to her, ready for the blow, but* LI FENG *withdraws her hand blushingly. Four beats on the drum, diminuendo. She goes right.*) Ai-ya-ya! (*Shyly, the index finger of her right hand lightly touching her left cheek, she lowers her head.*) I dare not do it.

CHENG TEH Why not?

LI FENG I'm afraid you'll be angry with me.

CHENG TEH I promise you I won't be angry.

LI FENG If you won't be angry, then (*drum, three quick beats*) . . . I'll (*drum and small gong, one beat, as she strikes* CHENG TEH) . . . hit (*drum and small gong*) . . . hit you (*drum and small gong*) . . . (*She runs, crosses the threshold, and exits upstage right to clapper, two beats; drum and small gong, one beat; clapper, three beats; and drum and small gong, one beat.*)

CHENG TEH (*bursts into laughter*) Ha! Ha! What a smart girl this Li Feng is! Playing tricks on me! Let me sound the wooden horse again.

294

He sits down and knocks on the table with the wooden horse.
LI FENG *enters to drum and small gong beats.*

LI FENG (*walks downstage; to the audience*) The wine must be cold and the tea icy.

CHENG TEH (*calling*) Miss Innkeeper! Miss Innkeeper! (*Clapper, three beats; drum and clapper, one beat.*)

LI FENG (*stepping over the threshold and entering the room*) Yes, Mister Soldier? Is your tea icy?

CHENG TEH My tea isn't icy.

LI FENG Then is your wine cold?

CHENG TEH My wine isn't cold.

LI FENG Huh! Your tea isn't icy and your wine isn't cold. Then why did you beat on our table? If you break it, you'll have to pay for it.

CHENG TEH You think I can't pay for the damage of a table? I can even pay for the damage of a person! (*Big gong.*)

LI FENG Then which one do you want to pay for?

CHENG TEH Erh . . . (*Stroking his beard and fanning himself. Four beats of the drum.*) I want to pay for this table.

LI FENG In the first place, sir, let me ask you, Why did you call me? What can I do for you?

CHENG TEH Big Sister, who set the table for dinner?

LI FENG I did. Wasn't it beautifully set? (*Looking proudly at table.*)

CHENG TEH Yes, beautifully set, but it's a pity it lacks two things.

LI FENG What two things?

CHENG TEH Plum blossoms and white turnips! Or (*drum, one beat*) powder and rouge! Erh . . . (*Embarrassed; drum, three beats.*) I mean, a beautiful lady of the moon!

LI FENG Oh, I see, sir. So you want some carrots and turnips. Wait, I'll get them for you. (*Starts walking forward; drum, one beat each step.*)

CHENG TEH Not those!

295

The Price of Wine

LI FENG (*stops and turns toward him, impatiently*) Then what do you mean?

CHENG TEH Ah, I mean those in pink aprons and green trousers like you.

LI FENG Oh, those! We used to have them around.

CHENG TEH How about now?

LI FENG Now the government prohibits them. It is said that there are none, but there are still some. However, where can I, a girl like me, in the dark of night, find one for you?

CHENG TEH (*moves his head in a circular movement and strokes his beard*) That's right; how and where could you find one in the dark of night? Since this is the case, Big Sister, I'd like to discuss something with you.

LI FENG What is it you want to discuss with me? (*Goes to him.*)

CHENG TEH Will you do me the favor of pouring a cup of wine for me?

LI FENG I just sell wine. (*Waving her handkerchief toward him.*) I don't pour it like a paid entertainer. (*Angry and proud, she puts both her hands on her hips.*)

CHENG TEH Oh, do pour!

LI FENG (*turning and taking a step away from him*) No, I won't.

CHENG TEH Are you going to pour or not?

LI FENG No! (*Clapper, putting her right hand on her hip.*) No! (*Clapper, putting her left hand on her hip.*) No! (*Clapper, one beat; drum and gong, one beat, putting both her hands on her hips.*)

CHENG TEH All right, give me back the piece of silver!

LI FENG I'll get it. (*Moves toward downstage center; drum and small gong.*)

CHENG TEH (*stands up*) Wait! (*Drum and small gong, one beat.*) I've eaten your dinner and drunk your wine. If your brother comes back, he'll ask you for the money. What are you going to tell him?

LI FENG (*drum, one tremble; drum, two beats; small gong, one beat; clapper, three beats; drum and small gong, one beat;*

worried, she walks downstage and speaks front) Let me humor him awhile. (*Goes back to him.*) Sir, what color are the rats in your village?

CHENG TEH   Our rats are gray.

LI FENG   Ours are white.

CHENG TEH   Really? Where are they?

LI FENG   There! (*Drum and small gong, one beat; she points under the table.*)

CHENG TEH (*looks*)   Where?

LI FENG (*swiftly pours wine into his cup*)   Here! (*Drum, three beats; drum and small gong, one beat. Pointing to the cup of wine.*)

CHENG TEH   Who poured this wine for me?

LI FENG (*triumphantly and coyly*)   I! (*Left hand on hip and right hand pointing to herself below the chin.*)

CHENG TEH   Huh! Such style of pouring wine! And only one cup! Even ten or twenty cups don't mean much poured in such style!

LI FENG   Then how should I pour wine?

CHENG TEH (*sits again*)   I want you, my dear Big Sister, to pour wine into my cup with your own beautiful hands, and with your beautiful hands put the cup in my hand. Then guide the cup of wine to my lips. After I finish this cup of wine, I'll leave. (*Waving his left sleeve.*)

LI FENG   Is there sugar on my hands?

CHENG TEH   No, there isn't.

LI FENG   Is there honey on my hands?

CHENG TEH   No, there isn't any honey on your hands, either.

LI FENG   Since there isn't any sugar nor any honey, why do you want me to pour wine for you? (*Turns away and puts her hands on her hips.*)

CHENG TEH   Men who are spendthrifts desire such comforts.

LI FENG   Such comforts I hate to give.

CHENG TEH   Are you going to pour or not?

LI FENG (*takes a step away toward the right and puts her right hand firmly on her hip*)   I still refuse to pour.

CHENG TEH   All right. You'd better return the piece of silver to me.

LI FENG (*going downstage center, accompanied by the drum*) I'll get it for you.

CHENG TEH   Wait a moment. (*Drum and small gong, one beat.*) Do you know where I got the money?

LI FENG (*surprised, turns toward him*) You probably robbed a house!

CHENG TEH   Exactly. (*Big gong.*) I broke into the royal house. (*Big gong.*) If I'm not arrested, everything will be all right. (*Big gong.*) But if I am arrested, then you and your brother will be involved in the crime. (*Big gong, two beats.*) I don't want the piece of silver now. I'm going. (*Stands up and starts to go; drumbeats.*)

LI FENG (*excitedly and perplexedly following him*) Sir, please come back and talk it over with me.

CHENG TEH   There isn't anything to talk over.

LI FENG (*greatly frustrated*) Talk it over! (*Two beats on the drum. She puts the back of her right hand on her left cheek.*) Talk it over! (*Two beats of the drum. She puts the back of her left hand on her right cheek as she lowers her head.*)

CHENG TEH   With whom do you want to talk it over?

LI FENG   My heart wants to talk it over with my mouth.

CHENG TEH (*goes back to the table and sits down*) Hurry up and talk it over, then.

Worried, she moves slowly downstage right, her steps marked by four beats of the drum and small gong, ending with one beat on the small gong.

LI FENG (*aside*) Ai-ya! Let me see! (*Makes a circular movement with the third finger toward her right temple, accompanied by the drum and the small gong.*) His silver was stolen from the imperial palace. If he is not arrested, everything will be all right. But if he is arrested, my brother and I will be arrested, too. What am I going to do? (*Drum and small gong, four beats, ending with a heavy beat on the small gong.*) Oh, my brother. (*Weeps, with her handkerchief over her eyes and shaking her head.*) My dear brother! (*Two beats of the drum, one beat on the small gong.*) Is this the way we'll end our business of selling wine? (*Dejectedly and helplessly, goes back to* CHENG TEH, *accompanied by drumbeats. She pours the wine.*) I, Li Feng, pour out a cup of wine and ask the Lord Soldier to accept it graciously and drink it.

CHENG TEH   I am going to tease her to see if she has any feelings. (*Touching the back of her hand with his fan and looking at her jokingly.*) Dry cup! (*He holds up his left sleeve in front of his face, downs the wine, and tickles* LI FENG's *palm. Four beats of the drum and the small gong.*)

LI FENG (*jumps up, turns away, stamps her foot in protest, and snaps vulgarly at him*)   Dry cup to your mother!

CHENG TEH   Why do you curse at me like that?

LI FENG   If you want to drink, go on and drink. Why did you have to scratch my palm? What for?

CHENG TEH   Oh, since I haven't been hunting with my bow and arrows these days, my nails have grown. Accidentally, I must have touched you a little with my fingernails.

LI FENG (*pleased, but pretends to be angry*)   My nails are long, too; but they aren't touching you. (*Points coyly at him.*)

CHENG TEH (*stands and walks up to her*)   I can see Big Sister likes to take advantage of others. Come here, come here and tickle my rough hands if you like, Big Sister. (*He stretches out his palm for her to tickle.*)

LI FENG   Sir, if you ask for it . . . (*Drum and small gong, four beats, ending with one beat on the small gong.*)

CHENG TEH (*holding out his right hand to her*)   Come on and tickle me.

LI FENG (*takes a step away from him, to the right*)   No, I won't. (*Shyly lowering her head, the back of her right hand on her left cheek.*)

299

CHENG TEH (*desiring to be touched by the girl, stretches his right hand toward her*) Why not? (*But at the same time, he is afraid of being tickled and runs away to the left.*)

LI FENG Look at you! I haven't started tickling yet and you are running away already.

CHENG TEH (*comes back to her with his hand outstretched*) I promise I won't run away.

LI FENG If so, I'll tickle (*drum and small gong, one beat*), tickle (*drum and small gong, one beat*), tickle! (*Drum and small gong, one beat. She flirtatiously tickles* CHENG TEH's *hand.*)

CHENG TEH (*laughs*) Ha, ha, ha!

LI FENG (*dreamily and romantically singing "Hsi-p'i-liu-shiu-pan," a light and free aria in* hsi p'i, *the other main mode of Peking opera*)

> The silvery new moon
> Is shining over the earth.
> Where do you come from,
> My good sir?

CHENG TEH (*singing*)

> Big Sister, don't ask me questions.
> I live on earth and beneath the sky.

LI FENG (*speaking*) You fool! Everybody lives on earth and beneath the sky. Do you suppose anyone can live above the sky?

CHENG TEH Ah, Big Sister, my lodging is different from anybody else's.

LI FENG (*innocently*) How different?

CHENG TEH Far, far away in the city of Peking (*waves his long sleeve to the left*), there is a large circle (*makes a large circle with his folded fan; small gong and cymbals*), within which there is a small circle (*small gong and cymbals as he makes a smaller circle with his fan*), within which there is a yellow circle (*making a still smaller circle with his fan; followed by drum and small gong, two beats*). And it is within that yellow circle that I live. (*Two beats on the cymbals; drum and small gong, three beats; followed by one beat on the small gong as he points with his fan.*)

LI FENG Now I know who you are.

CHENG TEH Who am I?

LI FENG You are my brother . . .

CHENG TEH Ay!

LI FENG (*rudely and impishly*) . . . my brother's brother-in-law.

CHENG TEH Huh! What nonsense! (*Disgusted, he waves his right sleeve at her and turns away to the left. Drum, two beats; clapper, two beats; drum and small gong, three beats; drum, soft taps; drum and small gong, one beat; drum, soft taps; drum and small gong, one beat.*)

LI FENG Mister Soldier's manners are really too outrageous. You shouldn't try seduction of a decent girl.

CHENG TEH (*turns back to tease her and sings "Hsi-p'i-liu-shiu-pan"*)
Decent girl! Oh, what a decent girl!
You shouldn't wear a cherry-apple blossom in your hair,
Or smile and giggle to attract a person's love,
But it all comes down to this cherry-apple blossom.

Points with his fan at the flower in her hair.

LI FENG
Cherry-apple blossom!
Oh, what a cherry-apple blossom!
(*Takes the flower from her hair and looks admiringly at it.*)
How it makes you tease me so!
Let me throw it on the floor.
(*She angrily throws the flower on the floor. Three drumbeats.*)
Throw it and stamp on it.
(*She stamps on it. Two beats of the small gong.*)
From now on, I'll never wear this cherry-apple flower!
(*Big gong.*)

CHENG TEH
Li Feng's manners are really too outrageous,
To destroy this cherry-apple flower!
Let me pick it up for you.

301

The Price of Wine

*(He picks it up. Four strong beats on the drum; two pauses;
one soft tap on the drum; one heavy beat on the drum; and one
beat on the clapper.)*

　　Let me put *(drum)*, put *(drum)*, put *(drum, two beats)*
　　On you this cherry-apple flower!

*He puts the flower in her hair to show their intimacy and love.
Drum, two heavy beats; clapper, two beats; drum and small
gong, three beats together; drum, soft taps; drum and small
gong, soft taps; drum and small gong, one beat.*

LI FENG *(very pleased but shy)*
　　I am so upset and frightened.
　　I'd better run away and escape into my bedroom.

*She runs away, crosses the threshold, and exits upstage left,
accompanied by drum, three heavy beats; clapper, one beat;
drum, one heavy beat; clapper, one beat; drum, one heavy beat;
drum and small gong, three beats.*

CHENG TEH *(following, crosses over the threshold, his eyes not
　　leaving her)*
　　　　　Let her go *(waving his left sleeve)*,
　　　　　Let her run *(waving his right sleeve)*,
　　　　　May it be as far as to the sea or the ocean
(Waving both sleeves, one after another),
　　　　　I can always catch her,
　　　　　Follow her even to the end of the earth!

*He walks leisurely as he fans himself and then points with his
fan to the audience. Exits to the left, to beats of the small gong.
The* PROPERTY MAN *appears from upstage left, puts the chair
in front of the table. Soft playing of the cymbals. Then drum,
three strong beats; clapper, one beat; drum, one strong beat;
clapper, one beat; drum and small gong, two strong beats, one
soft, one strong. Repetition of the percussion, ending with the*

drum-and-small-gong strong beats for LI FENG *to enter in the next scene.*

Scene 2

The setting is the same. Center stage, however, is now LI FENG'S *bedroom. Enter* LI FENG *from the right, to drumbeats.*

LI FENG (*downstage center*)   Here comes Li Feng.

CHENG TEH (*entering from the right*)   With Cheng Teh follow-ing close by!

She circles once around the stage, followed by CHENG TEH. *She steps over an imaginary threshold into her bedroom, downstage center, and mimes closing and bolting the door.*

LI FENG   I must shut the door. (*She carries the chair downstage center and places it with its back toward the audience, to close the door tight so that he cannot enter; drum and gong, one beat.*)

CHENG TEH (*mimes knocking on the door with his fan, each knock accompanied by two beats of the wooden clapper*)   Big Sister, open the door! Quick! (*Knocks again.*) Open the door, Big Sister! (*Knocks again to two beats of the clapper.*)

LI FENG (*stands facing the audience with her hand on the back of the chair, the invisible door between them*)   No, I won't. (*Small gong.*)

CHENG TEH   Why not? (*Cymbals.*)

LI FENG   Not until my brother comes back. (*Small gong.*)

CHENG TEH   Your brother won't come home tonight. (*Big gong.*)

LI FENG   Then I will not open it tonight. (*Small gong.*)

CHENG TEH   He won't come home in ten days. (*Small gong, two beats.*)

303

LI FENG Then I will not open it in ten days. (*Big gong.*)

CHENG TEH He will never come home. (*Big gong.*)

LI FENG Then I will never open it! (*Small gong; then big gong.*)

CHENG TEH (*moves downstage right, thoughtfully strokes his beard and taps his temple with his index and third fingers, and speaks aside*) Hm-m, let me see. (*Drum, two beats; pause; small gong, one beat.*) This lass won't open the door until her brother comes back. What shall I do? (*Drum, three beats; clapper, one beat.*) I've got it. (*Small gong. Pointing with his fan; excitedly and decidedly to the audience.*) Let me play a trick on her. (*Aloud and toward* LI FENG.) Oh, Mr. Li Lung! So you're back at last. The food is cold, the wine is bad in your hotel, and there is no service whatsoever. Please give me the check, and I'll leave here at once!

LI FENG Oh, my! My brother is back! Let me open the door. (*She carries the chair back and places it in front of the table to drum and gong beats. She returns downstage center and mimes opening the bolt to beating of the gong. She opens the door. The gong is beating furiously. She steps over the imaginary threshold and goes to the left, looking for her brother.*) Where is my brother? (CHENG TEH *quickly crosses over the imaginary threshold, indicating he has slipped into her bedroom. When she returns, she is surprised and then furious to find him standing there with the fan in front of his face. Drum and small gong accompany their movements.*) Where is my brother?

CHENG TEH (*lowering the fan, triumphantly and proudly*) Here. (*Big gong.*)

LI FENG (*spitting at him*) Ah tsui! You rascal! You followed me from the front room to the back yard, and from the back yard to my bedroom. Why? (*Small gong.*)

CHENG TEH I want you to give me something to send me off with.

LI FENG Oh, so you are a beggar! Just a minute. I'll get a penny to send you off. (*Goes to the table.*)

CHENG TEH (*following her*) A big girl like you should know what to send me off with.

LI FENG (*going around table and to center stage*) I understand, but I'm frightened. (*Drum, small gong, and clapper.*)

CHENG TEH Frightened of what?

LI FENG Of my brother coming back.

CHENG TEH Oh, I'll be here if he comes back.

LI FENG Exactly! If you're here, then I'm not! So you'd better leave, quickly! (*Drum and clapper.*)

CHENG TEH (*puts his hands behind his back*) I refuse to go. (*Big gong.*)

LI FENG If you don't, I'll scream! (*Small gong.*)

CHENG TEH Scream what?

LI FENG Scream that you're killing people! (*Small gong.*)

CHENG TEH Without any weapons, how can I murder anyone? (*Big gong.*)

LI FENG (*points at him*) Your heart is sharper than a knife! (*Cymbals.*)

CHENG TEH (*stands firm with hands on back*) I won't get out. (*Big gong.*)

LI FENG (*comes downstage*) Then I'll scream for help! Ahhhh!!! (*Two small gong beats, cymbals.*)

CHENG TEH Wait! Just a moment.

LI FENG (*waving her handkerchief at him*) Then get out at once! (*Big gong.*)

CHENG TEH (*crossing downstage left, raising his right sleeve to the level of his head, and speaking aside, to drum, two beats; clapper, one beat*) Now, if this girl should really scream, she would wake up all the people in this town. (*Drum and clapper, one beat.*) That would be quite inconvenient. (*Drumbeat.*) Ah, well! (*Two drumbeats and one beat of the clapper.*) If she has good fortune, she is going to be a lady in my court; if not, I will leave here at once. (*Drum and clapper, one beat, as he goes to the chair in front of the table and sits down.*) Big Sister, do you recognize me?

LI FENG You are a little brother of a number-one house (*puts up her right thumb; small gong*) and the big brother of a number-three house. (*Puts up the first three fingers of her left hand.*) You are a number-two ass! (*Two drumbeats and one small gong and clapper beat as she points at* CHENG TEH.)

CHENG TEH Ay! Stop cursing. I am no other than the Emperor, Cheng Teh! (*Two beats of the big gong and cymbals.*)

LI FENG Go on! (*She shoves him from the chair and sits down herself.*) Do you know who I am?

CHENG TEH Of course I do. You are a wine girl in the town of the Plum Dragon.

LI FENG Huh! I am no other than the mother of the present Emperor, Cheng Teh. (*Small gong, cymbals, big gong.*)

CHENG TEH What an imprudent and outrageous remark, you country lass! Ever since the beginning of time an emperor has always worn precious things.

LI FENG Then show your precious things.

CHENG TEH If I don't have any——

LI FENG Then show your mother's.

CHENG TEH Don't curse, Big Sister, but look! (*The* PROPERTY MAN *enters from upstage right and helps* CHENG TEH *take off the hood while* LI FENG *gets up and watches in utter surprise.*) Taking off my hood and opening my gown to show the imperial dragon robe, I ask Big Sister to look. There are dragons on my head, dragons on my gown, dragons left and right, front and back. There are, altogether, nine dragons on my robe—golden dragons with five claws, too. Now am I not the Emperor, Big Sister? (*Big gong.* CHENG TEH *puts his right foot on the chair to show his dragon robe, emblem of the Chinese emperor.*)

LI FENG (*amazed, moves to him*) Ah, what precious things! (*She tries to feel his robe, but he mimes that boy and girl should not touch each other. Then he sits down and she walks downstage right. Cymbals.*) No wonder last night I had a dream about a golden dragon with five claws descending on this room. (*Sings an aria in moderate tempo in Erh-huang-ping-*

pan, with hope and delight.) Allow me to come forward and kneel, so this slave can be pardoned and be ennobled. (*Walks toward him. The* PROPERTY MAN *puts a red cushion on the floor in front of* CHENG TEH *for her to kneel on.*) Long live the Emperor! (*Drum and big gong. She kneels facing* CHENG TEH.)

CHENG TEH   Who is this that is kneeling before me?

LI FENG   Li Feng, your Majesty. (*Small gong.*)

CHENG TEH (*waving his sleeve*)   What is your wish? (*Big gong.*)

LI FENG   That I be granted the title of a lady in your court, your Majesty. (*Small gong.*)

CHENG TEH   Just now you offended me by saying I was your brother's big brother-in-law, so I am not going to ennoble you. (*Big gong.*)

LI FENG   If you make me a lady, then my brother will be your big brother-in-law. (*Small gong.*)

CHENG TEH   Not even to become a younger brother-in-law! (*Big gong.*)

LI FENG   Oh, your Majesty, please do make me a lady, even if it's of lowest rank.

CHENG TEH   No, I won't. (*Big gong.*)

LI FENG   Just a tiny bit of a lady, please. (*Cymbals.*)

CHENG TEH   No. (*Big gong.*)

LI FENG   Just a wee-wee bit of a lady, please. (*Cymbals.*)

CHENG TEH   No, not even that. (*Big gong.*)

LI FENG   All right, if that's the case . . . (*Gets up and starts to go, to drum and small gong.*)

CHENG TEH   Wait. (*Big gong.*) If I don't grant you the title of a lady, what a disgrace it will be to you, my dear girl!

LI FENG   It's all your fault.

CHENG TEH   My three palaces and six courts are all full, but I can squeeze you in somewhere! All right, come, come, I'll ennoble you. I, Emperor Cheng Teh, hereby proclaim you a lady of the Sixth Court of the Third Palace! (*Big gong, two beats.*)

The Price of Wine

LI FENG (*kneeling before him*)   I kneel and kowtow to show my respect and gratitude.

CHENG TEH (*standing, helps* LI FENG *rise*)   With my royal hands I help my darling lady rise from the floor.

LI FENG (*rising*)   May I ask where your Majesty wishes to go?

CHENG TEH   Take me to my horse and let us leave for the palace. (*Big gong.*)

LI FENG   Your Majesty has certainly honored our humble town of the Plum Dragon tonight. (*Small gong.*)

CHENG TEH *and* LI FENG (*speaking together*)   A real dragon has descended on a pair of golden cups. (*Small gong, cymbal, big gong.*)

LI FENG   Your Majesty, this way, please. (*Pointing left.*)

CHENG TEH   Where to?

LI FENG   To my bedroom.

CHENG TEH   Ai-ya-ya. I'm frightened! (*Three drumbeats, followed by one beat of the wooden clapper.*)

LI FENG   Of what?

CHENG TEH   Of your brother, who'll come back soon.

LI FENG   But now you have me, an empress, to protect you.

CHENG TEH   That's right. As long as I have you, I have nothing to fear. So let's go, my dear Li Feng. (*Small gong, two beats.*)

LI FENG (*curtsies, with hands folded on the left side*)   Your Majesty! (*Big gong.*)

CHENG TEH   My empress! (*Big gong.*)

LI FENG   Long live the Emperor! (*Big gong, two beats.*)

CHENG TEH (*laughing*)   Now to our palace!

CHENG TEH *follows* LI FENG *off upstage left to the alternate beating of the small gong and the wooden clapper. Curtain.*